# In the Shadow
# of Race

*Growing Up As a Multiethnic, Multicultural, and "Multiracial" American*

# In the Shadow
# of Race

*Growing Up As a Multiethnic, Multicultural,
and "Multiracial" American*

## Teja Arboleda

**LEA** LAWRENCE ERLBAUM ASSOCIATES, PUBLISHERS
1998 Mahwah, New Jersey            London

Lawrence Erlbaum Associates, Inc., Publishers
10 Industrial Avenue
Mahwah, New Jersey 07430-2262

Cover design by Teja Arboleda

**Library of Congress Cataloging-in-Publication Data**

Arboleda, Teja.
    In the shadow of race : growing up as a multiethnic,
multicultural, and "multiracial" American / Teja Arboleda.
        p.  cm.
    ISBN  0-8058-2574-6  (alk. paper).  --  ISBN  0-8058-
2575-4  (pbk. : alk. paper)
    1. Arboleda, Teja.  2. Racially mixed people--United
States--Biography.  3. Pluralism (Social sciences)--United
States.  4. United States--Race relations.  I. Title.
E184.A1A747   1998
305.8 ' 00973--dc21                                          98-16200
                                                                 CIP

Books published by Lawrence Erlbaum Associates are printed
on acid-free paper, and their bindings are chosen for strength
and durability.

Printed in the United States of America
10  9  8  7  6  5  4  3  2  1

# Contents

# Preface

The most complicated thing about writing an autobiography at my age is that because all my immediate family members are still alive, there is rarely agreement on the memories. Naturally, my own memories are colored by my own perceptions, which undoubtedly change over time, as does everyone else's. In the process of obtaining "permissions," researching the "truth," and creating the "story," I ultimately had to average out what I had learned from others with my own experiences to come up with a story that has at least some measure of consensus.

Four years ago I attended my first annual National Association for Multicultural Education conference, which took place in Detroit, Michigan, where I presented my one-man show, *Ethnic Man!* A woman by the name of Naomi Silverman approached me and asked me if I would be interested in making my play into a book. "An autobiography?" I asked her. "I'm only 32." A woman who overheard our conversation butted in, "Hey, I know a young nun who wrote an autobiography, a compelling story, and she was only 25." "Well," I said, "I'd better write an official autobiography before someone writes an 'unofficial' biography."

I had been performing *Ethnic Man!* around the country for 1 year already and continued to wonder (as all artists do no matter how successful they are) if America would really be interested in reading about me or even attending my performances. I mean, who am I? I'm not famous, nor am I rich, I'm not a Kennedy, nor am I a mass murderer, I don't have "dirt" to sell and I haven't been abducted by aliens.

I am engaging in a cathartic, absorbing analysis about life on an often racist, sexist, homophobic, religious elitist, class-obsessed planet that has been cheaper than seeing a therapist, for sure. In the process of regurgitating my story, in small towns and big cities across the country, I have learned that in reflecting on my experiences, no matter how vibrant or vague they may be, they change over time, giving me constant alterations in my under-standing of who I am. I am also resolved to the fact that they will continue to change and that possibly I will never really understand who I am.

But I do understand *what* I am.

So I started writing this book, which was originally titled *My Kind,* fashioned after an encounter with a racist in Woburn, Massachusetts who told me, "Go back to where you belong, we don't like your kind here!" Not wanting it to sound like a celebrity "tell-all" (i.e., *My Life*), I thought of how a person like myself, with a mixed heritage that some Americans like to call "messed-up," is often in the shadows—not quite perceived as a "whole" anything and yet not completely detached from the "real thing."

*  *  *

I remember back when I was a child in New York, there were posters and buttons that read, "Black is beautiful." Then there was the counterpro-clamation, "White is beautiful." After college, I noticed an increase in non-White awareness, and I considered launching a mock "multiracial is beautiful" campaign, where I would host parades and the "Miss Multira-cial American" contest. The desire to make light of my dilemma didn't last long, however, as I became more serious about what had become a predicament—a seemingly impossible task of defining who and what I am in the context of the status-quo world around me. I started questioning: What have I gained by being of mixed heritage, ethnicity, and culture? Do I really *have* all these things in my *blood,* physically, or are we what we are based purely on our experiences and upbringing? What race am I? Does race exist? Are the spirits of my ancestors, my guardians, watching over me, or has my connection to them crumbled with their bodies in the soil? Do I carry any legacy outside of the advice and teachings of my immediate family and friends, or am I in fact, in sense, a reincarnation of the souls of former fellow human beings? Can an adopted child be proud of her heritage without knowing anything about it? Can an American be proud of his German heritage without ever having been to Germany?

And although I've traveled a lot and seen more than most people will ever see of the world (I have been extremely lucky, even privileged to have done so, and don't deny the advantage I had in that respect), those places seem like a blur to me now. Most of the "tours" took place when I was much younger, and completely uninterested in things like the Sphinx or the Eiffel Tower. I only remember snippets, and honestly can't say much about them other than I have *been* there. *Been* there, not *known* the place. Therefore, I don't mention them in detail in the book because they were not as relevant in constructing my identity as were the places where I lived.

The most important thing to me, as I wrote this book, was trying to be as honest as I could. Not honest in telling the absolute truth because, as I said earlier, I don't know what the absolute truth is, but the truth in my *perceptions* about my memories and what I've learned. I have made many mistakes in my life and will continue to make many more. That is as important as *hansei* in Japan, when individuals in a group confess or "reflect" on shortcomings or wrongdoings. The most I could do is try to tell the story in a way that resonates with the ever-changing history of my grandparents, parents and myself.

In understanding *what* I am, I am free to search the infinite possibilities of *who* I am. What I am is human. A high schooler might groan over that statement, but it is after all, the only truth. Everything else is political. This simplistic answer doesn't mean I'm *happy* only with having to say I'm human because I find myself frequently jealous of people who can comfortably, knowingly proclaim they are Jewish, Filipina, African, Black, Black-Jewish or African-Catholic, for that matter, but I must be at least satisfied. This is what the book is all about—my *perceptions* about *who* I am. Hopefully, this might encourage others to reflect on who they are outside of the limited categories of race, ethnicity, gender, religion, class, and all those other things that politically fragment *what* they are. After all, the basis of discrimination is sociopolitical—we, as humans, intellectualize our differences.

It all started with the simple question we all ask, *Who am I?* It continued to, *where did I come from?* It then branched off to, *what can you assume by looking at me? Does my face tell a story, or should I tell you my story, myself?*

Sometimes after a performance of *Ethnic Man!*, I ask audience members what they thought I was when I first came out on stage. The answers are always as colorful as their perceptions. "I don't know, Hispanic?" "I thought you were Black." "Egyptian, Moroccan, Lebanese?" "A White guy with a great tan?" "You look like you're from Brooklyn."

I began to question: *What's in a face? Where does Black begin? Where does Asian end? Do all Jewish people look like Woody Allen? Do all Asians look like Judge Lance Ito? What does a Muslim look like? What does a poor person look like? What does an American look like? In the early 1950s, could a citizen of the newly formed Pakistan be proud of her Pakistani heritage? How long and what does it take to belong to a place, to form national heritage, ethnic pride, or racial identity?*

\* \* \*

In the process of writing *In the Shadow of Race*, I have learned that I am vulnerable and still quite like a tourist, looking for a "family" of people and trying to make sense of my constantly changing surroundings. I have tried to expose my own stereotypes and mistreatment of others, and hope that *how* I've learned to better myself can serve as an example for overcoming the barriers that separate us all. The process is, nonetheless, a lifelong journey and I continue to try to unlearn the prejudices I was taught at an early age, or even ones I concocted on my own as an adult. I heal myself through educated guesses and organic experiences. I hope we all learn to step outside our circles, for that brief moment where discoveries are made, to touch and be touched by that which connects us.

We are not isolated, for even islands are mere tips of underwater mountains and valleys. My family has known isolation, but like islands they connect, somehow, deep below.

In the end, my intention for this book is to allow all of us to realize that there is no such thing as a pure culture or pure race, completely devoid of connection with another, isolated as a whole and disconnected from the web of human existence. We are more than anthropological, socio-logical, pedagogical, psychological, philosophical, political details. We are born, become, change, and move on. The common thread may be a tangled one at times, but when woven together, the resulting tapestry can only be fully appreciated when observed as a whole.

\* \* \*

I thank my parents, Marilis Jörgensen Arboleda and Amadio Arboleda, for raising me to keep an open mind and teaching me to be proud of my heritage; my brother Miguel for guiding me since childhood; my wife Barbara for her love, support, encouragement, willingness to temporarily take over some of my share of household duties, and her tolerance for my workaholic tendencies; my grandparents who have passed away but still watch over me; Christine Clark for her knowledge of the issues and for taking on the arduous task of creating the Study Guide to facilitate this book as course text; my Aunt Soli and Uncle Gene who have supplied me with stories and photographs to help me learn about my heritage; my editor, Naomi Silverman, for believing in this book and for her friendship; my loving friends who continue to remind me that what I do makes a difference in some people's lives; my mother- and father-in-law who have become family to me; our two long-haired cats, Sneakers and Sheila, who have complained of my unwillingness to let them sit on my lap while I type because their fur gets in the keyboard; all the individuals in the story who have given me the impetus, good or bad, to write about how their actions or viewpoints have affected me and how I have affected them; the skunk in my old neighborhood in Somerville, Massachusetts, that re-minds me of how a stinky situation will last as long as we let it linger;

Murray and Herstein who proved to me in less than 1,000 pages that they were wrong; and Al Franken, who negatively imposed on me what became my stage name, *Ethnic Man!*, and whom, for the rest of my career, I will use as a point of reference for my battle to help end discrimination and the negative effects of media.

—*Teja Arboleda*

# Race Is a Four-Letter Word

I've been called *nigger* and a neighbor set the dogs on us in Queens, New York.

I've been called *spic* and was frisked in a plush neighborhood of Los Angeles.

I've been called *Jap* and was blamed for America's weaknesses.

I've been called *Nazi* and the neighborhood G.I. Joes had me every time.

I've been called *Turk* and was sneered at in Germany.

I've been called *Stupid Yankee* and was threatened in Japan.

I've been called *Afghanistani* and was spit on by a Boston cab driver.

I've been called *Iraqi* and Desert Storm was America's pride.

I've been called *mulatto, criollo, mestizo, simarron, Hapahaoli, masala, exotic, alternative, mixed-up, messed-up, half-breed*, and *in between*. I've been mistaken for Moroccan, Algerian, Egyptian, Lebanese, Iranian, Turkish, Brazilian, Argentinean, Puerto Rican, Cuban, Mexican, Indonesian, Nepalese, Greek, Italian, Pakistani, Indian, Black, White, Hispanic, Asian, and being a Brooklynite. I've been mistaken for Michael Jackson and Billy Crystal on the same day.

I've been ordered to get glasses of water for neighboring restaurant patrons. I've been told to be careful mopping the floors at the television station where I was directing a show. Even with my U.S. passport, I've been escorted to the "aliens only" line at Kennedy International Airport. I've been told I'm not dark enough. I've been told I'm not White enough. I've been told I talk American real good. I've been told, "Take your humus and your pita bread and go back to Mexico!" I've been ordered to "Go back to where you belong, we don't like *your* kind here!"

I spent too much time and energy as a budding adult abbreviating my identity and rehearsing its explanation. I would practice quietly by myself, reciting what my father always told me: "Filipino-German." He never smiled when he said this.

My father's dark skin told many stories that his stern face and anger-filled tension couldn't translate. My mother's light skin could never spell empathy—even suntanning only made her turn bright red. My brother Miguel and I became curiosity factors when we appeared in public with her. During the past 34 years, my skin has lightened, somewhat, but then in the summers (even in New England where summers happen suddenly, and disappear just as quickly), I can darken several degrees in a matter of hours. This phenomena seems a peculiar paradigm to which people's perceptions of my culture or race alter with the waning and waxing of my skin tone. I can almost design others' perceptions by counting my minutes in the sun. My years in Japan, the United States, Germany, and the numerous countries, cities, and towns through which I've traveled, have proven that my flesh is irrelevant to the language I speak, to the way I walk and talk, or the way I jog or mow my lawn or to the fact that I often use chopsticks to eat. It is irrelevant to *who* or *what* I married, my political viewpoints, my career, my hopes, desires and fears.

I don't remember being taught by my parents never to *question* skin color, yet when I compare the back of my hand to these pages, I cannot help myself—I must know. Like a sickness coursing through my veins with the very blood that makes me who I am, I ask: What color am I? And, what color was I yesterday? Tomorrow? There is also that pesky, familiar feeling I get when, in the corner of my eye, I catch passing strangers with judgments written on their brows. Maybe paranoia, maybe vanity, but the experiences and memories of too often being "different" or "undefinable" have left me with a weary sense of instant verdict on my part. And sometimes I study their thousands of faces, hoping somehow to connect. I know that they ask themselves the same questions, as they are plagued by the same epidemic, asking and reasking themselves, ourselves, "Who and what are we?"

Overadapting to new environments has become second nature to me, as my father and my mother eagerly fed me culture. As a child I felt like I was being dragged to different corners of the planet with my parents, filling their need for exploration and contact, and teaching us the value and beauty of difference. Between packing suitcases and wandering through unfamiliar territory, all I had ever wanted was to be "the same."

They were successful in some respects—I do believe I am liberal in my thinking—but inevitably there was a price to pay. With each step, each move, each landing through the thick and tenuous atmosphere of a new culture, my feet searched for solid ground, for something familiar. The concept of home, identity, and place become ethereal, like a swirl of gases circling in orbit, waiting for gravity to define their position.

In a sense, I have been relegated to ethnic benchwarmer, on a hunt for simplicity in a world of confusing words that deeply divide us all. In response, I learned to overcompensate. New places and new faces have rarely threatened me, but I have a desperate need to belong to whatever group I'm with at any particular moment. I soak in the surrounding elements to cope with what my instincts oblige, and deliver a new temporary self. I am out of bounds, transcending people and places. I carry within my blood the memories of my heritage connected in the web of my mind, the marriage of history and biology. I breathe the air of my ancestors as if it were fresh from the sunrises of their past. I am illogical, providing argument to traditional categories of race, culture, and ethnicity. I am a cultural chameleon, adapting out of necessity only to discover, yet again, a new Darwinism at the frontiers of identity.

"What are you, anyway?" sometimes demandingly curious Americans like to ask. "I'm Filipino-German," I used to say. I have never been satisfied with abbreviating my identity to the exclusion of all the other puzzle pieces that would then be lost forever in shadowy corners where no one ever looks.

Do I throw a nod at a Black brother who passes me on the street? And if I did so, would he understand why I did? Do I even call him "brother?" Does *he* call *me* "brother?" If not, should he call me a "half-brother," or throw me a half nod? In the United States do I nod or bow to Japanese nationals in a Japanese restaurant? Would they know to bow with me? In Jamaica Plain, Massachusetts, if a Hispanic male gestures hello to me, is it a simple greeting, or a gesture of camaraderie because I might be Hispanic? Do I dress up to go to a country club because, in the eyes of its rich White men, I would otherwise live up their idea of the stereotypical minority? Should I dance well, shaking and driving my body like Papa's family afforded me, or should I remain appropriately conservative to preserve the integrity of a long-gone Puritan New England? Do I shave for the silver hallways of white-collar high-rises so as not to look too "ethnic?" Do I agree to an audition for a commercial when I know the reason I'm there is just to fill in with some skin color for an industry quota?

"I know you're *something*," someone once said. "You have some Black in you," another offered. "He must be ethnic or something," I've over-heard. "I've got such a boring family compared to yours," another confided. "You're messed-up," an elementary school girl decided. "Do you love your race?" her classmate wondered. "*What* did you marry?" I've been asked. "*Who* did you marry?" I've been asked. "Is she just like you?" I've been asked. "You are the quintessential American," someone decided.

\* \* \*

America continues to struggle through its identity crisis, and the simple, lazy, bureaucratic checklist we use only serves to satisfy an outdated four-letter word—*race.* Like the basic food groups, it is overconsumed and digested, forming a hemorrhoid in the backside of the same old power struggle. I am only one of many millions of Americans, from this "League of Outsiders," demanding a change in the way we are designated, routed, cattle-called, herded, and shackled into these simplified classifications.

The United States is going through growing pains. The immigrants coming to the United States and becoming citizens are no longer primarily of European origin. But let's not fool ourselves into thinking that America is only now becoming multicultural.

In 1992, *Time* magazine produced a special issue entitled, "The New Face of America" with the subtitle, "How immigrants are shaping the world's first multicultural society." The cover featured a picture of a woman's face. Next to the face was a paragraph that suggested her image was the result of a computerized average of faces of people of several different races.

The operative words on the cover are "races," "culture," and "first." Race and culture are very different words. Race in America is predominantly determined by skin color. Culture is determined by our experiences and our interactions within a society, large or small.

Then there is this idea of being "first." Are we to say that this continent was never populated by a mix of people? Are we to say that the Lacota and Iroquois were of exactly the same culture? What about the different Europeans who settled here later on? Of course, African slaves were not all from the same tribe, and they certainly were not of the same culture as the slave traders.

In the middle of the magazine, there was a compilation, more like a chart of photographs of people from all over the world. The editor and computer artist scanned all the pictures into a computer. Then, by having the computer average the faces together, they produced a variety of facial combinations. Remember, however, they said on the cover, "People from different *races* ... to form the world's first *multicultural* society." But in the body of the article and its accompanying pictures, many people were not identified by their *race,* but rather by their *nationalities*—such as Italian and Chinese—in other words *citizenship,* a very different word.

Through it all, *Time* was trying to educate us, but at the same time, we're miseducated. The world—not just this country—has always been and always will be a multicultural environment. So what is it about the words *multicultural* or *diversity* that is confusing or overwhelming?

In the next 20 years, the average American will no longer be technically White. This will have to be reflected in the media, in the workplace, and in the schools, not out of charitable interest, but out of necessity. More people are designating themselves as multiracial or multicultural. People continue to marry across religious, cultural, and ethnic barriers. A definition for "mainstream society" is harder to find.

\* \* \*

My mother's father, Opa, died a year after Oma passed away. The day after the funeral in Germany, my mother's relatives told her, for the first time, that her father was not really her father (i.e., biologically). All the people who knew the true identity of her father have long since passed away. So, if my mother's biological father was, let's say, Italian or Russian, does that make her German-Italian or German-Russian? She says no. German, only German, because that's how she was raised.

My brother, Miguel, married a Brazilian. (*Pause.*) Do you have an image in your head of what she looks like? I did when he first told me about her over the phone. Well, she is Brazilian by culture and citizenship, but her parents are Japanese nationals who moved to Brazil in their early 20s to escape poverty in Japan after World War II. So she *looks stereotypically* Japanese. But she speaks Portuguese and doesn't interact socially like most Japanese do.

\* \* \*

I offer myself as a case study in transcending the complex maze of barriers, pedestals, doors, and traps that form the boundaries that confine human beings to dominant and minority groups.

I am tired. I am exhausted. I am always looking for new and improved definitions for my identity. My very-mixed heritage, culture, and international experiences seem like a blur sometimes, and I long for a resting place. A place where I can breathe like I did in my mother's womb: without having to open my mouth.

# 2

# Among the Trees

In the summer of 1986, Papa sent me a miniature family crest. He had just returned to his home in Japan from a business trip to Spain where he found the keychain-sized pendant with a picture of a bear standing upright, pawing at the branches of a tree. Arboleda means "among the trees" in that southern region of Spain. The name conjures up images of roots, tree trunks, branches, twigs, and leaves, the very symbol of stability, growth, and the cycle of life. When he handed me the pendant, he didn't explain what it meant, and at the time I wasn't interested enough to ask. Months later, I found it in a drawer and I wondered how Grandpa could have been so proud of the name, knowing it went all the way back to his Filipino ancestors during Spanish colonial rule. And I wondered why Papa would go to such great lengths to retrieve an emblem of that oppressive history. I began to consider the relevance of this historic symbolism of our name, or any name for that matter.

My first name, Teja, was picked from my German grandparents' *Stammbuch*, something that Germans automatically receive at their wedding. In this ancestry logbook, during Hitler's regime, true Aryan names were listed in the back for the purpose of naming offspring. So, in the wrinkles of old-world fascism and a neo-Nazi surge, it gives me great pleasure to know that I am quite possibly the only non-Aryan-looking Teja of German heritage.

A year after Papa handed me the crest, Mama found an article in *The New York Times* describing an Indian man of royalty by the name of Teja Singh Swatantar, who had traveled to Germany in 1916 and played an active role in early efforts to legally liberate India from the British Empire.

The article and the pendant served to remind me of my tenuous hold on ethnic and national identity. My father had tried, just as his father had tried, to keep it simple for me. Only a couple of years before he gave me the pendant, Papa revealed his Black heritage to me. I was beginning to question the depth and number of secrets that were still being held hostage. How many voices could there be, desperate to legitimize the complexities of their heritage? To find the root of these fears, I needed only to look at my own history. And to discover my history, I needed only to look within myself.

* * *

Grandpa, Federico Arboleda, was uninterested in the intellectual pursuit of tracking his heritage—he considered himself simply Filipino. But his parents' heritage, like that of many Filipinos, was a mix of southern Chinese and several other Southeast Asian ethnicities and cultures. He was born in 1914 in a town called Kalibo, on the isolated island of Panay, and grew up speaking Spanish, Visayan, and Tagalog. A simple industrial valley surrounded them, a medley of rice and barley farms, the wooden browns and metallic grays of coconut and sugar cane refineries, and a sisal hemp mill. They lived in a thatched Nipa tree leaf house built on stilts in the water-flooded rice fields; underneath them lived the water buffalo they used to plow their fields.

As the *Kuya* (oldest son), Grandpa was oldest of 13 children, and was expected to oversee the farm activities and land after his parents' death. It was also his responsibility to help educate his brothers and sisters. He was very short, but he was a tank of a man. In a way, he was a rebel, a nonconformist, and tough. He was the only one of his generation in his immediate family to ever leave the Philippines.

When the Philippines was no longer dominated by Spain but by the United States, military tactical advantage was exchanged with a temporary "favor" to the "disadvantaged natives"—the legal status of "White." So, Grandpa switched from Yellow to White overnight. Promises of streets paved with gold were the incentive to buy into the American Dream politics. He was told he could have it all.

So, at age 17, he broke from family tradition and left for the United States to look for a better life. Before he boarded the steamer destined for America, his mother had asked him, "When will you return home?" He searched deep inside himself for an answer, held her hands close to his heart, and said, "when I become a real American."

He arrived in Seattle, Washington, in the middle of the Great Depression, where he connected with the small Filipino community. They helped him find odd jobs and eventually full-time work in a salmon cannery. He then moved to San Francisco where he learned that as a Filipino, he could automatically become a U.S. citizen by enlisting in the U.S. Armed Forces.

He was too short for most military service except the Coast Guard, so he joined and worked first as a steward, and then as a petty officer. He believed he could make a home on the west coast, maybe even eventually send for the family. After all, many of his Filipino friends had done the same.

Arboleda: among the trees. Lost in a cultural forest, Grandpa tried to find his way out for most of his life. America had given Grandpa the opportunity to gain much, yet he had lost his identity. He underwent a lifelong struggle to become what he perceived to be a mainstream American. Growing relatively comfortable with this status quo, he promised he would never travel again, unless it were to return to his family.

But his traveling, even if only in his heart, would never be over.

* * *

Grandma, Isabella Driessen, was born on Hilton Head Island, South Carolina, to a light-skinned Black man and Native-American woman. It was 1916, and Grandma's mother, a Seventh Day Adventist, raised her daughter in the strong African traditions of her husband's Gullah community. Closer to her roots now than she would ever be again, Grandma absorbed the vibrant culture surrounding her. Her grandfather, Henry Driessen, was a French-German who had children with one of his slaves, then subsequently left the country. It was on these sea coast islands where only a generation before, during slavery days African cultures mixed, a result of the island's relative isolation. The mixing produced a strong identity and language. Like most of her relatives, she never spoke of her Native-American heritage, and although she was raised Gullah, she would remain an outsider, her fairer skin like the permanence of an unwanted tattoo.

Her father died when she was only 5 years old. Several years later, her mother left the island for a man who lived in rural Georgia. It is not all too clear or precise perhaps, but it is said that Grandma was then cared for by great-grandma who worked as the personal maid to the mayor's wife in Savannah, Georgia. In the confines of a fenced-in, all-White world, Mrs. Hitch apparently took to Grandma, seeing promise in the feisty girl whose skin tone boarded on the brink of Black and White. She trained Grandma to sneak the liquor from the cellar to her private bar, and in return promised to educate her.

Mrs. Hitch saw Grandma as one of her own daughters and was determined to mold her in her own image. She disciplined Grandma's speech, excising the Gulluh accent from her tongue and replacing it with the Queen's English. She straightened Grandma's back and disciplined her mannerisms. To Mrs. Hitch, Grandma would be no less than a proper young woman, even if she was Black, and the transformation would prove that Negroes could be educated, given the right circumstances.

When she felt Grandma was sufficiently adjusted for formal education, Mrs. Hitch arranged to have her chauffeured to middle school and later high school. Eight years after Grandma first arrived at the mansion, the willow trees and ferns along the front garden had grown along with her, like a delicate compliment. She could have all but forgotten her heritage, now showered in a world designed and fitted to the liking of her guardian. Nevertheless, Grandma developed into an intelligent, strong, and attractive woman. But Mrs. Hitch wasn't finished with her yet. She sent her to Oakwood Junior College in Huntsville, Alabama, where Grandma obtained a nursing degree.

It was there, on the campus and away from the protection of a familiar environment, where she was confronted with harsh words and confusion. The enigma of racial identity confronted her undeniably—she was not White enough and not Black enough. Finally, within the comfort of a small group of light-skinned Black, female colleagues, she settled into a comfortable state, flirting with both sides of the spectrum. Graduating with highest honors, she returned to South Carolina and took a job as a nurse in a local hospital only miles from the bridge to Hilton Head.

Now a professional adult, a model minority in the eyes of Mrs. Hitch, Grandma paid her respects and absorbed more advice from the woman who had helped to mold her. Mrs. Hitch's last concerns were the most critical, the most difficult, and the most painful. Grandma had reached the age of marriage, and Mrs. Hitch wasn't going to let that go easy.

"You must better your race," she would say. "You must not marry a Black man. A fine woman like you deserves a White man."

The seed of self-destruction had been planted long before that, however. It had been 10 years since she left the culture of her roots on Hilton Head, and the brainwashing would never cease to control her self-image. Society had made its demands, and living beyond that was a challenge only a few could afford.

* * *

In 1927, the ship on which Grandpa was serving was making its way north from the Caribbean. Off the coast of South Carolina, he was injured in a mission and landed in the hospital, under Grandma's care. He was attracted to her, and after one date, they fell in love. His ship wouldn't be back for several months, so he requested shelter from the local Filipino community. There he reconnected with his roots in the cramped quarters of his countrymen. But when they learned of his involvement with a Negro woman, they criticized him. Sad that he couldn't share his life with his own countrymen, he decided to keep his personal affairs to himself.

Soon Grandma introduced her new boyfriend to Mrs. Hitch, who blessed their relationship. "He seems like a nice Chinese man," she declared. "Chinese are close enough to White, and far enough from Black." Within a year they were married. They lived in Savannah, Georgia, where they had their first child, Freddy. A year later my father, Amadio, was born.

On some occasions, Uncle Freddy and my father stayed with relatives on Hilton Head while Grandpa went hunting and fishing on the island with some of Grandma's relatives. By then the Arboleda family had become curiosities, the subject of family stories and gossip—the "Chinese" element of their already-mixed history.

Millions of heartbeats away from where he was born, Grandpa struggled to belong, pushing up through complicated layers of values and customs. Buried under his isolation lay a secret too raw to acknowledge. He never could accept Negroes as equals. He had become used to making derogatory remarks about them, but tried hard not to express this to his wife or family. Nevertheless, the Arboledas would take that last, precarious step away from the truth, where the foothold is weak, and the bind breaks the ties.

As legs grow feeble in the presence of the enemy, Grandpa's weakness seeped through his staunch facade. He was 5'2" and wore little boy's shoes. And even though he was legally White, his sea-faring skin was in fact darker than Grandma's. By law he was granted access to the White world, but his skin always proved different. No argument, no demands would suffice, and with his wife at his side he was relegated, just like she and the children, to "colored only." The lesser fountain, the back of the bus, "Yes sir, yes m'am." He learned to blame Grandma for their bad luck and unresolved cultural differences. The lack of communication tore at their roots, tying simple links into unforgiving knots.

In public, or even in the privacy of his home, Grandpa rarely smiled; his brusque mouth gave cold orders even in the warm glow of his living room. To the world he was nothing but a short, dark, Chinese man. His fellow sailors called him "boy," and "chink." To them he was a brave anomaly—all they knew of Filipinos was that they were houseboys or servants. Sometimes he felt lucky, being spared the term "nigger." Maybe it was the straight hair that saved the Filipinos. He grew angrier, frustrated by the limitations set for a man of his measure. He missed the Philippines and his family—America had proven itself farther away from home than he ever imagined. Maybe the north would be kinder.

A transfer to New York was granted, and in 1940 he packed up his family and moved to a little apartment in the borough of Queens, New York. In 1942, his ship was torpedoed by Germans in the Atlantic, and the Coast Guard didn't know if he was alive or dead. Grandma didn't give up, looking for hours on end out the window, then taking her two young boys to walk the streets in search of the man they hardly knew.

When he finally did return, uninjured, Grandpa moved the family again, to the sparsely inhabited borough of Staten Island, New York. There, Grandma began working in a hospital. Her qualifications were impeccable—a college degree and years of experience proved valuable, taking her far beyond the credentials of even some of the White men she faced. Eventually she moved up to become the head nurse. Sometimes, like in the flash of a brief encounter with one's mirror image, Grandma would remember her other life on Hilton Head. It seemed so long ago and so alien, and she might have wondered what life would have been like had she had never left.

On Staten Island they lived on the second floor of a two-family house. Below them lived a childless Italian couple. The wife depended on Grandma for her daily gossip and support. The island was safe and quiet, a haven, Grandpa thought, ideal for the raising of children.

But Coast Guard missions took Grandpa far from home, leaving Grandma to raise the children by herself. They were one of the very few "colored" families in the neighborhood, a peculiarity like the only two Black families. Grandpa regarded their predicament as lucky, because their darkness was seen more like a condition. "Look at those two Black kids in that yard" a passerby once pointed out. "They're not Black," another surmised, "they're just dirty." With time, the Arboledas learned that Black children were never invited to neighborhood parties and their families were rarely asked to barbecues. The Arboledas, the dirty Whites, felt lucky enough to pass.

"Why won't they invite them?" Papa had once asked Grandma.

In her mind, Grandma traveled the long path back to Hilton Head. She had been given the choice a long time ago: either protect her kids, or be despondent forever. She replied, "because they are different."

She tried to become comfortable, even functional with the overbearing White culture that surrounded her, but failed. She was lost in isolation and loneliness. Against her fundamental Baptist beliefs, she turned to alcohol, often becoming delusional. When Grandpa returned for shore leave, he grew more and more concerned and frustrated, watching her vitality dissolve in deep, shocking stages of depression. He eventually put her into a mental hospital where she was confined for 6 months, but her depression and alcoholism stayed with her throughout her life.

Several years later, Grandpa's parents died. It was official: His duty as the oldest son was to return and take over the family farm. Maybe he was hoping they would have chosen the next in line, but the moment of truth made it clear—to neglect this would be to relinquish his family and heritage. He hadn't managed to become the American he promised yet, and he was beginning to doubt that it would ever happen. It would be strange to return to the Philippines when countless others risked everything to stay in America. This new country and new life was at least comfortable. America hadn't really been touched by war, and his family was safe. Why go back?

His family urged his return. "You can live better than a senator!" they claimed. "Your children will learn to be proud of their heritage," they advised. True, he could retire early, live off his savings, pension, and the mighty American dollar. By returning, he would also save face as the oldest son and he would take his wife away from her desperation, away from this oppressive country, away from segregation and race politics. He took his savings and sent money ahead to his family in Calibo to have a house built on his own land.

Soon after their first daughter, Solidad, was born, he retired early from the Coast Guard and packed up his family once again. Papa, now 12 years old, for the first time saw the sights that Grandpa has spoken of: the distant shores of Central America and the Panama Canal; Grandpa's first American home—San Francisco; the endless quenching deep blue of the Pacific; the beauty of ocean Islanders; Hawaii, Guam, Jamaica, Japan. The world was beckoning him, and just like Grandpa, the itching need to see the world jarred his imagination. And although he was too young to understand, like father like son, his traveling would never be over.

As they docked in Manila, Grandpa vowed this would be the last time he would have to uproot his family to find a place that would welcome them. He was finally home again.

They never continued to Calibo. In Manila they stayed with Grandpa's uncle in the county of Baclaren. His uncle was surprised that Grandpa would take his family back to a place that was, in his eyes, primitive in comparison to the United States. He convinced Grandpa to forget the idea of returning home and to settle in the growing city of Manila, with more reminders of America.

Grandpa sent a message ahead to Calibo, stating his intentions. Then, during the next few months while they waited for a house to be fixed up in the city, they camped in a Nipa hut near the uncle's house. Eventually they settled in a modest house with servants and the only refrigerator in the neighborhood. Although materially they were well off, there were limitations. Grandpa recognized the warning signs: His wife was not fitting in, and his children were clearly not often accepted by his fellow countrymen. How could his own people do this to him? What would it take to be worthy of approval?

In his anger and frustration, he resorted to harsh punishment and discipline of his children. Ordering them to kneel on raw rice and slapping their legs with a belt were his only words of encouragement.

Grandma, now even more secluded than ever, fell even shorter of Grandpa's expectations. When their fourth child Consuela was born, they thought Consuela's presence would bring acceptance to their adopted new world. But Grandma's dark skin created an untouchable wall around her, maybe some of it imaginary, created by her insecurity and loneliness. She confined herself to the house and remained in the shadows of Filipino society.

Grandpa didn't like what the Philippines had become—his country was not at all the same as it was when he left it. His outspoken criticism became dubious to others, he fought back when challenged, and soon he became the local pariah. Political and social corruption angered him, and he wondered, now, why he ever uprooted his family from the United States. Feeling like a failure and unable to cope with the problems, Grandpa joined a merchant marine shipping company. His tours of duty took him far away, and he returned to see his wife and children in the Philippines only once during the next 12 years of their stay.

Uncle Freddy as the *kuya* became, by proxy, the head of the household, which he rejected. To their Filipino relatives, this outright defiance was clearly a mirror of Grandpa's neglect. By assuming the helm, Papa abandoned his own childhood by taking the reigns of responsibility. This would forever dictate his reserved nature, his strict commands, and his desperate longing to be the perfect father.

Grandma managed to periodically break from her bouts of depression, and even ran a neighborhood children's health clinic from the garage. And slowly, the neighborhood became familiar, even comfortable with this outsider family.

Despite the occasional juvenile mockery of their curly hair or their dark skin, Papa, Freddy, Soli, and Connie adapted to the local customs, language, and food. Through friends and classmates, by the pattern of environment, and the elements of society, they became, inevitably, Filipino. For this was their world now, no longer new, no longer different. Young enough to adapt, they wanted to be accepted, sometimes overcompensating for lack of direction. America became just a word, not eliciting a deep nostalgia, but the Philippines bonded with something inside them. They could feel in the swell of their chests, the rich presentation of a definitive Filipino culture, like the sweet taste of pride. These spirited resources remained impeccable—a true testimony to the nexus of heritage. To reneg on responsibility to their newfound culture would cause disrespect, leaving them *walang hiya*, or without shame. Their Filipino spirit would be dry, empty with *untang ng loog*, a serious debt of honor. This is how they absorbed the very essence of the Philippines, no less from books, the passing pedestrian, the trusting classmate, the familiar neighbor, the hand of a stranger, or the whisper of a passing spirit. No longer strangers, now they could feel the ground beneath them, soft and fertile, almost gentle in response, like a ripple to a wave.

* * *

At age 21, Papa received his bachelor's degree in biology from the Ateneo de Manila University. It was then that Grandpa returned, like a reluctant spirit. After 12 years of absence, and with no real attachment left to his country or to his family, he ordered them to move back to America, promising again, that this would be the last move.

Determined to find the idyllic suburban anchor, Grandpa chose to buy a house in an all-White neighborhood of Queens, one of the boroughs of New York City.

Papa anticipated the move. He would be glad to distance himself from the nagging presence of the Catholic church and the embarrassment of their overly privileged class status. The memories of his childhood in America were but brief memories, catalogued and cross-referenced, a jumble of mostly youthful truths and feelings, and the occasional invention. As he prepared to leave, he already craved the verdant, shocking green of the trees and plants; the grand Manila sunsets, quivering through the evaporating ground moisture from afternoon rain showers; the gracefulness of the market-goers; the evening fiestas, the exuberance and bright colors of Christmas and New Year celebrations; the elegance and charm of dance parties; the call of the early-morning rice cake vendor; the laughter of people enjoying the evening breeze after a long hot day. How long would it take to soak in every inch of earth, building, flower, and face he had become accustomed to, lest he forget a detail. Does one ever *really* know a place? Is identity like a tent, a temporary shelter from all that surrounds us, and are the stakes in the ground there only to be removed? Who would he be outside of the Philippines?

# Four Walls and a Cellar

In a large working-class neighborhood in a northern German city called Hannover, the Jörgensen/Lippelt family was born, lived, and died. The legacy of their struggle was paramount, fused by the members of this strong but devastated community like so many others, in a country left in shambles and war-torn poverty.

Opa, Hermann Jörgensen, was a tall, muscular man with blond hair, bright blue eyes, and a Danish heritage. He belonged to a lineage of indentured servant refugees who escaped the oppressive and barren Danish countryside when the harvest failed once again, only to land in a country that would soon be embroiled in the calamities of two world wars. He was born in 1914 into poverty, at the inception of World War I, but had the strength and conviction to make a better future. He spoke little of his past, with his eyes always set on the present and the future.

He left school at the age of 13 and had secured an apprenticeship to become a cook. Two of his older brothers had been killed in the war and the apprenticeship didn't bring any income, so his father needed him to bring home money for the family. So at age 14, he moved to the countryside and worked as a farm boy where his hands grew muscular and he had no time for dreaming. Later he worked in a factory doing hard, manual work that compromised his health.

Oma, Anelise Lippels, was born in 1916, in the same apartment in which her mother and her grandmother grew up. She was short but strikingly beautiful with brown hair and blue eyes. The building was owned by the Jewish family on the fourth floor with whom Oma shared an intimate friendship. She also left school at the age of 13 and was expected to go no further. She was full of life and mischief, and had a belly full of laughter, and her vivaciousness would be the weapon against the hard times and uncertain future.

Tante Luise, Oma's aunt, also lived with the family. In fact, the apartment officially was in her name. She would never marry and spent the most of her life between the factory job, the apartment, and the community garden. Like most of the neighborhood, she stood at an assembly line, for hours at a stretch, and later suffered from severe varicose veins and a stiff back. It was at the Balsen Cookie factory where she made it to Vorarbeiterin, a team manager, and eventually retired at the age of 65. Despite her somewhat debilitating loneliness, she had an incredible amount of energy that she expended on cooking, cleaning, baking, gardening, and mending.

Their life along the cobbled streets might suggest a classic nobility, not of aristocracy, but of the age of pride and resourcefulness. Arched and carved moldings framing large apartment windows, dignified carriage coves leading to the rear of buildings, humble gas street lamps, and manicured parks were reminders of a heyday long gone.

From a distance, the sandwiched apartment buildings along Köhtner-holzweg and Limmerstrasse made for conformity. The sea of basic clothes, the black, hard-leathered shoes, the language, and the flow of dark green bicycles might have made it seem as if all the pedestrians were all alike. But in the long, lonely, hard winters blanketed in frozen snow and complicated by basic survival needs, each had their own way of coping.

The community was comprised of simple people, with no chance of leaving their familiar town. Some were eager to cross the ocean to America, and even Oma dreamed of different life. But there would be no traveling, no escape, and certainly no chance for anything more than an honest life and a strong family. They were firmly rooted in German soil.

Opa and Oma met at the *Gesungfurein*, a local singing club on Limmer Street, where once a week they escaped from the routine of factory work. Oma loved to sing, dance, and celebrate. She danced on tables and flirted with men, and her laughter could clear the smoke-filled rooms. Opa was attracted to Oma's infectious smile—she was a vision of hope and freedom, both of which he found he craved but couldn't grasp. Here, after a few glasses of the local beer and an earful of gossip, the group congregated to debate politics, striking the chord against the oppressive class structure and building hope for a socialist government. The future as they saw it would have to be in the hands of the people, the workers.

But the treatise after World War I had a devastating affect on the general atmosphere of a country already starved, and the now fascist, central government looked for scapegoats. Soon, all aspects of economic, cultural, and religious life were brought under Nazi party control, manipulated by sophisticated propaganda. Hitler promised an end to unemployment and a better life and began his mass genocide, ingraining the freakish hell of concentration camps that burned through the heart of the continent. At age 20, Opa was dragged from his wife and sent to the trenches in Russia where he served as a medical nurse.

The Jewish family's movements had been restricted so they relied heavily on Oma for food and supplies. They feared the moment the family would be taken to the camps like so many others had. That day eventually did come, and as the family was led down the wide staircase and hallway, their fear echoed through locked doors of the other apartments, like frantic whispers in a nightmare. Only the mother and one child would survive.

Mama, Marlis, was born in 1941, in the middle of Allied attacks. By her first birthday, the steady shrill of sirens and thundering roar of low flying bombers were etched permanently in her memory. The cellar was the makeshift bomb shelter, with only an small iron grated window that blinked in the sunlight with the passing of scurrying civilians and black, buckled marching boots. Here, in the damp, cold darkness, next to the box of coal, some bottled preserves, and a pile of potatoes, they would wait for the ground to stop shaking and the dust to stop raining from the floor above.

Only Tante Luise was capable of bringing an income, continuing to work at Balsen. At the end of each day, while being checked by the door guards, she thought only of her family, and risked being fired to bring home the occasional bag of smuggled crushed cookies or dough to make bread, cookies, or even rarer, chocolate. She also made friends with the butchers for the occasional gratuity, and begged for potatoes from friends in the countryside. If it weren't for this, she knew they would not survive the war.

On a good day, before the sirens whined, Mama would climb on the chair to watch the neighbors hurry across the streets, bartering their wares and food, clutching what could have been their last pail of potatoes or milk. There were no trees or gardens showcased in the frame of the window, only one tenth of the sky and the blackened building across the way, like a faded mirror image. This would always be her window, and even later, as an adult, her childhood memories would creep through, like old movies. The face of the buildings seemed grayer back then, layered with the soul of ashes that floated freely, a tribute to the war's dead.

One afternoon, as the sun painted a lasting impression on the horizon, an encroaching drone of airplanes clashed with the screeching air-raid sirens. The dissonance was deadened by an occasional heart-stopping, ground level thump in the distance. The thumps grew closer and louder, and Tante Luise clutched Mama and stroked her hair. They waited for Oma to usher her grandmother out the door, then rushed into the basement cellar. It was suddenly quiet except for the siren. A few muffled wails persisted in the distant, sending a passing feeling of relief that they were spared, and then guilt. Then, a piercing shriek of an airplane engine passed overhead, sending shivers up their spines. Their arms and hands locked, and their eyes closed to a tight wrinkle. When the bomb hit the building next door, they couldn't even hear their own screams. Well after the explosion, the world faded in again with the clambering of survivors, their cries seeping in with the dust through the closed basement window.

The next morning, Mama picked up her doll and climbed down the stairs to the main foyer. The doors were open, and outside, basking in the warm sun, were the remains of the next-door apartment building. One of the neighbors grabbed her before she ventured outside among the debris and the danger.

Sometimes there were peculiar men who appeared at the doorsteps of the neighbors. Occasionally Oma spent some time away from home, leaving Mama in the care of Tante Luise. She came home with food, and sometimes money, but her face didn't reflect this good news. Rather, she had become quiet and not like herself. Mama can remember a strange man in the apartment, helping her mother to dress her in the morning. She would learn later, that he was an American, and only one of thousands of western foreigners who reciprocated with food for comfort to many German women. There really hadn't been a choice, and with Oma's charm and wit, the assistance came more easily. The American eventually fell in love with her and offered to take her and Mama back to the United States.

Opa's whereabouts were unknown, and they hadn't heard from him in almost a year. Whenever they learned of a new wave of returnees, Oma and the family assembled on the street, straining to hear the officials announce the names of survivors, injured, and the dead. When there were arrivals, Opa was never in the group, and Oma's faith diminished. Her husband was special, a man of peace, forced into war created by a devil he despised. It was war or death to his family. Working in the MASH unit, he wasn't even required to carry a gun. God would surely pardon him and bring him back.

Within time, after the war came to a lilting halt, Germany managed to break free of the rubble. Factories re-opened and hired those who were capable—Tante Luise helped Oma obtain a job on the assembly line at Bahlsen. They worked from 6:30 a.m. to 4:00 p.m. Unable to afford the streetcar fares they rode their bicycles to work, even in the winter, when the sun rose long after they started work, and set well before they would punch out.

The stark reality of yet another war lost, the newly installed German government tightened its belt and set out to repair the country. Families with empty rooms were forced to open them to strangers. *Schreber-gärten*—affordable community gardens—were rented, where families could grow their own food. Horses were commissioned as cheap available meat, and their manure scraped from the streets was used as fertilizer in the gardens.

Mama would join Oma to go to the local store to have their metal pails filled with soup and milk. Her grandfather took the tobacco from discarded cigarette butts he collected, and rolled them into new paper. Because their tenement building had no bathrooms, only toilets, once a week the family took turns washing at the local public bath. But what Mama loved most was to tend to their garden. She played for hours in the humble, fenced-in heaven with its short wooden shack and vegetables and flowers.

* * *

Mama kneeled on the rocking chair backward and traced the ice flowers with her finger on her favorite window. The trail of condensed water rolled down the window, blurring the image of the pedestrians and horses on the street. Earlier, Oma braided her hair and told her that there would be an arrival later that afternoon, and that this time, Opa was sure to be coming home. They layered their homemade sweaters and braced themselves in thick woolen jackets and headed outside to *Limmerstrasse*. A crowd had already gathered, and the anticipation that cut through the bone-chilling wind prompted a weary silence.

A few women wailed and broke from the group, and the front of the crowd stirred. Oma's hand gripped tightly to Mama's. Then suddenly she picked her up and ran around to the left where she thought she saw a familiar face. Near the front of the returns stood a thin and sullen man, his face sunken, unshaved, and his clothes shabby and torn. I imagine him holding his head high and tossing his blond hair back with his hand as I always remembered him doing. Oma screamed. When he saw her, his eyes flashed open and broke a smile for the first time in 3 years. They grabbed each other and broke into tears, clenching their teeth. She then placed Mama in his arms and took a deep breath. "This is your daughter, my love, Marlis."

* * *

Opa rose very early in the mornings, and might have wondered how he had been spared. Even after obtaining a demanding job at Continental's rubber tire factory, he still relived his secret terrors whenever he let his mind wander. In the heavy, blue darkness of the early winter mornings, he would lift the iron lid off the living room stove and stoke the coal. By the time the room had warmed up, the family would be awake. His time alone by the stove was served by purging his unwelcome instincts leftover from dodging combat, and the cruel, confined terror during his 14 months in an American prisoner of war camp. He'd rather flush the debilitating memories than resort to growing old giving endless dinner table speeches.

\* \* \*

Most of the school buildings had been bombed, so the remaining buildings had to divide the girls and boys into 3-days-a-week turns. Mama excelled in her studies and spent her afternoons and evenings reading and drawing by herself. She read about distant lands, fascinating people, and strange, wild animals. In her early teens, she was convinced she would find romance in traveling to exotic lands, and imagined herself as an explorer. Her history lessons at school stopped before the introduction to the Nazi machine. Hitler was never mentioned in school, at home, or among families and friends, and she would only learn about this dark past of the old German government much later.

Mama's interests in foreigners were partly initiated by the intriguing stories of Oma's friend, Sophie, who had married a Black American soldier. On her yearly returns to Germany, Sophie would come for coffee with Oma who would sit and dream while Sophie spoke about the United States. Mama listened in and envied her "high life" on the ships that shuttled her across the Atlantic Ocean. Although most of the neighborhood disapproved of Sophie's choice for a husband, she herself, it turns out, was afraid to be seen with him. All the stares and criticisms were too much for her, and she confided in Oma, concocting ways she could leave him.

But Mama was hooked, itching to visit distant lands. Her uncle Otto, her mother's brother who lived with them for a while, tickled her imagination with stories of cowboys and wild Indians. Most of all, he whispered excitedly with wide eyes about America, with its streets paved with gold and fountains of chocolate. Eventually, Otto was arrested along with a friend of his, after being found as stowaways on board a ship ready to leave the dock.

Mama's best friend was Marianne, a spry, outgoing girl who fueled Mama's attraction to foreigners and distant lands. Mama's shyness was of no consequence to Marianne who was capable of drumming up enough interest from strangers for both of them. Together, they frequented the

*Haus der Jugend*, a community house that brought together young Germans and foreigners. The two of them were particularly captivated by the stories and songs of Africans and Indians, often continuing their discussions in parks and coffee shops. Around the corner from the apartment, they played with the gypsy children, and near the local hospital, they confided in some local Persian nurses who eagerly told them stories of their lives in the middle east. When they felt daring, they approached the U.S. Army headquarters where the soldiers were stationed. The soldiers made them laugh with their casual remarks and carefree style. A year later they befriended some Greek and Turkish students with whom they fantasized young teenage, romantic adventures.

According to their families and school friends, their interests and escapades were not only strange, but somewhat forbidden. Foreigners were avoided by most of the local public, and the family of gypsies lived in an old bombed-out school down the street was untouchable. The Italians were pegged as too loud and the Turks were treated as lower class. So, certainly Marianne's unreserved approach to soliciting the friendship of dark-skinned foreigners was to be kept in check.

Eventually Marianne dated a Nepalese boy. As girlfriend and boyfriend, they tagged along another Nepalese boy for Mama, and the four of them took walks through the Victory Gardens and along the Leine River. When Marianne's parents found out, there was a big uproar after which she was grounded. But even during the subsequent quiet of the afternoons, she and Mama challenged each other by compiling huge scrapbooks filled with cut-out pictures and articles about the lands that seemed only a page away.

\* \* \*

Mama was encouraged by one of her teachers to switch over to middle school, and possibly high school, but Opa was deadset against it. He saw no reason for the daughter of a working-class family to pursue a higher education. He hadn't even been to middle school, and he would consider it already an accomplishment for her to obtain basic office work. In his mind, as his father had made so clear to him, the pursuit of a dream was unrealistic and a waste of time. He could not afford for her to remain at home at age 14 without bringing in an income.

But Mama's grades were exceptional, and her teacher, despite the flak she received from her colleagues, persuaded Opa and Oma to give Mama a chance. Tante Luise had been earning a little extra as a *vorarbeiterin* and offered to pay the hefty 5-mark-a-month tuition. Opa gave in, and Mama went on to become only one of two girls in the neighborhood to finish middle school.

She excelled again in middle school, and spoke vaguely of becoming a fashion designer, and even inquired about art school. It was made clear to her, however, from all angles, that it was already a luxury for her to attend school, and that she should be happy to settle, at very best, with all Germany could offer her—the product of a reluctant lower class family.

She dreamed more and more about foreign cultures and distant places. In her dreams she would run far with nothing left behind but the confinement of the four walls that made her room. With the help of Sophie, they located an American in the United States who offered to correspond. He was 7 years older than Mama and was just entering graduate school.

The letters were at first infrequent, and Mama thought nothing much of it. But gradually, as she matured, their formal interests turned from cordial to emotional. The American's English was superb and he was obviously very well educated. This intrigued Mama even more, and she was surprised she could at least understand most of his gentle, illustrative prose. Finally, they exchanged photographs, and although they were 6,000 miles apart, they held the image of the stranger across the ocean, no longer attracted by words alone.

A year and a half later, the man from America suggested a trip to Germany. He would be on summer break from college, and could be there in a couple of months. Most of his friends at the college were Jewish, and they emphatically suggested he not set foot in Germany, lest he risk severe residual discrimination and the torment of a latent Nazi state. At this point, he had it coming from all sides anyway, what would make this any different? Besides, the woman who was his faithful pen pal seemed more real than any stereotype. All Germans couldn't possibly be bad.

It was a while before she would break the news to Oma, Opa, and Tante Luise, but by now she had graduated and was working as office assistant. In her mind she was an adult and could handle this situation on her own.

*   *   *

She had memorized his itinerary. She knew the train from the docks in Hamburg would arrive not a minute too late. Waiting next to the car her friend had driven, she leaned nervously on the opened passenger side door. Periodic breaks in the clouds allowed playful stretches of sun to travel over the tracks and caress her face. Steam whistled carelessly from the joints of the train engine as it slowed to a stop. *"What am I doing?"* she thought to herself, trying to resurface all the positive points of which Marianne had reassured her. *"I don't even know this man."*

She recognized him the second he appeared at the metal door. There was only one dark-skinned man, and as he disembarked from the train, he was handsome and everything she imagined. Even her friend Gudrun, after seeing a photograph of her pen pal asked if he had a brother. She raised her hand and gave a shy wave. Papa tells me he had spotted her instantly as the train came to a halt, and now when he looked at her, the sun had just crowned her head.

# 4
# Checkmate

Oma and Opa liked him right away. It took Tante Luise a little longer, but she eventually took to him as well. Their concern wasn't so much the color of his skin, but rather his class. Opa tightened his lips and Oma and Tante Luise stood with their arms akimbo. Here was man who was getting a master's degree and was interested in their daughter, whose parents didn't even have a bookshelf. And even though there was no mention of even a casual courtship between the two, it was obvious that the involved correspondence and the magic of their meeting was telling of what was to come. But the expectations had to be kept under wrap, and Mama tried to pass the foreigner off as just a friend. Besides, she was only 17 years old, and the thought of a formal relationship, even marriage, was out of the question. Papa floated cautiously into this predicament, struggling with the knowledge that even in the Philippines, this arranged meeting would inevitably lead to marriage.

Mama gave him a tour of Hannover, pointing out significant buildings and bombed-out landmarks. As she labored over her limited English, she was reminded of the times she and Marianne spent befriending foreigners with whom they could barely communicate. This time it was quite different, however, the man she walked with was here to see her. Suddenly she realized how much she had learned about the outside world, but had never fully expected reciprocated attention. She was confident, for once, that she was doing the right thing on her own.

But all the hope in the world couldn't block the hostile glances from strangers on the street and in the markets. Their obvious fondness for each other seemed like a threat. But to what? She had not calculated the effect that race would play in Papa's arrival, and there was no language, no support for her to protect her guest. The reactions had never been so obvious when she galavanted with Marianne. This new awareness scared

24

her, suddenly needing to dodge snide and venomous remarks, sharp whispers, and heads cocked back with judgmental eyes. And even though it wasn't long before they held hands, sealing their affection, they remained guarded. She learned from Papa the fine art of suppressed emotions. Once, an old man spit on them as he passed, bracing his frail body, his knuckles clenched white with anger. Mama turned around to yell at the old man, but Papa calmed her. "Just pretend it didn't happen," he said, keeping his eyes ahead of him. "We are above that." Several times they were spit at, pushed, or mocked. And sometimes when a stare or a comment was not intended to be hostile, Papa found himself reacting defensively against his own better judgment. But mostly he bottled up his anger, releasing it in unpredictable spurts, such became the raw routine of survival for him. And for Mama, the romanticism and idealism of being with a foreigner had faded into the reality of a Germany she had never imagined.

Along the rivers and parks and away from the bustling city, they grew fond of each other. Mama's English improved, now that she could speak regularly, and Papa picked up German quickly. His knowledge and kindness, and Mama's gentle observations and creative aspirations made his visit seem shorter than intended. He played out scenarios in his head, of waiting for this young woman to come of age. Was he good enough for her? How would he survive in this ocean of White faces and blue eyes? How would it affect her life, if he were to come back for her?

It was after Papa returned to the United States to continue graduate school, that Mama started to realize how much she had changed during his stay. From across the Atlantic, they continued their letters, and considered carefully their next move.

In 1958, just before he graduated, Papa was issued a draft notice. The Vietnam War was not only something he vehemently opposed, but he saw right through the naive politics of America's involvement in the conflict. Besides, his country had betrayed him, his mother, and all other minorities with its racist agenda, why should he support a war against a country most Americans didn't even know existed? Like many Blacks, he had been picked for an early group of battalions and was sure to serve on the front lines. For him this was yet another reason to cast away any remaining respect he had for a democracy that considered him disposable. He opted to leave, and without hesitation returned to Germany. Here he would be back in the arms of his pen pal, and away from the madness that was America.

He stayed with Oma's friends, a family named Stahmer, and looked for work during the days. With his background in biochemistry, he found a job as a chemical lab technician at Kali Chemi. There he made friends and was often invited to their houses for dinner and parties. Gradually, Papa's evaluation of Germany changed for the better, although he knew he had to stick to a routine. He knew that the more one kept on course, the duller the edges got, and in his case, the stares and whispers diminished into a blind spot. Most of his friends outside of work were Egyptian and Arab immigrants, many of whom expressed their frustrations with racism. Although he did confront these issues with his friends, it nevertheless brought back harrowing memories that he preferred to leave behind.

And for Mama, at her typewriter in front of the little office, she rarely heard a negative remark regarding her boyfriend. But silence, she had learned, can be layered with opinions and emotions.

Papa joined the crew at the *Gesungfurein*, where Mama, Oma, and Opa taught him the waltz and the words to drinking music. Oma's uncle once leaned over to Mama and nodded toward Papa who sat at the end of the room.

"*Are Amadio's teeth as white as yours?*" he asked.

"*No, of course not,*" Mama replied. She was always armed with a snide remark. "*His teeth are black.*"

Engulfed in cigarette smoke and holding a glass beer mug, Papa tried his best to adjust to this alien form of entertainment. The beat was different and the dances were restrictive-looking. As the chorus belted foreign lyrics and swayed to the three-step rhythm, he soaked in the image of bobbing beer mugs, the men tall and weighted around the middle, the women rotund and loud. And he wondered seriously, behind his smile, if he could get used to this. There were some things that one could easily adapt too, and there were others that clashed with a spirit deep inside one's bones.

But the tenderness of lifelong friendships that the Jörgensen family had, touched a spot of envy in him. The connectedness and respect, even in the middle of heated arguments, was as clear as the faces that carried the smiles and tears. Great grandparents, grandparents, uncles, aunts, cousins, and friends frequented each other's homes and shared banquets and coffee and cake regularly. Maybe surviving the war had reminded them that family was all that there really was.

It is a gradual process to come into a family, any kind of family, and Papa could connect with this all too well. He was almost uncomfortable with the reality of this household and community, and he was certain he had missed something very important growing up, something he would never be able to hold. He even wondered if he was good enough for such a family that might look less than curiously at the history of his fragmented heritage. He didn't even know where he belonged on the planet, let alone what street. He could taste the need for stability, like the sweet and sour tastes of desire.

And everywhere he went, he was reminded, in not so many words, that to be a foreign man, a dark foreign man in Germany was not only a difficult task, but a risky one. This won him the respect from the family he fell into. They confided in him and listened to his stories and ideas as if he were one of the clan. Even the occasional disapproving comment reflecting earlier doubts was quickly passed and disregarded.

On one unforgettable afternoon, the surviving Jewish mother and her son came to visit from their new home in Israel. They had come to pay respects to the friends in the building they once owned. The terrifying march down the stairs and the hallway, lead by the S.S. still echoed in their waking moments. Oma and Tante Luise remembered seeing the truck pull away from the apartment building, an image they tried to block from memory. Papa, along with the rest, broke into tears as the mother recounted the years in hell, separated from every member of the family, not knowing who had been killed and when she would be next.

\* \* \*

Papa observed with amusement, the delicateness of Mama's family—almost a dance, with unbroken roots, a wisdom, old and tested. But he kept his mental diary to himself. Like the relationship with his own father, Papa's communication with Opa was basically nonverbal. They chose to build their trust and bond through the game of chess. Both men had spent countless hours improving their game on opposite sides of the ocean. Now, from across the thick, wooden table in the living room, they sat in silence contemplating the next few moves. The living room clock ticked, casting a deep rhythmic spell, and the hour hand dragged the evening into night.

This particular evening, Papa's moves were unpolished, and he was having a hard time concentrating. Opa was well ahead, and was considering issuing a checkmate.

Papa pushed up his glasses up with his finger and stole a glance at Opa. "I would like to marry your daughter."

Opa kept his eye on the chessboard. He couldn't afford to lose his concentration, and for once, he was so close to beating Papa. He casually held his cigarette between his index and middle fingers and raised it to his mouth. After a long drag, he released the smoke toward the ceiling, made his move, and placed his elbows on the table to contemplate the next. He was going to win this match, and he could see the path clearly.

The clock chimed the passing hour and then the ticking resumed noticeably. A rush of thoughts filled Papa's head. *He doesn't want an*

*American to marry his daughter. Is it the color of my skin? Is he afraid I might take her daughter back to America?*

Opa broke the silence.

*"Amadio. You are an educated man, from a very different life, a different class. We are just simple, working people. We do not have the means you do, or the education you do. And, mainly, she is too young. I'm afraid you might not be happy with us because of this, and in the end, you might not be happy with Marlis. Please consider this carefully. It's not that we don't like you, because we are very fond of you."*

Relieved that the issue of race hadn't come up, Papa relaxed a bit. *"I love your daughter, and I believe she loves me. I may have a college education, but we are also very simple people, and I hope you recognize my humbleness."*

Opa nodded his head, broke an unmistakable but rare smile, then focused on the board.

*       *       *

As they began their wedding plans, Mama learned she was pregnant. They had been living in a small room off the kitchen in an acquaintance's apartment. They knew they had to move out soon, in preparation for the baby, so they saved every mark they could, skimping on resources. But then the lab laid off Papa and he had to again take a deep breath and start over.

Soon after Miguel was born at the end of November, Papa obtained a low-paying English teaching position at the Berlitz school in Krefeld, 5 hours away by car. Mama had quit her job, and took to caring for Miguel full time. She would be the first in the family to move from the neighborhood, let alone the city. Tante Luise cried and protested, for this was exactly what she feared.

They rented a studio apartment and barely made ends meet. They cut back on heat and even the smallest of luxuries. New friends from the school invited them to the movies or restaurants, to which they begrudgingly turned down the invitations. Without the family support that Mama had been used to, and without the income to hire a babysitter she became lonely and depressed.

Their predicament left them arguing. Papa's mood was often sour, as he struggled with the demand placed on him to provide better for his family. Mama's self-confidence weakened, battling with the realization that she was still too young and that her world had become a blur of phantom realities.

*       *       *

Ten months after moving to Krefeld, Papa received another draft letter from the U.S. government. This time if he didn't return, he would be in deep trouble. He had promised Mama's family that he would take care of their daughter, but without an option, he knew that it was time to return to America.

# 5

# Carrots?

Papa boarded the steamer and waved good-bye to Mama who held their 11-month-old baby in her arms. Next to her, Opa, Oma, and Tante Louise waved and threw kisses to the man who had changed their lives forever. To them he was a courageous, loving man who defied all conventional cultural logic in determining war enemies and racial inferiority. The ship negotiated the cramped mouth of the Elbe, skimmed by the dotted Frisian Islands and ventured out to the open skies of the North Atlantic Ocean.

Like his father, Papa was leaving the place that had become his home to look for a better life. He was returning to America to find work and then send for Mama and Miguel. His art career, never realized in Germany, was gone forever, and he hoped his country would be kinder to him now. In a few short weeks, he would set foot once again in the United States to claim the rights given to him by birth and passport.

He had bought the cheap freightliner ticket under the agreement that he would work on board as a hand. But, anxious about the future, he spent the 3 weeks doubled over, nursing an ulcer and unable to sleep. He knew that once he was back in the United States, he would have to explain why he didn't register for the draft before leaving for Germany 2 years earlier. Tension was escalating in Southeast Asia and civilians like him were a perfect pick for frontline duty.

After arriving in New York City, Papa relaxed, finally able to communicate free of language barriers, and he convinced himself that everything would proceed smoothly.

Grandpa's house hadn't changed much. There were a few more decorations and some new clear plastic armchair and couch covers. A pleasant shiver rose up his back, and he smiled at the familiarity of the streets, the bend of the backyard trees, the smell of a Filipino meal. It was good to be back with family. Immersed once again in the loud, infectious laughter of his sisters and brother-in-law, and an abundance of food, for a short while, he could pretend that he had never left Queens, in the heart New York City.

He received a call from Germany. Mama was pregnant again, and he would have to send for her soon. Some friends advised him to approach the draft board at once to appeal for dismissal. According to law, a father with two children could not be drafted. All he needed was a letter from Mama's doctor in Germany vouching for her. The longer he waited for the doctor's report, the closer he was to being sent to boot camp, and ultimately the front line.

He remained confident that his master's degree and writing skills would land him a well-paying job and when he wrote to Mama, he promised them good news soon. But each interview and subsequent letter of rejection made it clear that his services were not needed, that he was overqualified, or that his qualifications didn't match employers' needs. A familiar feeling of hopelessness and anger consumed him again and manifested itself in fits of rage.

Even after he received the official draft pardon, he settled in his makeshift room in the basement of the house. There Papa would escape the brutal battles of the day by reading late into the night. Despite external discouragements, Papa was determined to continue educating himself. As he had done in the Philippines, Papa satisfied his healthy appetite for literature by finishing several books a week. His letters to Mama renewed the memory of their years as pen pals.

He felt different now—lonelier. He wanted to hold tight the son he hardly knew. He missed his wife's smell, her smile, her gentle outlook on the world, and her optimistic, engaging bewilderment about life beyond the boundaries of northern Germany. He craved the physical and intellectual closeness he found with her. And he scorned the possibility of becoming like Grandpa who had been an absentee father and husband for most of his life. He looked for solace in the hope that just maybe their arrival would bring good luck and greater incentive to keep searching for a livable situation.

Finally after finding a few menial, temporary jobs, he sent for them. Grandma made enticing predictions of the wonderful life Papa, Mama, and Miguel would have. Aunt Soli, Uncle Gene, and Uncle Freddy knew, however, that things wouldn't be easy. Papa would have to find a place for his family to live, rents were not affordable in the better neighborhoods, and landlords were unwilling to rent to minorities. Having been married in Germany where there were no laws against interracial marriage didn't make things easier either. Racial tensions were on the rise in the United States and Mama and Papa weren't shy about public displays of their love for each other.

* * *

In the fall of 1961, Mama and Miguel arrived in the United States. Leaning against the metal railing, Mama held Miguel and combed his hair, feeling the salty mist from the ocean between her fingers. The infamous Statue of Liberty was still a speck on the horizon, lost in the wall of the skyline that was Manhattan. As their ship sailed into New York harbor, the statue rose up from the water, green and majestic, staring at Mama like an old friend. Mama had deep apprehensions toward life in America, and now, under the bronze arm raised at the sky, she was humbled, and was confident that somehow they had made the right choice.

Their arrival was celebrated in true Filipino form: Big dinners were held in their honor, followed by dancing and storytelling, each member clambering over others in excitement, exaggeration, and laughter. To her, the lavish meals, their dance moves and mannerisms seemed flamboyant. In Germany, Christianity dictated that body consciousness was evil. But here in America, the gyrations and the pumping bodies of her Filipino family would generally be considered devil-motivated. She chuckled out of nervousness and struggled to understand and reciprocate conversation—it had been hard enough to understand Papa, and now she had to negotiate the complex rhythm of slang and colloquialisms and a Filipino accent.

Miguel, now 1½ years old, was Grandpa and Grandma's second grandchild, (cousin Dino, Aunt Soli's son had been born 1 year earlier) and another boy at that. Grandpa was proud that his name would continue. Mama cared for Miguel in the attic bedroom, bending under the sloped walls, whispering and singing to him in German and English. Although the days got colder and shorter, Mama made sure she took Miguel out into the new world regularly, convinced that her friends back home were wrong about the dangers of America. Moving to a country that was an enemy not long ago concerned Mama, but gradually, her vivid memories of allied bombings in her neighborhood seemed as distant as the exotic lands to which she dreamed of traveling.

Papa's temper worsened as his search for a better job met with no success. This sometimes cost him the opportunities he did find. He let his frustrations out at Mama, yelling and pounding on the kitchen table as much in response to his job situation as the racial injustices he read about in the newspaper. Mama didn't protest his disposition. She prepared herself carefully before he arrived home each day, smiling, holding Miguel in her arms, and showing him her expanding womb. Papa believed Mama didn't understand—he didn't want her to understand his rage. He didn't intend to bring them thousands of miles to this alien country without fulfilling the assurances he had made. America, the land of plenty had become as empty as a broken promise.

He barely remained one step ahead of breaking. With no choice but to put his dignity on hold, and without Grandpa's knowledge, he considered accepting a job where he knew he would only sit idle at an empty desk at the front of some office. With no paper, no typewriter and no phone, Papa saw himself folding his hands and rested them on the shiny table, fighting apathy and filling a quota. He knew these companies wanted to hire him as a token Black man, for a job where he would have to bury his humiliation and allow his mind to wander. He had been in these situations before in which, when someone would approach him with a question or a concern, he could feel the eyes of generations of oppression undressing him. When it was quiet, he daydreamed of the paintings he would finish and display in a famous museum in another world and another time. But he could never again take such a job. Grandpa especially would see it as a disgrace to the family.

Eventually, with the help of some of Grandpa's acquaintances, Papa was hired by a small textile manufacturer as an assistant manager of operations. The days went by a little more quickly, as he wasn't so visible to the outside world. At this point he knew wouldn't be able to handle sheltering himself from real or perceived threats by strangers. When it became clear the job was another equal opportunity setup, he quit, much to the surprise of the owner. "You're lucky just to have a job! I was doing you a favor!" he was told.

Papa was back on the streets looking for work again. Often at interviews, the prospective employers were quite blunt about their intentions to hire him in order to fill a quota. They praised his exemplary skills and master's degree, calling it "a curious accomplishment." He walked away, thanking them for their time, then cursed himself all the way home. Money was running low and winter was just around the corner. He would have to borrow warm clothing for his family, but promised himself this would be the last winter his family would have to suffer through.

Mama wrote to Oma and Opa in Germany, assuring her family that everything was working out fine, and informed them that they would soon be grandparents again. With the help of family, they barely made rent. Meals were limited to rice, eggs, and oatmeal.

Spring arrived and Mama was due. On April 11, 1962, in a gray hospital in Brooklyn, New York, I was born. Mama wanted to call me Alexander, but Papa offered that a German name would be a nice balance to the Filipino name Miguel carried. So I was named Teja-José Manuel Arboleda.

Grandpa was overjoyed that another boy had been born into the family. Grandma was concerned, however, about my failing health. With her nurse's training, she recognized my symptom: passing food quickly without proper digestion. A doctor was rushed to the house and promptly gave me a life-saving injection. I would have died within the evening had Grandma not acted on her suspicion.

Having almost lost a grandchild, Grandma demanded that Miguel and I be baptized before something tragic happened. She firmly believed that we would go to hell if we were not blessed and made official members of the Catholic church. At first Papa refused, having decided years earlier to split from the church. His relinquishing his religion had been very difficult on the family, and this time Grandma's demand became a mission. Long ago, Grandpa had imposed Catholicism on his family to ensure the strict lifestyle he had been accustomed to in the Philippines. It was ironic that Grandma, who had dropped her own Baptist upbringing in order to comply with Grandpa's wishes, was insisting that Mama and Papa not tarnish the Arboleda name by giving the devil a chance to claim our souls. As a nurse, she had seen too many children die unbaptized.

One afternoon Mama took me to the pediatrician for a checkup. The doctor's waiting room was full of mothers and babies. White mothers and White babies—except for me. There was a curious woman making her rounds, socializing. She went from mother and baby to mother and baby, praising the beauty of the children and attempting to gain recognition from the other mothers for her own precious boy. Then she came upon me. She looked at me, looked at my mother, looked at me again, then again at my mother. "His skin complexion … it's very nice! How did you get him to be so … dark? Do you feed him plenty of carrots? See, I was reading somewhere that carrots improve skin complexion, add color you know!"

In a jolt of cultural overcompensation, and armed with a box full of facetious remarks, Mama kicked into high gear with an American come-back, "Why, yes! Yes … plenty of carrots! Carrot juice, carrot cake, carrot pie … in fact the doctor was thinking of putting him on a carrot IV!"

Like most things that come in clusters, Mama was suddenly aware of the comments of passers-by on the street: "He's quite an interesting looking child!"; "Oh, that's darling of you to be taking your neighbor's kid for a walk!"; "You feed him plenty of carrots, huh!?" It became more and more apparent to Mama that Miguel's and my dark complexions next to her very fair skin was odd to those who didn't know that she was married to a Black man. Finally, when she began to overhear comments about her "dirty Negro children," she began to wonder if the environment in New York had become damaging for us. The few times Papa and Mama went out in public together with Miguel and I, usually to go window shopping in Manhattan, they returned home psychologically beaten by the many stares and comments they had tried to ignore.

Eventually, it had become too difficult to live by the strict rules of Grandpa and Grandma's household, so Papa decided that with minimal savings, they had just enough money to rent an apartment of their own. They found a small one-bedroom unit in a building that was part of a low-income neighborhood to the north of Queens Boulevard. Miguel and I were shuffled from one babysitter to another during the day while Mama looked for part-time work. The conservative atmosphere of the new neighborhood made life difficult for a mixed couple like Mama and Papa. The neighbors rarely acknowledged Papa, diverting their eyes and attention elsewhere when he passed by. The homemakers avoided Mama as well, making comments about her Negro husband when they spotted her shopping in the local stores. Their only friends were a Japanese couple, Iwane and Hisako Susumu, who lived in the same building.

The Susumus had also found that living in America as non-White foreigners was more difficult than they had ever imagined. At the time, most Japanese living in the area were lower middle class, blue-collar working immigrants who brought their families over from their homeland like most other immigrant ethnic groups. Once in America, they soon discovered that the promise of a better life was as unreliable as dreams can be.

Finally, Mama found a part-time sales clerk job at the Gertz department store. Convinced she would fit right in as a department store clerk, Mama proudly wore her blue uniform with starched white gloves. During lunch at the department store on one of Mama's first days, her co-workers started a seemingly innocent, friendly interrogation.

"So, do you like America?" one of the sales clerks asked.

"Yes, I enjoy it very much." Mama was proud of her English.

"Your English is very good. Are you married?" another woman asked.

"Do you have children?" yet another co-worker chimed in.

"Is your husband American?" the first sales clerk inquired, moving closer to her, studying her German accent.

Mama was very taken in by the forward friendliness they displayed. She began to think that maybe Americans weren't quite so cold after all. She smiled as she fancied all the friends she would finally make. "Yes, he's American." The others smiled in response. "He's part Black and part Filipino."

Their smiles dropped. One of them started to move away as the first clerk responded. "He's *Black*? How could you marry someone who's Black?" Her voice had become accusatory as she squinted and winced. "How could you do that!? How could you marry a Negro?"

One co-worker came from behind and looked at Mama wide-eyed. "Do you ... have children?"

Mama, feeling violated, was torn between speaking her mind and going against Papa's wishes to keep this kind of information off-limits. Finally, she straightened her back and looked up instead of fidgeting with her purse. "Yes, my husband and I have two wonderful baby boys." The others looked at each other, and some shook their heads. In less than 2 minutes she made and lost a fistful of friends.

Mama didn't want to tell Papa about her confrontation at work, but felt she had to. She wanted him to know that she could understand his pain.

Papa didn't know what to say when she told him. But what could he do? What control did he have over any of this? People would just see him as Black even though nothing was more certain to him than his Filipino identity. And damn if is family would always be seen as some societal anomaly. He looked at Mama and then dropped his head.

"Did they ask about he children, too?"

"You'd think they just saw a monster when I told them."

"From the time I leave for work in the morning until the minute I get home...." Papa could feel a part of himself dying, ashamed of his pain and helplessness. "Matters are just going to get worse."

A neighbor told them about a nearby attractive, developed neighborhood called Parkway Village off Queens Boulevard. Some friends had recently moved there and raved about the politically liberal and culturally diverse neighborhood. So, at the end of 1962, we moved to the village, and into an apartment module in a string of two-story buildings that formed a series of circular neighborhoods.

Among our immediate neighbors were two other mixed couples with children, like our next door neighbors, Paul who was Black and Judy Bristol who was White, and their two daughters who were the same age as Miguel and I. There were two Japanese families, a marijuana-smoking hippie Jewish family, a demonstrative Italian household, a proud Russian family, a quiet Indian couple, an obnoxious Australian couple, a childless, laidback White artist couple, and an Australian family with a terrorizing, overweight kid named Butch.

The apartment was more than Mama and Papa could afford, and the money situation was still the cause of most of their anxiety. By the spring of 1963 Papa and Mama felt that shuffling us between babysitters they couldn't afford, juggling work, and caring for us had become too much of a strain. After figuring that Mama would take a full-time job, they decided that Miguel and I should temporarily live in Germany with Mama's family, so that summer, Mama, Miguel, and I flew back to Hannover, then Mama returned by herself to the United States.

Once again, Papa felt his family fragmented by conditions outside of his control, and he promised it would never happen again.

# 6

# Plastic Armies

Although I can't remember, returning to America must have been odd for me. It had been 1½ years, a lifetime, settled comfortably in Hannover, away from Mama and Papa, only to be torn away again. These dramatic transitions set the tone for the rest of my life. And these many departures and returns would continue to be equally as jarring. Like stepping off a ship from a long voyage at sea, the world would seem to sway, and my feet would wobble curiously.

I wasn't even really aware we were in America, at least, it probably didn't really make a difference *where* I was, only *with whom* I was. Papa and Mama were almost like strangers. But the softness of Mama's hand and her gentle voice, and the smell of Papa's neck and his laugh was almost too much to bear at first, the connection between time and place, still, a foreign dilemma.

"I missed you so much, both of you." Mama grabbed me, cried, and held me tight. "We will never let you go again, we promise, okay? We missed you both so much."

Tante Luise was always close by, familiar and comforting. I reached for her desperately, the face and figure that had become so familiar and available. I have vague memories of how the tears dried on my cheeks and itched as she held me.

"*It will take time, Marlis, it will take time,*" she would tell Mama. I would never know how jealous she was now that she had, even if only for a brief moment in her life, her own children.

But Mama continued to cry, wondering if they had done the right thing. There was no way she could ever capture some of the most important periods of our lives. But we *were* German, now, in fact, at this point more than anything, and that was something with which she could live.

*"Did you miss me? I bet you missed Papa too."* Mama would ask, switching to German. *"Did you eat a lot of nice food? Did you have fun?"*

As Grandpa drove us from the airport, trees and buildings flashed by in the pale light of late autumn sky, creating an almost permanent brown haze. He steered and judgmentally peered down the road through his thick glasses, whispering curses at indecisive drivers ahead of us. He always drove with his right hand pressed down on the plastic red seat, sometimes clutching a paper note or a nail clipper. This obscure visual reminder reassured me that I had returned.

At Grandpa and Grandma's home, the family showered us with kisses and food, spoke loudly, laughed heartily, and screamed with excitement. I had become used to the relative quiet, reserved nature of my German relatives, the most raucous being a team of beer drinkers singing to a cranked up jukebox blaring German marching music.

The air was a little different, as was the water, and everyone spoke in English. It wasn't strange, however, like the adults would say: "It's strange being back" or "It'll be strange to be there again." For me, a shift in location will always be like walking into a dark, new room, and groping for the light switch.

In the mornings, as Papa and Mama got ready to rush off to work, I clung desperately to Tante Luise. With her we spoke only German, and spent most of our time in the yard or in the house. Tante Luise rarely left the neighborhood and didn't drive. She missed the streetcars and public transportation in Hannover. She even missed the few friends she did have back home. She simply nodded to neighbors, emitting a friendly little grunt, and always made sure her thick, black, hard-leathered shoes were shiny, and her long, loose-fitting dresses hung neatly. Here in America she was isolated, even shunned by some of the local boys on occasion, carrying the weight of Germany's horrific past, like a metal shield through the neighborhood. Miguel and I were like her own children, and she would protect us and make us proud. And although this was her way of surviving the next 12 months, she would tell us that her time in New York was one the highlights of her life.

As the summer approached, the severity of the winter, although nothing compared to the winters in northern Germany, was almost forgotten. Soon a neighbor would pull out a lawn mower or hedge clipper, and another would scrape last year's remnants off a barbecue grill. Windows were left open during the day, and curtains billowed freely in casual spring breezes. Somehow people turned nicer when the weather eased up—maybe that's why I always remember the winters to be so long.

Papa argued less, and he and Mama even held hands more often. There were Saturdays and Sundays where they did nothing but stay home;

Mama would make pancakes and Papa would scramble eggs while Tante Luise got us ready for breakfast. The smell of morning coffee brewing and the crisp waft of bacon frying reminded me bluntly that I was no longer in Hannover. We paraded the apartment in pajamas, Papa's face covered with stubble and Mama, as she would put it, not yet "made up." Occasionally, a neighbor would stop by, unannounced, with a story or a plate of food. This is how we were acquainted, and the English I heard became familiar. In the months to follow, I would speak more English than German, sometimes to the frustration of Tante Luise. She had a habit of reminding me years later that she loved when we spoke German with her as children, and that she wished we would have returned with her to Hannover.

That summer, Oma and Opa came to visit. Oma had never been outside of Germany, and Opa was intrigued, standing on territory of the country he had been forced to see as an enemy. But through the 33 years I knew him, he only spoke positively about Americans during the war. This was his way of protecting us from his true feelings about foreigners and how the war scarred him. We learned later, just before he died, that in fact the Americans treated him like an animal in the prison camps. The brutality he suffered would never leave his mind, always with him like a painful, growing secret.

America was indeed a strange country to them—all they knew was either what the news reported or gossip. In America, no one took naps, and there was rarely any silence. New York City in particular was like a 24-hour bowling alley, with neon lights flashing to swing and rock and roll music. Here, in what was called the *new world*, the young people were casual and outwardly free. Women swayed in tight jeans with flaring bottoms, with midriffs exposed, and men swaggered with long, gangly hair and large, amber sunglasses. Even Hitler's commissioned Volkswagen bug had become a symbol of freedom, ordained with bright stick-on flowers and peace signs. Across the yard were American-Jewish and Polish-Jewish neighbors, seemingly inattentive to the terror that had reigned on their people only a generation before.

But most of all, they wondered how their daughter had adapted, and worried that she wasn't being accepted. They were curious as to how, in America, their daughter was capable of transcending the class issue, when in Germany, as a child she could only be expected to obtain a job in a factory at best. They did know, however, that there was a terrible problem: even here, in the trenches of a burgeoning free-for-all lifestyle, was the fact that she was married to a dark-skinned man. This was America's problem.

But what a parade we made! A Black man, a White woman, two "something" kids, and three German adults, all speaking a mixture of

German and English, making heads turn and ears perk up. Curiosity seemingly followed us like a swarm of bees too temperamental to be shooed away.

In a restaurant overlooking Mystic Seaport in Connecticut, the five of us settled for a late lunch after a tour of the ships—"An emblem of our conquering, racist past," Papa had said, although I was still too young to understand the inference. A older White couple at the neighboring table eyed Miguel and I intently, and offered us smiles and encouraging words. Opa took this to be only friendly gestures—he had hope yet, for America.

The couple walked over after they finished their coffee. "I'm sorry to keep staring, but what beautiful children you have" the man said.

Papa translated the conversation into German for the others, who smiled accordingly.

The woman leaned down and patted my head. "Really wonderful little ones. We haven't been able to have children." The others made grave faces, understanding the implications.

"We were wondering," the man continued, "if we could buy them."

"You could always have more." The woman leaned down to touch Miguel.

Tante Luise, shocked by Papa's translation, shot up and scolded the couple, her voice cracking and her finger shaking. Mama reverted to German also, and complained to Papa. Papa pulled us away from the couple, his eyes darting with anger. Opa and Oma were now sure that something was deeply awry in their daughter's adopted country.

* * *

It wasn't until long after Oma and Opa left, then eventually Tante Luise, that my attachment to their presence had finally waned. With their absence, my speech had turned almost solely to English and without a German accent. The few memories of my life in Germany were revived with the occasional care package from Hannover, filled with cookies, chocolates, socks, underwear. Once, for Christmas, Miguel and I received *lederhosen*, traditional leather shorts with straps, accompanied with green knee-high socks with tassels. With pride, Miguel and I wore these outfits, imagining ourselves as handsome and proud as our uncles marching with their trusty hunting rifles in the annual *Shützen Fest* down the length of *Limmerstrasse*.

But some of the neighborhood kids didn't see it that way. All they knew was *Hogan's Heroes* and other stereotypical German-bashing television shows. To them we were easy targets—we dressed differently and spoke German—the symbol of a lampooned group of people, prime for ridicule.

We didn't even play war games, or Cowboys and Indians. We were pompous, Indian-loving, Nazi wimps for all they cared.

"Heil Hitler!" Butch the Australian kid would yell toward us, clutching his decked-out G.I. Joe dolls. "You wanna play? You be the Germans, and we'll be the good guys! Heil Hitler!" He motioned to his entourage to follow, like a true brainwashed officer. His fat thighs rubbed together as he walked toward us, squinting his light blue eyes in the sun.

Butch became ruthless, upset that we didn't stick up for ourselves. He even beat me up one afternoon, for refusing to play the bad guy. "You're not American, you're a foreigner!" he yelled. Papa emerged from the apartment, picked him up by the shirt collar and dragged him along the concrete walkway to his apartment, then deposited him on the front steps. Papa would rid the neighborhood of bullies single-handedly if he had to.

Papa had never let us accumulate plastic guns or let us watch war movies. He hated John Wayne with a passion and saw no reason for us to practice the art of pretend killing. "John Wayne is a racist," he would say. "He always wins and the Indians always lose, even though he is the bad one." He was clear about many things he saw. He huffed when Bob Hope adorned fake buck-teeth and knocked his forehead while bowing to the sound of a Chinese gong. His knuckles cracked under his tightening fists when White men painted their faces Black and jumped around, cracking their voices with their eyes bugged and mouths wide open in perpetual surprise. He hated Tarzan as a White man who tamed the jungle. He detested that Friday was a willing slave to Robinson Cruso. He scorned Elvis for stealing his moves and music from Black artists. He protested that the Japanese were always depicted as short, slit-eyed, and cunning; his relatives in the Philippines lived in trees; all Germans were Nazis; lazy, fat-lipped Negroes wouldn't amount to much; wild, intoxicated Indians were savages; and cold-hearted Russians were evil because they wanted to kill us all. How simple it all really was for Hollywood's producers—no proof, no facts, no guilt. Behind the curtain of certainty, these things, he knew, would haunt America for life.

But outside, the circular, grassy courtyard with its low, lumber fence had become the anchor for the neighborhood. Here, we learned of the good and the bad in life, the shortcomings and rewards of living in a community, a sustainable community, no matter what the differences were. In the summer it was a campground with barbecue banquets. In the winter it was a snow sculpture museum and angel-making paradise. We gained friends and respect, and slowly, we gained a home.

# 7
# Old Fence, New Paint

Mama dressed me on my first day of school. I was proud of my new clothes—my first pair of dress shoes with heels and my first pair of bell-bottomed jeans. The shoes felt a little tight, but they shined just like new shoes should. I studied Papa, dressed in a suit with a tie and his own black shiny shoes. He always shined his shoes meticulously, with a clean cloth, creamy shoe polish, and spittle. I looked down at my shoes, tied tight like Grandpa tied them for church on Sundays. I studied the ends of my pant legs. They met the lips of my shoes with only a hint of a bend. I felt, for a moment, like I was a grown-up and on my way to work.

"Papa corrects books at American Heritage now. And I used to be a secretary at the television station, NBC." Mama had explained this to me several times, but I was still trying to grasp the concept of why a person would be correcting books. I had seen secretaries before—they were all women, and they sat up straight at their desks and they wore eyeglasses and their hair puffed-out and curled at the ends. Their fingernails tapped the keys of their typewriters, creating rhythmic clicking sounds. But I had never seen a book-corrector. So every time I saw a man wearing a suit, carrying a briefcase, I was sure he was off to correct books somewhere. An awful number of books with mistakes in them were out there floating around! Suddenly, the world was made up of secretaries, book-correctors, and mailmen. Now in my own little suit, I thought I would go off to school to learn how to do the same, just like Papa, and come home upset, just like Papa.

When I was much older, I would learn that specifically, Papa had been a lexicographer for the *American Heritage Dictionary*, helping to define scientific language for the next edition. Mama worked for WNBC on the fourth floor, in the library. One afternoon, the tall and loud sidekick from a famous late-night talk show leaned up against Mama's desk and pointed to a newspaper photograph and article featuring a long line of dark-skinned people waiting to enter an unemployment office.

"Those Blacks are so damn lazy," he said, shaking his head.

"Why do you say that?" Mama replied.

"Look at them just standing there," he said, then laughed like a drunken Santa Claus, from the pit of his stomach like I had seen him do on television.

"Well, I think you're wrong."

"How am I wrong?"

"I'm married to a man who's half-Black."

He raised his eyebrows and cleared his throat. Mama half expected one of his standard comebacks, but he left her desk without a word.

\* \* \*

The climate in New York was changing rapidly, and a strange energy filled with confusion incubated in our neighborhood. Dr. King's assassination in April, coupled with escalating deaths of American soldiers in Asia, lead to protests, riots, and sit-ins. These had become daily events, working their way around the country. Television images of thousands of people marching on Washington, DC; riots in Newark, New Jersey and Chicago, Illinois; and the devastating race riots in Detroit, Michigan were the foreshadowing of events that would follow. It was also around this time that New York City began experiencing a surge in anti-war demonstrations.

Racial tension became as ugly as politics, dividing the country over proposed legislation that would enforce integration by ordering the busing of students to different school systems. On many afternoons and weekends, Papa and Mama bundled up Miguel and I and stood outside for hours campaigning to end the war and to support the mandate for busing within the region. Some of our neighbors were ashamed of Papa and Mama for their support of forced integration. Most, however, showed their concern by marching alongside us, making signs and obtaining signatures for petitions. Many neighborhoods began splitting over these issues, new enemies were made and there was talk among the teachers of going on strike.

\* \* \*

A big yellow school bus was scheduled to pick up Miguel and I in a half-hour to take us to PS 117. After pleading with Mama, I had permission to open a new box of corn flakes. I reached all the way in looking for the prize, crushing half the flakes in the process. My heart was set on the Winnie the Pooh spoon-attachment doll that never seemed to be in any of the boxes, yet was always featured on the front and side panels. I got another Christopher Robin, although this time he was green. Then I heard Papa start up our white Volkswagen bug outside. He always came back inside for another sip of coffee while the car warmed up.

I stood in the pantry holding up a bottle of Flinstones vitamins, looking for a Dino. "Mama?"

"What is it, dear?" she asked as she kneeled down to help me open the bottle.

"I don't wanna go." Flashes of anxiety weakened my knees as I thought about big classrooms, new faces, and new teachers. I stood up and began fidgeting with the edge of the counter. I had to go to the bathroom again—my nerves had already sent me to the bathroom twice that morning. Papa ran into the kitchen and gave Mama a kiss. He reached down for me and gave me a hug.

"Bye! Have a good time in school! You're a big man now—be good!" With that he raced to the car. Through the window I watched him speed away.

Mama tried to comfort me. "You don't want to go to school? You'll meet so many other nice kids there. You'll see. You'll make a lot of nice friends. I think you'll really like it."

I heard the bus rounding the corner. My intestines loosened and my legs curled. Mama pulled my jacket from the closet and wrapped it around me. Then she handed me my Batman lunchbox and put her warm hand on the back of my neck. "You'll tell me all about your day when you come home, okay? Now let's get to the bus before it leaves without you!"

The next thing I knew I was sitting next to a girl at the back of the bus. I almost forgot about Mama until I saw her waving good-bye as we drove away. The girl next to me didn't look up from her lunch pail and started to cry.

By the time we pulled up to the school building, I was so desperate to get to the bathroom that my legs were shaking uncontrollably. Seeing all the other kids lined up outside made me realize it would be a while before I could get to the bathroom. As soon as I descended the stairs of the bus, the man who helped us down stopped me. "Are you okay?" My knees locked as I looked toward the building. He took my hand and led me inside, past the other kids and to the bathroom. The big hallways smelled of old radiator steam. I grew smaller as the sound of hundreds of kids echoed from around the corners. The bathroom was empty and all of a sudden I didn't have to go anymore.

In the classroom, we were seated alphabetically, so I was in the first row. As Mrs. Davidson introduced herself, I looked around the room and recognized a couple of kids I had seen around my neighborhood. Finally, Mrs. Davidson asked each of us to introduce ourselves to the class. I dreaded the moment I would have to open my mouth and began to cry. When it was my turn, I stared at Mrs. Davidson and froze. She smiled at me and looked at her pad. "Boys and girls, this is ... Teh ... Teija ... T.J. Abo ... Abode ... Arbleedah." A couple of the kids behind me laughed nervously.

"*Teya* Arboleda," I corrected her, turning my red pencil case over on itself with one hand and wiping the sticky tears from my chin with the other. One boy behind me tried in vain to repeat my name and made a comment on how stupid it sounded. I listened to the other kids' names, and thought many of them were also pretty funny-sounding. The girl whose name got the biggest laugh out of the class was Andrea Slobo-donkin. She was a cute girl who was proud to mention she was born in Yugoslavia and had come to the United States only a few years before. I liked her immediately.

From there, Mrs. Davidson herded us to the gymnasium. We sat on cold, gray metal chairs as the principal and his staff stood next to the flag on the stage and introduced themselves over a microphone. Their voices reverberated, doubled, and tripled, giving no more color to the dull gray support beams under the ceiling. I spotted Andrea a few rows back and wondered if she was sad from being laughed at. I looked to the rear of the room and noticed a bunch of older kids laughing, making noises, and throwing balls of paper at each other. From the sidelines, teachers tried to quiet them down. One of the kids was hauled off by a teacher who grabbed his ear and pulled him through one of the side doors. Laughter broke out and one teacher raised a large wooden ruler, ordering everyone to pipe down.

The principal asked us to stand and a group of students and some teachers behind him began to sing. I recognized the music when I noticed some of my classmates and all the teachers had their right hand on their chest. I had seen crowds of people on television sing this song before the boxing matches that Papa didn't like us to watch. The whole gymnasium swelled with singing, which was louder toward the back where the older kids sat. Mrs. Davidson was a good singer, so I watched her and tried pretending to sing for fear of being laughed at again. I had no idea what the lyrics were and felt so embarrassed and scared that I had already let down my teacher and the rest of the class.

Back in the classroom, Mrs. Davidson picked up her long wooden pointer and tapped on the display of letters above the blackboard. She moved her pointer from left to right, stopping briefly at each letter. "Repeat after me: A, apple. B, boy. C, candy. D, dog ... " Papa and Mama had already started teaching me the alphabet, and I remembered that *Teja* had a German spelling where the "j" is pronounced like a "y." When we got to the letter "j," I whispered to myself, "J, Te-*ja*."

Mama waited for me at the corner where the bus dropped us off. She kneeled down, took my lunchbox and held my hand. "How was school? Did you make any friends?"

"It was okay." I looked around for Andrea and then remembered she had gotten off a few stops before. I wanted to tell Mama that I didn't like my name. I had thought about it every time the teacher called on my classmates by name. I could still hear some of the kids laughing each time she mispronounced mine.

Mama had milk and cookies waiting for me every day when I came home from school. She sometimes sat in front of the television with Miguel and I as we snacked and watched cartoons. When evening rolled around, Papa came home, quiet and stern as usual and we knew not to bother him. At dinner he complained about his day. Not about his actual work, but things that happened on the way to the office, in the hallways, during lunch.

One evening after dinner, Papa found us watching a cowboy and Indian movie. His face crinkled up when he saw John Wayne sitting on a horse next to a pile of Indians he had single-handedly massacred. His voice got louder as he lectured us about racist TV shows. After he grew tired of yelling, he apologized to Mama and hugged her. When they started kissing, I looked away, embarrassed to be caught staring.

In bed that night, I lay on my stomach looking out the window at the big willow tree. Its long, graceful branches rolled to the rhythm of the breeze. The window was open slightly, so I could hear the leaves clapping against each other softly, maybe even for me. Then I thought about the next day at school. I dreaded my classmates laughing at my name. I imagined Andrea Slobodonkin was sitting next to me, smiling. I pulled the covers over my head and chuckled because her name did sound funny. Then I curled myself up and fell asleep.

As the weeks passed by, I became more comfortable with school. I made a few friends: Andrea became my best friend, and one boy I liked, David, sat a few seats over from me, but was usually very quiet. He spoke to me but none of the others. Some of the kids taunted him and excluded him during group activities, matter-of-factly claiming that their parents didn't want them to play with "the Negro kids." David's serious expression reminded me of photographs of Papa as a kid.

One afternoon we were asked to draw a crayon-colored picture of our family. We were each given a sheet of white paper. On my sheet of paper I drew a house with a chimney, Miguel, Papa, and Mama and me in the middle. The house I drew was made of red brick, the smoke from the chimney, black. The sky was a squiggly light blue with straggly white clouds and the jeans I wore were dark blue. I colored Mama in with Crayola's choice of "skin color," Miguel and I were "burnt orange," and Papa was "brown." Carl, sitting next to me peeked at my drawing and warned me, "You're not supposed to use brown for the skin." I studied my picture and then looked at his. All five members of his family were the color of my mother. "Is your Daddy Black?" Carl asked. I thought about the word "Black," and stared at my picture again. "Your daddy's Black," he concluded, and went back to drawing the brown dog in his yard.

That afternoon when I got home, before having my milk and cookies, I sat down next to Mama at the kitchen counter and placed my arm next to hers.

"I wish I was your skin color ... ."

Mama's face changed, and there was a significant pause before she spoke. Suddenly I felt I had said something terribly wrong. "Teja ... you're very beautiful the way you are! I wish I had *your* color skin, hair and eyes. You have beautiful dark brown eyes and golden skin and very nice dark hair. Besides, why do you think I lie out in the sun?" She knew that I was beginning to understand the concept of race for the first time, and there was nothing she could do to shield me. I would find out only as an adult, that although he was always darker than I was, Miguel had never approached her with these concerns.

Early that October, during one of our regular weekend get-togethers at Grandpa and Grandma's house, Miguel, cousin Dino, and I went to play around the neighborhood while the grown-ups settled in for the afternoon. We ran and kicked up layers of dried fallen leaves and dove into the piles, laughing hysterically, choking from the powdery dust. We finally ending up in the backyard of one of the last remaining White families in the neighborhood. A man leaned out the window of the house, holding a rifle, aiming it at us. "Get outa my yard ya goddam niggers!" he yelled. I saw his face shake and turn red as I scrambled onto my feet. "Get out or I'll set the dogs out!"

I spotted two dogs snarling at us, tied to the handrails on the back entrance staircase. Miguel struggled out of a nest of leaves and began to run to the opposite side of the yard. Dino and I followed. As the neighbor stumbled down the steps past the dogs, yelling and shaking his rifle, we tore out of that backyard so fast it practically drained most of my color.

When Grandpa found out what had happened, he and Papa exploded into tirades.

"I'll beat the living shit out of him!" Papa shouted, as he frantically searched for a loose brick. Grandpa dashed inside to get his own rifle.

Papa rolled up his sleeves up and checked his glasses. "Which one is he, the blue house?"

Grandpa emerged from the house with his rifle. Papa grinded some large rocks in his hand. "The goddamn neighborhood is becoming one big war zone anyway, so what difference would a little more bloodshed make!" Uncle Gene and Uncle Freddy grabbed Papa and Grandpa, fighting to hold them back.

That evening, Papa sat in his parents living room, looking for answers hidden in his oil paintings that hung on the wall, and thought of how all he wanted was for the rage and hate to stop.

* * *

In the shadow of Manhattan skyscrapers, Grandpa's short stature was more pronounced than ever. He was compelled to stand straighter, demanding respect even as he was relegated to buying shoes in the boy's department at Macy's. And he never lost his strong Filipino accent or his anger. When his patience was tried, he was never afraid to chastise us: "Conpoundit, guards dey meet! Acting like pools! You don try my pehshients!" Then he would fall silent again, still commanding us with his grunts as he watched his favorite pro-wrestlers on his 4-foot high, carved-cherrywood television set. Grandpa rarely spoke without strong emotion. And he was angry often. With each fading layer of memories of the Philippines, his homesickness became more unmanageable.

Catholicism was forced onto the Filipinos along with their names—one legacy Grandpa carried well. On Sunday mornings he spot-checked me before church, inspecting my fingernails for mud and my collar for dirt rings. He straightened my tie until my pleas for him to stop made me sound like a munchkin. He spit on his hands to flatten my hair and wipe jam from my cheeks. The final and most painful procedure was his tying of my shoe laces. He spoke even before he looked into my eyes, "You look soo rediculus! You don go to cherch looking so sloppi! You mus tie your shoos tite! You don go to church looking so stupid!" With his thick-muscled hands he placed my right foot between his knees, the ends of the shoelaces in each hand. First he pulled them toward himself, bringing every millimeter of the black leather lapels over the tongue. Curling the lace around, he pulled up again, overlapping the lapels, squeezing the veins on the top of my feet. While he finished the knot, he ordered me to show no pain. He wanted us to look good for God, and he needed us to be the best citizens on the block.

Grandpa's attempts to be accepted as a perfect American were in our opinion, sensational. To him, American cars were more like wild horses than necessary utilities. His cars had left so many visible reminders on tree trunks, fences, neighbors' cars, and school buses that his insurance company refused to increase his coverage. Eventually Papa and his siblings were forced to keep an open escrow account to bribe the injured victims of the many accidents Grandpa caused or *would* cause. Luckily, Uncle Gene, a used car salesman, could always provide another automobile for Grandpa to drive. Still, for Grandpa, as long as his tie was straight, his suit pressed, and shoes tight, he was, in God's eyes, acceptable.

On barbecue days, meat was king. Grandpa would haul sides of cow from the Coast Guard commissary to the backyard, light the grills, and gorge the family with another feast. The portions of spareribs, steak, and hamburger he shoved on our plates hung over the edges, sweating in defeat. I remember standing between my grandparents' porcelain lawn donkey and plastic windmill at age 5, watching Uncle Gene devour a steak he named "Elvis."

When Grandma and Grandpa entertained in the living room, guests would compliment their large collection of framed pictures. Papa's early paintings and drawings depicting suffering dark-skinned men hung on the walls next to photographs of cheery-eyed relatives in wedding gowns and tuxedos. "Amadio is quite the talented artist, isn't he!" newcomers would exclaim, rarely seeing the pain behind the layers of oil paint. Grandpa never encouraged this discussion. He wanted more than a poor artist's life for Papa, so he never acknowledged Papa's talents. He had displayed them, and that was enough.

Grandpa watched television on his own terms. In his version of channel surfing, he called one of us to turn the dial until he found what he wanted to watch. He believed pro-wrestling was real, that Americans wouldn't fake it. He grunted and yelled at the wrestlers as he perched on his end of the clear plastic-covered recliner, chiseling with a small knife the hardened skin from the soles of his feet and the crevices under his toenails. I laughed with Mama about these calluses, claiming they were the result of his shoe tying techniques, and that God was angry with his feet.

\* \* \*

Halloween activities had been all but canceled due to reported incidents of candy and fruit stuffed with broken razor blades and glass. Papa and Mama worried for our safety more and more and began telling us to stay away from strangers. By Thanksgiving, the atmosphere nettled the neighborhood like an old promise. Toys were brought in before dusk, doors were shut and locked and even the bird feeders hung empty.

Something had changed in the atmosphere, and the grown-ups were finding it difficult to explain.

When Papa received a call from the Democratic Campaign Headquarters, he knew something was up. A prominent politician needed a well-spoken, non-White man to help him in his election campaign. He had been directed to Papa not only for his impressive command of English and level of education, but because Papa was married to a White woman—he exemplified the crux of the spirit of the 1960s. When he tried to flatter Papa with talk of exposure, big shows, celebrations, and campaign glitter, Papa realized he was being bamboozled. The issue of race was a mere playing card, a hand for yet another politician's career. Papa's concern about racial issues was not rooted in politics, and he wasn't going to let the blood of rhetoric muddle the cause of his own public battle and private struggle.

By then, the national debate on school integration became a neighborhood concern. In the early part of December, most of the teachers at PS117 and members of the PTA signed a petition to withdraw a court order to begin busing. When the state refused to comply, the educators began what became the massive New York City teachers strike. Mama helped form demonstrations in front of the school and Papa joined when he could. When it wasn't too cold, Miguel and I were brought as models for the cause. I remember hundreds of parents and teachers shouting, chanting, and marching in circles. Sometimes there was pushing and shoving and people yelling racial epithets. It was during these demonstrations, Mama recalls, that she felt for the first time in her life there was a real cause to live. "People may say nasty words," Mama would say, "but we are proud of who we are."

During the first few weeks of the strike, Mama and Papa discussed the question of where we should be bused. They agreed that it would be best for us to attend a predominantly Black school so that we might become positive agents of integration. They also determined that we wouldn't be welcome at predominantly White schools anymore.

Neighbors who had been supportive of busing were now changing their minds. They wanted an end to the strike and for their kids to be back in school. A White woman who had moved up from the south, and with whom Mama used to petition, confronted Mama. "No more. Now it's your turn to get your children involved in busing and discrimination issues. Both my sons had to go through it for years, bearing the brunt. It made life very hard for the whole family."

"Well, that's the way it has to be," Mama confirmed, knowing she might be losing another friend. "It's just as much up to Whites to fight the system, because life for them is already *easier*."

"Our little daughter is Teja's age and I'm going to protect her. I'm not getting involved anymore. I've done my part, and now it's up to you. Think about it: Teja and Miguel already have a difficult life, why make things even harder for them?"

Mama was sure of herself. "Miguel and Teja are not really threatened now—it will come later in life for them. Hopefully they will grow up to be strong."

* * *

Winter came early that year, bringing with it biting cold storms that dumped record amounts of snow on the region leaving New York City crippled.

Months went by without any word from officials about which schools we could attend. I thought about Andrea and some of my other classmates that I liked, and wondered if I would ever see them again. Mama and Papa were teaching us at home in the evenings, using the textbooks we had from the school and borrowed books from friends, neighbors, or the library.

Except for the snow storms that we had grown accustomed to, Christmas was relatively quiet. I received a bright red Schwinn bicycle with training wheels that I could only sit on in the living room in anticipation of the spring thaw.

Then one evening in February, while lying in bed, I saw the night sky swell with wind-driven snow that whipped through the air like a white flag. I cringed as my favorite willow tree submitted to the wrath, bending and flailing like a woman who has lost her child. When I woke up the next morning, the willow lay on the ground defeated, its lower body snapped in half and its branches strewn all over the yard.

An option for schools was finally officially released. When the day came to go back to school, Mama came in to get me ready, and she reminded me that I would be taking part in an experiment. I would be taking a new bus to a different school in a place called Bedford-Stuyvesant. Mama and Papa and their new colleagues were convinced that Miguel and I, along with some other kids, could be living proof that the integration of White and Black schools was possible.

The gloomy sky looked just like the porridge I had for breakfast. It prompted a sinking feeling about changes and moving that I still get today. I thought about this new school and ran to the bathroom.

Bundled up and nauseated, I boarded the bus, waving good-bye the best I could with my thick, woolen mittens. The bus grinded away along the half-plowed roads, negotiating the moguls with its jingling, chain-wrapped tires. No one spoke. My new schoolmates wiped holes in the fogged windows and stared out. As we rounded the corner, I saw the willow tree dead on its side. No longer would my friends and I gather at its feet, hammering away at pink taffy and playing hide and seek.

As the bus made its way across town and through Brooklyn, the buildings looked increasingly depressing. Many had broken windows. There was garbage on the street and men in tattered overcoats huddled around smoky drumcan fires. Most of the people I saw in the neighborhood were Black and I wondered if most Blacks lived in areas like that.

We arrived at the school and were greeted rather cautiously by the principal, then hastily shuffled into the school. I found myself sitting in the middle of a classroom with mostly Black kids. There was only one White girl with red hair and one Asian boy. From the minute I arrived, every eye was on me. One boy asked another, "What, is he Black? Is he White?" I was used to being stared at, so it didn't bother me much. Still, I wondered, "Am I Black?" If Black kids think I'm Black, then I must *look* Black.

Mama came to pick us up after lunch. The kids poured out of the school and spotted Mama with her pale White skin and (dyed) blond hair. Some of them stopped to eye her. One girl approached Mama cautiously. "Excuse me, may I touch your hair?"

Mama smiled, "You want to touch my hair?"

The girl confessed, "I've never touched a White person's hair before."

"Of course you may touch it." Mama kneeled down and tilted her head forward.

"It's very soft. It's pretty. I want hair like yours." She ran her hands through Mama's hair and giggled.

Mama looked at her straight in the eyes and encouraged her the way she encouraged me. "Well, *I* think your hair is *very* beautiful, and you're a *very* pretty girl!" With that the little girl smiled and turned around to join her friends who were already boarding the bus.

I didn't see much of my new school. We attended infrequently, due to obstructions by protesters, threats, and lingering mandates by the courts. By spring 1969, I had the equivalent of only 2 months of schooling. Mama and Papa started talking about moving far away, maybe to another country where it would be safer and less tumultuous. Mama had been spending afternoons with some of her Japanese friends who encouraged her to try Japan for a change. "One day we will return to Japan," they promised.

Mama was intrigued by Japan, and enthusiastically suggested a move there. Papa objected at first, remembering the horror stories about how the Japanese treated his Filipino relatives during the Japanese occupation. But what options were there? America had become as effective as bad medicine. Would he have to escape again to find peace and acceptance? He looked around and was quiet, just like he was every time he knew that very soon he and his family would be displaced again.

# 8
# Paper Houses, Horses, and Swords

I thought maybe I liked her. I don't think she really knew why I always ended up following her on foot as she rode her bicycle home from school. Junko Minamoto was a couple of years older than I, but I liked her because she was friendly and her laughter sometimes made me choke with excitement. The routine I got into was embarrassing, but the only Japanese words I could remember were the first ones she taught me: *Moshi moshi*. I knew it meant "hello" when answering a phone—maybe she would get the clue and ask me to call her. "*Moshi moshi! Moshi moshi!*" I'd tag alongside her as she pedaled faster than I could walk comfortably. I just wanted her to stop so I could ask her to teach me some more Japanese words.

When I had been at school, some of the kids would tease Junko with jeers that at first didn't seem to affect her. "*Chinga chinga ching ching ching!* Hey Junko, do people in China still ride horses and carry swords? Better not throw any rocks there—the houses are made of paper!" Once I saw her emerge from a crowd of onslaughts and I could tell she was good at keeping a straight face.

After the school succumbed to the strikes, we didn't bump into each other much. Then I heard that her father's company moved the family back to northern Japan. Occasionally, at home when the phone would ring, I would repeat out loud the only two Japanese words I knew. Mama and Papa didn't seem to care what it really meant, they just wanted me to stop obsessing on the words.

I began to wonder if it was true that Junko's people might still ride horses and carry swords, and make houses out of paper. The Susumus across the courtyard didn't seem un-Japanese—they just seemed *normal* to me. Since Junko never really said much, I thought maybe she was hiding something about herself, and that just maybe the kids at school were right.

Weeks after Junko left, some of the kids still made fun of her. Maybe their parents figured Junko's feelings couldn't be hurt now that she was gone. But, I thought of how it was probably better that she was back in Japan with her people, far enough away so that I would have to call her on the phone.

*     *     *

"Japan! We're going to Japan? Isn't that the place where they ride horses and carry swords and you can't throw rocks because they live in paper houses?" I waited to see if Papa winked at Mama as he often did when he was fibbing, but he just chuckled at my response.

"They ride horses and carry swords? Some of them do I suppose. But most of them have lazer guns and personal rocket ships."

Mama pinched Papa. "He's teasing you, Teja. Where did you hear that, anyway?"

"At school."

"At school, huh?" Papa scoffed. "Well, it's a good thing you're not going to that school anymore."

I was upset. "We're not going back to the school?"

Mama reached her arms up into the air and produced a big smile. "We're really going to Japan! Isn't that great?"

Miguel's eyes were big. "Why are we going to Japan?"

"Just for a year. Papa got a job in Tokyo, a really nice job. We'll go for a year and then we'll come back. And don't worry—both of you will really like it there."

Papa nudged up his glasses and smiled. I didn't remember him ever having been giddy, so I searched his and Mama's face for more answers. They held each other around the waist as they described to us the adventure on which we were about to embark. Mama gestured excitedly as she spoke. Papa attempted to contain his grin and pride, and his mind was traveling fast because his eyes were darting about. I tried to listen, but my heart and mind were racing and I kept getting these images in my head of a buck-toothed karate expert jumping and kicking upside down on the other side of the planet. In some movie I had seen the Japanese were clearly a vicious enemy, so why were we going to live among people who wanted to kill us?

Papa had two job offers: one as an editor at the University of Pennsylvania State and the other as chief editor at Tokyo University Press. Mama was eager to travel and experience a totally different culture, and the job perks in Tokyo were very nice. Maybe Papa felt that finally he had gained the recognition he deserved and besides, after working abroad as chief editor maybe he would have better opportunities when we returned.

A year seemed like an awful long time. My stomach would cramp up every time I thought of the neighborhood kids ridiculing me for going to Japan. I tried to keep it a secret, but I knew I was doomed when I heard familiar voices scoff and sneer at me in cartoonish voices imitating what even *I* thought was authentic Japanese.

Even at the good-bye picnic that Grandma and Grandpa held for us, I worried about the move. Uncle Gene tried to cheer me up by asking me to help name his steaks, and Aunt Soli and Aunt Connie urged me to join in on the dancing, but all the food and noise and laughter made me dizzy with anxiety.

"Better eat up, Teja!" Uncle Freddy nudged me. "I hear they don't have much meat in Japan. In fact, that piece of juicy, sumptuous prime slab of steak you got there on your plate next to the mmm-mashed potatoes and those garden-picked green beans? Only the Emperor gets that. I'll take it if you're not going to eat it! That's probably the last piece of steak you'll have 'til you get back here! A year is quite a long time you know! That's 365 days of fish, fish, fish, rice, fish, and then more fish!"

* * *

Within 2 weeks, most of our things were packed in boxes and shipped off. We moved into Grandpa and Grandma's house while we waited for one more thing: Miguel's citizenship papers. Since his birth, immigration offices in both Germany and the United States spewed forth legal snags as to why they couldn't grant him citizenship. Grandma tried to keep the family active and positive, but bureaucratic clutter always tied Papa into a tight knot, and the tension filtered down until I felt guilty for having a citizenship, a concept I didn't even understand. Papa knew he could not lose the great opportunity that was waiting for him in Japan, so his face remained stern.

In March, Tokyo University Press managed to obtain a temporary visa for Miguel. Then the University of Pennsylvania offered Papa a job once we returned from Japan a year later.

The good-byes were quick and unfulfilling and no one seemed concerned that I was terribly frightened about moving to what might as well have been another planet.

Mama was frantic during the hours before going to the airport. We were told not to get dirty otherwise we would have to bathe again before getting dressed. She had picked out matching blue suits for Miguel and me, told us to get dressed and wash our hands and faces. Grandma cried in the living room while Grandpa tied my shoes extra hard to last the long journey over the oceans. Miguel and I bickered on the living room couch, gradually loosening the constricting jacket, tie, and shoes. Papa secured the suitcases with elastic straps and checked the name tags. Grandpa started up the car and then Grandma joined him outside, standing on the front steps already waiting for our return.

\* \* \*

Eighteen hours had passed and we had touched down and taken off in Philadelphia, Denver, Los Angeles, Hawaii, and Guam. Using a balled-up napkin, Papa explained how the world was divided into 24 hours and that as the plane passed between zones, the time changed. In this case it went backward until we passed over the international date line at which point time jumped ahead. He told us that night was day in New York and day was night in Japan. I mused at the fact that all my old friends would be sleeping when I would be playing outside.

As we cleared a storm the captain announced landing preparations for arrival in Tokyo. When I heard the word "Tokyo," my stomach rolled and I eyed the bathroom. Then, out of the window I witnessed what looked like a giant, flashing pinball machine emerge from under the dark shadows of the storm clouds. The captain spoke proudly as we began the descent into an amazing rainbow of blinking lights. "If you look out the left side of the plane you will see Tokyo—the city of lights." I couldn't tell if any of the houses were made of paper, and I imagined the city full of people on horses, carrying swords. Mama gave us one last smile before the plane touched down.

\* \* \*

I woke up on the floor next to Miguel, under a thick-cushioned blanket. Papa was unpacking a bag as Mama put on makeup. A strange combination smell of fish and grass made me a little nauseated, and through the open window I could hear heavy traffic and a light drizzle. I noticed I was lying on a thick mattress, and right next to me was another mattress and blanket. The floor was a beige straw-like material that smelled like a combination of freshly cut grass and hay.

"Miguel, Teja! Time to get up." Mama peeked at us in the mirror she had propped up on a short wooden table pushed up against a window. "Breakfast is here."

Miguel shot straight up out of sleep and inhaled. "… Fish?"

"And some other stuff. Eat up. Mr. Minowa, Papa's boss, is coming to pick us up in less than an hour."

Mama instructed us to fold up our mattresses, then pull the ankle-high table to the center of the room. Papa picked up a shiny wooden tray of food off the dresser and placed it next to the table.

"Look at these!" Mama admired the ornate bowls with matching covers. "Let's see, what do we have for breakfast?" She placed the bowls neatly on the table and removed the covers. A cacophony of smells from ocean food to raw eggs, seaweed, rice, oranges, and bananas hit me all at once like a brick.

"Wow. O.K. Anybody want to go first?" Papa chuckled, picking up a pair of chopsticks.

Miguel reached for his chopsticks. "How do you use these?"

"I guess they don't have any forks. I'm not exactly in the mood for rice and … raw eggs." Mama looked at Miguel and me as if we would be happy with her share.

"Can I have the yellow thing?" I picked up a soft, bright yellow cake in shape of a banana.

"I guess that would be O.K." Mama poked at her raw egg that rested in its own little porcelain bowl.

I bit into the banana cake. As I spat it out, I realized it was not that it tasted badly, it just didn't taste right. I looked inside the piece I was holding and saw a dark reddish-brown paste slowly oozing out of the opening.

Papa poured some hot tea into each of the ceramic cups. "Well, someone has to eat breakfast." He took a bite of the fish that looked up at him from its perch next to his bowl of rice. He kept his face straight while swallowing. "Well, Teja. How's the banana thing going down?" I reached for my tea and took a sip. The scalding bitter liquid ripped through my esophagus, and again, my senses tensed up with conflicting messages.

\* \* \*

We waited in the lobby of the hotel for Mr. Minowa. Two desk clerks spoke quickly with each other, one giving the other some directions. Their language didn't sound at all like what I thought was Japanese. When the phone rang at the counter, one of the clerks answered the phone. "Moshi, moshi." As she continued her greeting, I had a sudden longing for home and Junko. I remembered my friend. Then I was reminded I was supposed to look out for the horses and paper houses.

I stood in front of a large window that looked out onto the main street and watched pedestrians with umbrellas, cars, and streetcars streak by. A three-wheeled pick-up truck pouring white smoke from its tailpipe sailed past a tiny, slow-moving bus. The buildings were all different shades of gray. I couldn't make out any of the words on the billboards and everyone seemed to have exactly the same kind of black hair. Most of the men wore blue or brown suits and carried black umbrellas, while the women wore American style dresses. I caught a glimpse of a group of women in long, bright-colored robes, and wooden clogs. Their hair was piled up with long pins poking their heads sideways. Their robes came together at their ankles restricting their mobility and they waddled as they crossed the street. The taxi drivers wore suits, caps, and white gloves. A woman flagged down a taxi, and when the taxi came to a stop, the back door opened for her automatically. After she got in, the door closed by itself. Then all of a sudden I realized something was terribly wrong but I couldn't figure it out what it was.

"Mama!"

"What is it?" Mama came toward me.

"There's something wrong with the cars."

"Something wrong with the ... oh, yes, they drive on the other side of the street here. See, they're driving on the left side."

"Why?"

"That's just the way they do it."

I watched a shiny black car stop in front of the hotel. A man emerged and walked in through the revolving door. "Aruboreeda-san! Mr. Arboleda!"

Papa got up from the couch and walked briskly toward the man. Mr. Minowa bowed, then held his hand out to Papa. After they shook hands and bowed, Papa called us to be introduced. Mr. Minowa wore a big smile as he bowed and shook our hands and repeated our names. Under Papa's directions, I bowed quickly but awkwardly.

As we were escorted into the car, a bellhop wearing black pants, a red jacket, and white gloves packed our bags in the trunk. Mr. Minowa asked Papa about the flight and our first night's stay. The driver maneuvered swiftly, passing cars and trucks and meeting traffic lights while they were still green.

"In Japan, we say the traffic light is *blue*." Mr. Minowa gestured ahead at the seemingly endless intersections. He pointed out important landmarks and curiosities he thought would be of interest to us. Concrete buildings pressed up against wooden stores and crowds of people made the city look tangled up, but clean, nonetheless. I saw no boarded-up buildings and trash. "Oh, look! Welcome to monsoon season!" A thump of heavy rain crashed on the windshield. A sudden, heavy wind swayed the car to the left just before we pulled into a crowded, but quiet-looking neighborhood. "I hope your new home is not too moldy yet!" A couple of kids were throwing a pink rubber ball while an older woman ushered them into a store front. The driver made a right onto what looked like an alley. I clutched the handle on the door and he made a left onto another, narrower alley that was barely wide enough for the car. Mr. Minowa turned to us, "This is a two-way street—plenty of room to play!" We came to a stop in front of a gate to a light gray three-story apartment building. "Welcome to your new home!"

Mr. and Mrs. Okino greeted us in Japanese at the gate. Mr. Minowa turned to us, "Okino-san welcomes you to the apartment building and hopes it is not too small and inconvenient."

Papa laughed nervously. Inside the entrance to our first floor unit we were instructed to take our shoes off and put on house slippers that were arranged in a row.

"This area is called the *genkan*." He then took our shoes and placed them neatly a small closet on the right side of the genkan. "You can keep your shoes in there."

The living room had wall-to-wall straw mats. Mr. Okino took a deep breath and looked pleased, as Mr. Minowa interpreted, "Fresh *tatami* mat." In the middle was a short table, about a foot and a half off the floor. The kitchen barely fit a stove and a refrigerator that was slightly taller than me. We entered the bathroom through a sliding glass door. The bathtub was deep enough to stand in. Mr. Minowa warned, "You must wash yourself and rinse before you enter the tub." Next to the bathroom was a closet sized door. Mr. Okino opened it and showed us the toilet room. He flushed and proudly nodded as a spigot produced a stream of water into a basin on the top of the tank. "Also, a western style toilet! You're lucky!" On the tank, a decal with cartoon stick-figure images instructed the proper way to use the toilet seat for urination and defecation. The bedroom was divided into two rooms with large wooden sliding doors. In one corner at the end of the room was an oil stove. "Mejiro is a very nice neighborhood. Many stores and many children to play with!" Mr. Minowa put his hand on my shoulder. "I will leave you with Okino-san and pick you up for dinner. Chinese food!" Mr. Minowa bowed. The Okinos bowed. Papa bowed. Mama bowed. I wondered, "Chinese food?"

"By the way," Mr. Minowa added, leaning toward Papa and lowering his voice, "your English is very good, Mr. Arboleda. I'm surprised because Whites usually speak English much better, but I see I have nothing to worry about!"

*   *   *

The next day Mama took us to our new school by train. My jet lag made my initial contact with this new, alien society even more surreal. The sheer number of people funneling into the station reminded me of Yankee Stadium, only everyone here looked the same. It wasn't until we were waiting on the platform that I realized a woman was staring at me. Then I noticed a group of kids whispering and pointing at me. One of them said out loud, "*Gaijin da!* " A man with a suitcase cocked his head forward and observed me like Grandpa did when he caught me disposing of food I didn't care for into my pocket. Mama guided Miguel and I to stand in line with a group of people who stood parallel to a white diagonal line. A green train packed with faces and hands pressed against the windows squealed into the station. A voice on the loudspeaker rattled some directions. Two uniformed men waited for the doors to open, then peeled out the first layer of travelers. As the passengers emerged, our line stepped to the side to make room. When the last passenger passed us, the first in line led the others into the train and moved to the center of the car. What I didn't realize was that behind us a long line had formed so that as soon as we got through the doors, we were propelled into a consuming crowd of warm bodies where my face was caught between a woman's belly and a man's briefcase. The train lurched forward, the crowd moved and I caught glimpses of faces peering at me through sweaty arms, bags, and newspapers. A mother standing next to me spoke to her baby as she pointed at me, "*Gaijin. Hora, gaijin desu yo!*"

Minowa-san called to see how the apartment was. We told him about being called "*gaijin.*" He laughed and explained, "that means 'outside person,' or foreigner, that's all. You are *gaijin* in Japan. You'll get used to it."

St. Mary's International School is an all-boys school run by Canadian Jesuit Brothers who vehemently enforced uniforms and prayer. Miss Takagi, my first grade teacher, introduced me to my new class. There were about 30 boys all wearing blue blazers, gray pants, and red ties. I didn't have my uniform yet, so I felt embarrassed and out of place. Unlike the world outside, there were very few Japanese-looking kids. In fact, many of them reminded me of my neighbors in New York.

In the cafeteria, the noise and bustle of people mixed with the daunting smell of industrial food. The teachers stood at the end of the tables and ordered us to rise. The room fell silent. Then, in unison, hundreds of voices chanted a prayer. I tried to follow those next to me and put my hands together, tilted my head down, and moved my mouth pretending to know the words and hoped no one would suspect me of offending God.

The hallways were lit with large frosted, glass lamps surrounded by ornate designs, and remained on all day to compensate for the lack of sunshine. Torrential rains persisted, and the blurred windows reminded me of going through a car wash in Parkway Village, Queens. The gales tossed around anonymous, mangled umbrellas that showed up on the playground and other unsuspecting places, and bent the trees in submission. I thought of the willow tree in our old backyard, and my friends, my goldfish, and my red bicycle. At my desk, I traced the names that were carved into the wood with my finger. Some of the names were funny sounding to me, names I had never heard before. And then I thought of Andrea, and I wished hard that Miss Takagi wouldn't ask me to repeat my name, but everyday at roll call, she pronounced it flawlessly.

After a month Miguel and I were allowed to travel the 1-hour trip to and from school by ourselves. One day, as we walked home from Mejiro train station, a group of girls from the local school crowded around us, screamed, and patted our heads. "*Kyaaa kawaii, kawaii janaino, kono gaijin boiya tachi wa! Kyaaa! American boi desuka?* Ah yu Amerikan boi?"

Miguel covered me like a secret service agent, and squinted his eyes in defiance. "Yes. We're American."

"*Kyaaa!* Yu ah so kyuuut! Yu lukku laiku Mahikeru Jakuson!"

Whoever Michael Jackson was, I didn't want to look like him, if this is what he did to school girls.

*   *   *

At home in the small apartment, with no place to roam around unlike our neighborhood in Queens, Miguel and I fought and bickered incessantly. Mama encouraged us to make friends with some of the neighborhood kids. But how? A couple of times we had seen a boy observing us through the bushes in his backyard, only to run away when he realized we had spotted him. Then one afternoon after school, his softball landed suspiciously outside the bedroom window. By that afternoon Miguel and I were playing "monkey-in-the-middle" with Kazu, and by that Saturday Miguel and I were invited over for *hotto kehki*, a 1-inch thick, distant cousin of American-style pancakes.

Mama shopped at the market near the train station, often upset with the lack of supplies of familiar ingredients and the price of meat. The one-story building housed more than 30 small stores divided only by plastic tarps. The fish market was next to the cosmetics counter, which was next to the bread and cake store. Mama tried her best to communicate with the store clerks, and they enjoyed her attempts to illustrate what was on her shopping list. She pantomimed with hand gestures, and they triumphed in unison at her brief successes as she expelled a mouthful of words from her pocket English-Japanese dictionary.

I looked forward to Sunday mornings again, when Papa made scrambled eggs and pancakes, which I shoveled in so voraciously Mama was convinced I would eat my way back to America. It didn't phase me, the irony of sitting on our knees on *tatami* mats eating Parkway Village food Japanese style. "We should try eating the pancakes with chopsticks!" Papa would joke. He missed the weighty decadence of the Sunday edition of *The New York Times*, and tried to fill in the empty spaces with conversation. But we were in Japan now, and he would adapt, slowly and correctly.

But as the monsoon season waned, making way for an oppressively humid summer vacation, I began to forget my old neighborhood in New York. Even the overwhelming fog of incomprehensible street signs, advertisements, and the drone of train station crowds no longer affected me. I listened, observed, and most of all did not want to stand out. Nothing in our neighborhood, except for an occasional makeup or Coca-Cola ad featuring a blond woman, or the rare smell of beef could remind me of the willow tree, the riots, and the cold, snow-packed winters from months ago.

Even St. Mary's, with its American textbook and Crayola-crayon curriculum couldn't transport me back to PS 117. The majority of my classmates were not from America, or even English-speaking countries. Sometimes Ms. Takagi would ask one of us at random to approach her desk and point to the globe, to the country of our origin. I placed my finger on the United States and then asked her to help me find Germany and the Philippines. The others didn't laugh as I feared—sometimes their fingers touched many more parts of the globe.

At night, Miguel and I shared a *futon*. Sleeping on the floor made the wooden ceiling and lantern seem much higher, a reminder of how I hated being so small and skinny. As the steady buzz of cicadas, crickets, and frogs put me to sleep, I wondered if a Japanese frog would understand an American frog if I took it back to the field in Parkway Village.

# Squares in a Circle

"You have Coca-Cola in America?" Nishikawa-san looked at us curiously. She had studied English at a local college before she got married and laughed at her possible ignorance. "No, Coca-Cola is best Japanese drink. You are very funny!" She opened a small porcelain container in which a tiny spoon rested in a familiar-looking pool of dark red goop. "Do you also have ketchup?" As she served us dinner, I felt strangely comfortable, as the warm moist smell of freshly cooked rice made my stomach tickle. Papa used to boast that Filipinos eat more rice than anyone else. So far we had had rice everyday, and although we were in Japan, I didn't care who ate more, I couldn't get enough of it. "You will be a strong boy, eat up!" Nishikawa-san added a whole cooked fish, eyes and all on my plate. "Be careful for bones!" The fish stared at me curiously like subway riders, but in this case without fingers.

Occasionally, during dinner, we would watch TV. There were eight channels, two of which were educational, featuring math study shows, foreign language, and science. From what we could gather, a viewer could buy an accompanying study guide to any of these programs. Sometimes we watched samurai movies, in which the hero, sometimes blind or one-armed, would single-handedly slaughter an enemy troop of 50 or more. Heads went flying, blood splattered, and limbs plopped on the ground. In war movies, Westerners were always the evil enemies, threatening the peaceful Japanese masses. But for the most part, variety shows were the most entertaining. When the farting, slapping, burping, kicking, slapstick skits began, no translation was needed. But for some reason, Mama's sense of humor didn't quite match ours. Papa, Miguel, and I would end up on the floor, choking on our food in hysterical laughter. One time Papa's chuckling was cut short when some actor in black-face entered the stage wearing only a grass skirt and carrying a spear. The audience roared and edged away, playfully terrified as the jungle man ran up and down the isles. On other nights, comedy shows ridiculed Americans as stupid and loud, to which Mama reminded us to behave and speak softly when in public.

Mama often sent one of us to go shopping at the market. One afternoon, a curious store owner lured me into a corner of his bread and pastry stand. A group of women surrounded me, smiled, and nodded their heads approvingly. The store owner picked up a bag of Wonder Bread and squeezed it. "American, yoah mahzah, she lukku laiku Wundah Breddo!" The women cupped their mouths and giggled. As I walked home with the groceries, I couldn't help wonder if he meant that my whole family looked like Wonder Bread, or just Mama. And Mama is not even American. Papa had always directed us to say "Filipino-German" when people asked us what we were. But in Japan, the bold ones who dared to approach us assumed we were American and could speak English. It wouldn't be until after the mass influx of Southeast Asians and Africans crowded into Japan in the mid-1980s that the issue of skin color suggested anything other than Western. But for now, unavoidably, the Arboleda family represented, unconditionally, the United States, and with it the rest of the Western world. When Papa and Mama failed to elaborate on things like marijuana, LSD, The Beatles, miniskirts, streaking, big breasts, and rock and roll, the investigating individual would look at them dispiritedly, as if my parents had casually deserted their culture.

* * *

After school Kazu would come to the front of the building and call for us. "*Migueeru, Tehyah! Asobimasho!*"

"*Hai*, Homework ... finish ... first!" Mama would lean out the window and respond to Kazu's familiar request, trying to make her English comprehensible. Kazu couldn't have understood her, but he waited patiently, rhythmically bouncing his softball against the stone wall as Miguel and I worked feverishly to finish our homework.

Summer arrived, and Miguel and I, with our days now free for 3 months, watched Japanese kids shuffle off to school with only a 2-week break to look forward to. The neighborhood store clerks remained suspicious of our free time as the summer progressed without seeing us return to classes. In the afternoons we played and explored the parks and streets with Kazu and the others. We had become buddies, so it was easy for me to retain many of the words Kazu used, and when I repeated them, he would break into a smile.

And so continued summer, with all its indolence and exploration. Every morning we woke up sweating and somewhat debilitated. The humidity hung like a wool sweater in a sauna; people walked slower and even traffic seemed sluggish. Shoes and books became sudden hosts to a white fuzzy mold. Mama wilted in the outside blaze, and even more in the tiny kitchen, and often wished out loud for a quick winter. She tended to her White arms and legs, now reddened in protest, and was frequently jealous of our browning skin. Miguel, hunched over in some bush or on the banks of the pond down the street, introduced me, like an old friend, to his praying mantises, Helmet Beetles, and Scissors Head Beetles.

I watched the local elementary school kids and staff exercising in unison on the school grounds. They stretched and did jumping jacks according to the gym teacher who commanded every move and turn. I had been told that this was the case every morning, and the discipline was the key to a good education and a strong community, and that the police department, many companies, and factory workers continued this tradition in parks and in the workplace through adulthood.

The neighbors acknowledged our presence with a simple bow or a smile, a sign that were now officially accepted. Occasionally something reminded me of the impending new school year, the gray hallways, the musty smell of textbooks, and the looming drudgery of homework. I deeply dreaded going back to school.

* * *

The hallway and bathroom lights always seemed dimmer during my second-grade school year. Miss Pedro (who was nicknamed "The Witch") was never without her long, wooden ruler that she carried in her left hand, knuckles white as her fingers clutched it tightly, ready to subjugate. Each morning, under the carved-wood statue of a bleeding Jesus hanging straight above her head, she began with a stern order to stand straight like her ruler and recite the Our Father. When Papa learned of this, his face puffed up and he argued with Mama. "I don't care if he's only in second grade, he'll just have to tell Pedro he won't do it! Or I'll go there and tell her myself!"

Mama usually tried to quell Papa's arguments with shots of logic. "Well, it's a Catholic school, after all, you knew that when you decided to send them there and not the American School."

"I wanted to get them away from those loud American kids and from discrimination."

"So let the kids pray! After all, there is a god! Besides, they might be faced with racism and loud Americans at St. Mary's anyway."

The next day I took it upon myself to tell "The Witch" that I wouldn't be praying anymore. I sat in defiance through the morning and lunch prayer, an action The Witch awarded me by cracking her 24 inches of pinewood on the back of my hands.

She once gave an impromptu sermon in which she told us of her missionary visit to a remote village of China where the townspeople burned her Jesuit sister on a cross. As she recounted the horror, she shook with anger, and I watched the ruler bend in submission. "They didn't want Christ in their hearts! Heaven has no place for animals like them!" She terrified me, her face scrunched up in perpetual hate. Once, she stood behind me and breathed down my neck as I copied words off the blackboard into my spelling workbook. I was so nervous my head spun, and as I wrote my fingers became numb. "Jesus ... is ... the ... son ... of ... gog."

"G-o-g? g-o-g! What is wrong with you, Arboleda? God is looking down at you right now and he's very angry!" She grabbed my hair, pulled me up and snapped my head against the table behind me. My father rushed to the school as soon as he heard about this. Brother Andrew, the principal, had to hold him back at the entrance to the school. "I'll beat the living hell out of that bitch!"

Although China was far away and a very different place, I often wondered if Miss Pedro was still being hounded by some spirits of that remote village. I imagined that she wasn't a good example of a Westerner, as Mama always reminded us to make a good impression of all foreigners by remaining calm and keeping to our own business.

I did everything I could to avoid being different. Within time I made some more friends in the neighborhood, some who taught me about television characters like Godzilla and Ultraman, ball games, funny phrases, and secret paths in the nearby park. Occasionally I was tested for my bravery by eating dried, slated cuttlefish strings and seaweed-covered rice crackers. To the amazement of the others, I could swallow anything. *"He's very Japanese,"* they would muse. I liked the attention, especially when they forgot to remind me that I was a *gaijin*.

After pleading with Mama, she bought me a Godzilla and an Ultraman action figure, now my heroes from what became my favorite TV show. Now, just like on television, I could reenact the daily destruction of Tokyo with my German-made Lego set. In the little neighborhood market, I demonstrated one of these reenactments and received less than enthusiastic responses. It must have meant something completely opposite to what I intended because toy store owner, who cringed when I rabidly stomped Lego-Tokyo with the plastic Ultraman, offered to replace my offending toy with a mechanical plastic beetle kit. I took the gift home, assembled it and was amazed as to how real-to-life the beetle looked. Mama was scared of bugs, so I let it loose on the kitchen floor behind her. The beetle's motorized mechanics created a horrific dissonance when combined with Mama's scream as she stomped the life out of it. The next day when I passed the toy store cubicle, I gave the owner a dirty look. He just nodded his head and bent over in laugher.

Although general comments about us being foreigners made by familiar people on the street became more frequent, they still prefaced their observations with a light bow and a hint of embarrassment. "American crazy? American crazy!"; "You no take bath?"; "American fat! Eat vegetable?" Their observations seemed strange because no one in my family fit any of these descriptions. They didn't upset me though—somehow I sensed that these neighbors, who had become my friends, meant only to communicate and knew no other way. "American long leg! Japanese tanasoku—short leg!"; "American blond, brown hair—interesting! Japanese only black hair—no good. Teja mother, very beautiful! Little Teja, Teja-*kun*, interesting, not look American, but yes, American!" I didn't sense hostility, and I laughed with them, and understood only years later the sadness in what had become a national self-denigrating fad. Usually I was glad I didn't have blond hair, knowing that then I would be ogled over, touched, and talked about even more. At least I was skinny, so from behind no one could tell I wasn't Japanese.

And in the madness of Tokyo crowds, there was even less of a chance of calling attention to myself. Sometimes I liked to stand in the middle of a train station foyer during rush hour and feel the hoards of people rush in and out and around me like herd of eager spirits too busy for earth. Maybe only a flicker of a response, a peripheral interest in my presence was all they could give me. Besides being at home, those were the moments I felt safest.

And when I did speak Japanese, store clerks looked shocked, not at my often feeble attempts, nor the fact that I didn't really have an accent, but rather the fact that a foreigner could speak Japanese at all. Their response in English was usually equally as pitiful, but they were adamant—an American could not speak Japanese.

"*Irrashaimase!*" a clerk at the local bakery once responded without looking up, as he heard the sound of the store door opening. "*Hai doozo, goyukkuri.*"

"*Sumimasen,*" I asked, picking up a small loaf of bread without a price tag near it. "*Kore ikura deshooka?*"

After seeing my face and realizing I was not Japanese, his face froze and his eyes darted around for help.

I repeated my question. "*Kore ikura deshooka?*"

"Ah ... herro ... ah ... I'm sorri, I donto undahstando. *Soo danee, doshioka,* ah ... I don'to speaku Engurishu."

I slowed my question and repeated again. "*Kore ... ikura ... desuka?*"

He continued to stare, then suddenly turned around and yelled for someone. A woman came out from the back room and stopped in the door frame and stared at me, wiping her hands on her apron. The clerk asked her some questions, then made breathing noises through his teeth. He cocked his head to the side, then looked back at me. The woman walked over to me and raised her eyebrows.

I held up the bread and repeated the question to her. "*Kore ikura deshooka?*"

She also cocked her head to the side a couple of times and nodded very quickly.

"How muchi?" she asked. "How muchi?"

I nodded, then said in English, "Yes. How much. How much is this?"

"Ahh! *Wakarimashita!* She nodded along with me. "*Sore wa* one hundoreddo fiftee *en desu.* One hundreddo fifty!"

"One hundred-fifty yen?" I asked.

"Oh! *Eigo wa umaineeh!* the clerk cheered. "Yoah English berry guddo!"

\* \* \*

I began to observe the little things that pleased Mama. "They are very proud of their work and their neighborhood. Look, just yesterday she swept in front of her store, and her neighbor's too. Today again, see?" I thought about the garbage and broken glass on the streets of New York. "Bow, Teja, she's saying hello!" Their eyes wouldn't meet ours, but their action was automatic. We exchanged bows everywhere and with everybody we came into contact with. "*Irrashaimase! Hai, gaijin no okyakusama, doozo!*" A store clerk at the fish store would lure us in, making it known that the foreigners had arrived, like a circus sideshow. He would briefly bow, then perform three functions quickly in succession: wrap a sale neatly, calculate the sale on an abacus, and exchange cash for the sale. Then with a heartfelt *Doomo arigatoo gozaimasu!* the clerk would thank the customer, followed by an exchange of a bow each. The sounds of the market became more real as I attached the words and actions to their meanings. A routine for everything, with enthusiasm and efficiency, and I never saw a slouching figure, feet propped up on a chair, or the American noncommital eyeroll. Change was placed carefully in a customer's hand, with cash neatly flattened and face up. If butter was not available, deep apologies. If the customer considered the piece of fish too small, a quick exchange with deep apologies. Policemen were neighborhood-friendly, slim, in shape, and courteous. Train conductors spoke intelligibly over the intercom, wore uniforms and white gloves, while station managers swept the platforms frequently. Passengers always went up staircases on the left and down on the right. When stopping at a red light at night, headlights were turned off so that drivers ahead and pedestrians would not be blinded. Gauze masks were to be worn in public when sick with a cold or flu so as not to spread germs. "Never serve yourself first. Share everything. The last gum in your own pocket is not your own." This energy, this awareness of "the other person" filled me, and the countless routines were oddly welcoming.

"You will learn discipline here." Papa felt right at home. "There's no room for laziness."

Nevertheless, the stares continued, the comments prevailed, and no matter what I did, I looked like I didn't belong. The word *gaijin* rang in my head, and I walked quickly in public with my eyes down, wanting desperately to hide my face. I squirmed when Mama spoke English with me in public, especially when I was being scolded. In English! What else could embarrass me more than loud, judgmental English! My name should have been like Kazu's or Yoshi's or Hiro's. Heads wouldn't snap around to gaze at me curiously if we were Japanese. And what started to make things more confusing was that I missed my friends back home, but I couldn't really remember them clearly.

*   *   *

The shape of the backyard, the walk to the train station, the bustle in the school halls, the family at dinner, the occasional weekend outing—these sweet everydays in Tokyo became comfortable, normal, and expected. And with each passing day I was reminded in subtle ways that I could still feel at home knowing that Parkway Village and its presence had slipped further away. Then gradually, but with only subtle hints, the refreshing chill of winter quelled the tangy smell of *ginko* trees: a clue to the arrival of Christmas.

It was no surprise to me that Santa Claus traveled to Japan. In fact I expected no less. Bogged down with blinking lights, tinsel, and shiny ornaments hanging from undersized Christmas trees, the multitude of store fronts beckoned the masses who mobbed the Shibuya shopping district with unabashed curiosity. Short and skinny Santas in baggy red and white costumes handed out coupons at store fronts, "Mehree Kurisu-masu! *Hai, doozo irrashaimase!*" In the windows at Seibu Department Store, White-skinned mannequins in mini Santa-skirts tugged delicately on the reigns of an embalmed mountain deer. Metal speakers hanging on telephone poles blared overmodulated Paul Anka and Harry Belafonte Christmas carols like a piece of home on full blast; Mama hummed along. A confusing mix of sugar-coated fruitcakes, fried noodles, and soy sauce hung in the air, and I wondered if this was the perfect combination platter for Santa when he came to deliver.

The Christmas tree bowed slightly in our living room as if in constant appreciation, and the familiar tinsel and ornaments we brought from America, now crowded on tiny limbs, smelled distinctly of Grandma's basement. Mama and Papa toasted with wine, and Miguel and I with our milk. "Well, we may be far away from home, but home is here with us. Here's to a Christmas without the rest of the family!" Papa turned up Nat King Cole's "White Christmas" and took Mama's hand. They danced and held each other close as if to seal some gap, somewhere near me in the room. Or was it something I had felt before? Miguel and I mocked their affection as we jerked awkwardly to the music. The melody, a faint remembrance of snowflakes and America.

On Christmas morning (Christmas Eve in New York), we exchanged repetitious greetings over the phone with the family who were all gathered in Grandma's living room. The sound of the phone changing hands was more telling of the distance between us than the faint, crackling of their voices. Our good-byes were short and uneasy.

The wrapping paper seemed almost unnecessary as I tore it off; there couldn't be any more surprises.

\* \* \*

Miguel and I wanted so badly for it to snow that winter, but it didn't. And rather timely was spring, a keepsaker and somewhat familiar—a reminder of our first day in this new country. Fresh, new smells and the hum of vigorous growth and insects were vibrant and passionate.

"We've been here almost 1 year, can you imagine that?" There had been a down note in Mama's comments lately. Months earlier, Papa traveled to Pennsylvania to meet with potential employers who had been interested in hiring Papa after his year in Japan. He returned disappointed with America. The racism, the riots, the hostility wore on him like a blister. He decided that staying in Japan would be better for us. Then there were fights; for the most part Mama had come to like Japan, but was looking forward to returning to America. She had grown to hate the humidity and the crowds and she was isolated. Although she did have friends, the foreign ones didn't stay in Japan for long, and the Japanese ones continued to bombard her with inferiority–superiority complexes. For her there was nowhere to escape from the discrimination she felt. The groping hands on her buttocks and breasts in the trains; the comments and gazes, like sharp teeth behind a smile. Once, a man in a train pushed up her hat to inspect her blond hair, then pointed downward. "Excuse me," he belted in Japanese, "is your hair down there the same color?" Mama was angrier than I had ever seen her when she recounted the incident. "I should have planted my knee in his crotch—made his hair down there turn *red!*" It was more difficult for Mama, as a foreign woman in Japan than it was for Papa. Mama urged a return to the United States where she wanted to finish college. Even Miguel, who hadn't gained friends in the neighborhood or at St. Mary's, was willing to forgo the fascinating wildlife for America. Miguel and I had been excited to go back to America, but somewhere along the way, I lost touch with how long we had been here. "Just one more year," is what we were told. Just one more year, again and again.

But escaping riots and hostility, one of Papa's arguments against returning to the United States, was not exactly an option. A build up of thousands of anti-American leftist demonstrators shut down parts of Tokyo. Shouting, rock-throwing college students clashed with shield-toting riot police. They often occupied university campus buildings like the one right across the walkway from Papa's office. Their demands were simple—less Westernization. They would confront Mama, the most Western-looking one, demanding apologies. Mama would be silent, which she was criticized for being a stupid American. We watched the news for riot forecasts and avoided target zones. The neighborhood housewives opened up to Mama only when she indicated she was German, not American.

Papa's jaws remained tight, and laced with occasional smiles. Even when the protests faded the air was different. The damage had been done. Daily language, in mockery of the Western world, if only for pure sensationalism, surfaced in commercials, comedy shows, and on the streets where little boys challenged us with name calling. In an instant, and then to change as if a tide, my anchor of reference to place and purpose flickered in and out.

But I still had the neighborhood. And the bows were still genuine and the smiles were still warm. We were not strangers here, just strange. And I had Kazu and the others.

But not this summer. Mama announced Miguel and I were going to spend the rest of the summer with Oma and Opa in Germany.

# Shuffle 10

We hadn't been back to Haneda Airport since we arrived 1 year earlier. The echoes of service announcements and the crowds brought back memories of old feelings, like the anticipation of a cold, rainy day. The rapid flipping of the departure charts caught my eye. "Well, it looks like we're on time." Papa said. I then realized I was in a swirling sea of foreigners. We all stared at one another, looking for familiar faces, like eager ghosts searching for ancestors. Here in the confines of a concrete block, strangers let down their guards for smiles and communication.

"Now be good and don't let them feed you too much candy and chocolate," Mama said, checking our ties. "Give them all a big kiss for us, okay? You have all the information you need pinned inside your jacket if you need it. The stewardess will help you, we made sure of that."

This formal event reminded me of dressing up for church, and I suddenly realized that my shoes were not tight enough, and for once I wished they were.

"Listen carefully." Papa had a softness in his voice that I can still hear today. It was the kind of effort one puts into a speech when it is intended to place serious responsibility for something sacred. "Miguel, you are the older one. You are *kuya*, so you must take good care of Teja."

Miguel puffed his cheeks nervously and led me to the security desk where an agent checked passports. The crowd flow was smooth, and I turned around and waved to Mama. Papa's face became stern, but he wasn't looking at me. When I turned back to Miguel, he was being ushered away from the line of travelers and into an isolated curtained booth.

"What the hell is going on?" Papa yelled, entering the security zone. "That's my son, get your hands off him!" Two security guards rushed over and grabbed Papa's arms. "Get your hands off him now!" My heart raced and I felt tears swelling up in my eyes. A half a minute later Miguel emerged from the booth, eyes big with confusion. Then one of the agents grabbed my arm and maneuvered me through the curtains. He told me to lower my pants and take off my shirt. I could hear Papa's voice booming with anger. The guard searched my clothes and my body. My heart was still pounding when Mama leaned down to straighten my clothes and asked, "Are you okay?" She turned to Papa, "They thought they were what?"

Papa grinded his teeth. "Arab terrorist bomb carriers."

"They think Miguel and Teja are terrorists?"

"Kids have been known to be trained bomb carriers on suicide missions. They obviously suspected Miguel and Teja."

With one last hug, Papa tried not to show his humiliation. As Miguel led me across the tarmac and toward the plane, I turned around frequently to search for something in the shrinking faces of Mama and Papa. At the top of the steps to the door to the plane, we waved one last time.

\* \* \*

There were only a few reminders of Germany, a smell, the touch of an insignificant object. It was almost new, being here with our German family. Miguel and I slept on the fold-out couch in the living room. In the afternoons, this would become Tante Louise's domain, a permanent fixture with her television shows. Opa and Oma would retreat to Mama's old bedroom in the rear of the apartment to watch their own programs. Oma sliced a peach or a pear while Opa folded the newspaper and took a drag from his cigarette. They both easily finished off one and a half, maybe two packs a day, leaving Opa's teeth yellowed, while Oma's dentures remained intact.

Everyone congregated for dinner at 12 p.m. followed by a quiet hour, then coffee and cake at 3 p.m. On Tuesday nights Oma and Opa let loose with the *Gesungfurein* followed by wine and beer at the local bar. Weekends were busy with visits to a cousin or an uncle's house or Great-Grandma's apartment that housed a talking canary. They filled us with cake, chocolate, and cookies, their affection and love overflowing. Germany, once more, was a solid place and not just a story or a thought. Leaving, as always, was to be stripped of some familiar security blanket.

\* \* \*

We returned to Japan speaking German again. In the apartment there was a calm, vaguely settled feeling I hadn't noticed before. Mama was resolved for now to the fact that she would never belong in Japan, or that any of us would. I would only understand, years later in my 20s, life in an alien world that will never include you can be seen as a freedom. But freedom, of course, is relative.

The end of the summer was earmarked with the yearly district *matsuri* festivities. Everyone was expected to cheer as this year's group of men, wearing only *fundoshi* to cover their privates, carried a large red and gold portable shrine through the streets. Locals joined in the traditional neighborhood dance, some even signaled for us to join. But the Arboleda family just sat on the sidelines like benchwarmers without a chance to participate.

Just as I was preparing to enter third grade, Papa enrolled us in Rikkyo Gakuen, a Japanese Catholic School one train station away from our home. We were to first attend on Saturdays only (Japanese schools operate 6 days a week), and then eventually switch to a full-time schedule. My stomach burned and I complained. It wasn't the thought of switching to a Japanese school—I just couldn't imagine going to school 6 days a week! "If a Japanese kid is transferred to the United States, he doesn't go to a Japanese school," Papa argued, "he goes to an American school. We are in Japan now. And you'll need to learn Japanese fluently." The principal agreed to take us, but we both had to step back a grade.

So, once a week, wearing a standard Japanese school uniform, I learned the general routines. At 7:30 a.m., the entire student body and faculty stretched in unison and performed aerobic exercises in the field. General announcements were taken seriously, especially when the school monitor announced special orders for the two *gaijin*. Sitting in the middle of my first grade class, I struggled with the reading while sweating under my collar and shaking with nervousness. I was eventually allowed to be aided by Shin-chan, who sat on my right. Between classes, Shin-chan grilled me on the *hiragana* and *katakana* alphabets. I found it much more difficult to pick up on the set of complicated Chinese characters called *kanji*.

The most confusing thing about the classroom setup was that the teacher spent a lot of his time in the back of the room, allowing the students to choose the day's class leaders, assist each other in problem solving and lead group *hansei* (apology or self-reflection) at the end of the day. The teacher seemed almost secondary to the workings of the class, submitting only suggestions or encouragement when needed. I had expected the teacher to be strict and commanding like the those I had known in New York and at St. Mary's. When a question was posed, all the hands shot up. The class leader or teacher would pick a student and the student would answer the question. If the answer was wrong, another would shout *wrong!* and proceed to answer the question correctly. I felt compelled to raise my hand in unison with the others and hoped I would never be picked. I understand now that it was important for me to look eager and involved, but it wasn't necessary that I knew the answer.

In the classrooms and along the hallways, slogans lined the walls and were often chanted out loud, like prayer before lunch at St. Mary's. "Active and Cheerful, Friendly and Helpful," or "Doing Our Best in Everything." We took turns bringing food from the cafeteria and serving lunch to our classmates, then cleaning up afterward. Before leaving school, we were given more chores. My first duty was to scrub the hallway floors on my hands and knees, while Shin-chan and Eriko-chan washed the windows.

I shouldn't have told my St. Mary's classmates about my Saturday at Rikkyo. "You're stupid!" Mark yelled. A couple of the other Americans guffawed and pointed at me like I was a bug. Mama reminded me to pay them no heed, besides, Shin-chan and Eriko-chan and the others at Rikkyo seemed to look forward to their duties. Although our *sensei* (teacher) didn't smile at us with encouragement, he heartily displayed satisfaction. It was our duty, especially as foreigners, to learn humility and respect. There were no exceptions, no special situations, no slouching, no diversion. Studying and hard work was a directive, not an elective, and we were reminded even at this early age that college and a good job were the goals. I knew it then—my fellow first graders were already far ahead of me.

In the end, we would be at Rikkyo for only 1 year. After considering the implication for a realistic future, it had become obvious that if we were eventually going to attend college in the United States, we should learn in English.

Just as we settled back into a normal routine at St. Mary's, the grounds were sold to a bank. While we waited for the new school to be built, the bank moved into the building that housed our cafeteria. The school struck a deal with the local McDonald's and Kentucky Fried Chicken: 4 months of Big Macs and chicken legs. "Why junk food? Why not a variety, Japanese food, or something else!" Mama and many of the Asian parents were furious and argued against the plan, but the American parents generally endorsed the arrangement whole-heartedly, and won. "Real food!" the kids would cheer, no doubt reflecting the very sentiments of their parents. This daily trophy, the smell of ground red meat and greasy fries became tired like the stained, crinkled wrapping of a cheeseburger.

* * *

My homeroom teacher, Mrs. Glauche, was married to a German. "I'm a Filipina, and Mr. Glauche is German." She said this in front of the others. "Your mother is German and your father is from Manila. We're much the same. You should be proud to be a Filipino." *Filipino?* I didn't know anything about the Philippines. We didn't practice any Filipino culture at home, at least not any that I knew of. Not only did I feel guilty about not being able to live up to Mrs. Gluche's expectations, but I thought that maybe there was something I was supposed to know about, like I did in respect to Germany or the United States.

Mrs. Glauche was a severe and harsh woman, whose unpredictable mood swings left us constantly on the edge of our seats. The half-moon blemish on her cheek waned and waxed with her moods, but her grip on our attention remained steady. I was a nervous third grader and she made it worse. I stumbled over words when she called on me, and I imagined I was her only constant in a classroom full of non-Filipinos. She picked on me to be the perfect substitute for her childless marriage, and once clamped a stapler on my ear because I stuttered instead of answering her question. Luckily the stapler was empty, but I was filled with humiliation of not measuring up, and I perspired more. "You ought to be ashamed to be Filipino!" she scolded. I could sense Mark Corkum, the class bully, laughing under the wiggling weightiness of his gelatinous double chin. From then on I could see only his chin; to this day I cannot remember his eyes.

Some deep disenchantment filled the hallways that year. In late April, as the school wound down for the summer, we were called to an emergency assembly. Brother Andrew spoke at the podium, solemn and reserved. One of the seniors had committed suicide; his brother found him hanging from a rope. A note indicated he couldn't bear to part with Japan for college in the United States. Japan had become his home, and no one seemed to understand. I remember thinking that just because he didn't *look* Japanese that didn't mean he didn't *love* Japan, with the strange, wonderful tingling inside when you really sense the beauty of something. When I thought about his death, I felt his presence—the United States was barely a whisper for me, too. And although I couldn't comprehend a struggle so desperate, so heart-wrenching, I imagined myself facing a window of uncertainty and becoming the next casualty. It was then I decided that I would live in Japan forever.

I regretted Papa and Mama's announcement that we would be moving to a new place, a new neighborhood. The thought of packing all my things in boxes and saying good-bye again was exactly what I feared. I remained silent, my stomach sour with thoughts of having to make new friends.

Papa spoke encouragingly about their choice—a big house in a quiet neighborhood that was closer to the school. At least we would have a backyard, most Japanese couldn't even dream of such a luxury. Miguel was especially looking forward to this because he would be able to catch and study insects without having to travel to a public park. Mama, who had by now resolved herself to the fact that we would not be returning to America soon, hoped that she would be able to go back to school to finish her bachelor's degree. Tokyo University Press had just given Papa a new, extended contract and a substantial raise.

Mr. and Mrs. Okino, our landlords, came over to our apartment a few days before we moved out. Mrs. Okino wore a red and orange silk *kimono* and Mr. Okino wore a dark and light blue *haori*. We sat across from each other, with our legs folded on the floor pillows in the living room. *"We will never have better renters,"* said Mrs. Okino. Mr. Okino nodded his head in agreement. Facing Mama and Papa, Mrs. Okino produced a small box wrapped in brightly colored silky cloth and tied with a bow at the top. She placed it on the tatami mat and with both hands, pushed it toward Mama. She then closed her eyes, bowed her head slightly and spoke slowly. *"Totemo tsumaranai mono desuga ... doozo ...* we aah sad you go."

Mama had spent many afternoons learning basic Japanese cultural etiquette from Mrs. Okino. She tightened her lips and cleared her throat. *"Ieh, ... mm ... watakushi totemo osewa ni narimashita ... "* Mama fumbled for the right words, trying to express, as is expected in Japan, her matter in not having been a good renter. She closed her eyes, bowed, and pushed the box back toward our landlords. Papa cleared his throat to make sure Miguel and I were paying attention.

Mr. Okino nodded his head again in approval. Mrs. Okino bowed lower and pushed the package back toward Mama. *"Ieh, tondemoni. Taihen osewa ni narimashite ... doozo ...* please, take." Mr. Okino bowed and Mrs. Okino bowed even lower.

I studied Mama, then looked at Papa who was bowing with her. As she pushed the present toward Mrs. Okino for what should be the last time, she began to chuckle nervously. She kept her head down and began fumbling for words. "Ah ... mm ... (chuckle) ... *watakushi* ... ah ... I don't remember ... um ... we have been very difficult guests ... ."

Mr. and Mrs. Okino chuckled with her and bowed down to the floor. "Please ... for Arboleda family ... ." This time she pushed the small package one last time right into Mama's hands.

Mama steadied her fingers on either side of the box. "I'm embarrassed ... *arigatoo gozaimasu.*"

Mr. Okino motioned for Mama to unwrap the present. As Mama untied the bow, I leaned forward to see what was in it. Papa glanced at me, indicating that I should return to my position. After the silky cloth gently unraveled onto the tatami, Mama straightened it out. She then opened the flaps of the cardboard box and made a hole in some shredded, colorful plastic packing strips. Pulling out a apple-shaped gold-colored fruit, she smiled and showed it to Papa, Miguel and I.

"It's yoah faborit fruuts. You rike *nashi*, yes? From auah tree." Mr. Okino gently pointed his hand, palms up, toward their backyard.

"Thank you very much—it's beautiful!" Mama exclaimed, still holding the *nashi* in her hands. Papa coughed, looked at Mama and then at the *nashi*. "Oh ... I'm sorry, *sumimasen*." She picked up the box and dashed into the kitchen.

"Yu ah nice boi ... " Mr. Okino gestured toward Miguel and I with both palms of hands facing upward. I looked at Papa who bowed his head slightly, clueing Miguel and I. We bowed. I didn't know how low to bow or what to say, but when I came up, Mr. and Mrs. Okino were both bent over lower than I had been. I bowed again, even lower. When I straightened, they both smiled contentedly. A tear rolled down Mrs. Okino's face.

Mama came from the kitchen with the washed and cut *nashi* neatly arranged on a small plate. On the edge of the plate were six toothpicks. Mama returned to her place on the floor and offered the plate to the Okinos. Mrs. Okino nodded and took a piece. Then, Mr. Okino rolled back the right sleeve of his *haori*, nodded and took a piece. Taking turns, Miguel, myself, Papa and finally Mama took a piece. I was about to bite into mine, but Papa glared at me. The Okinos looked at Mama, indicating she should take the first bite.

Mama stuck a toothpick into a piece and then bit in. "Mmm ... vrygd ... (slurp) ... expushmi ... ."

The Okinos laughed, took their bites and mumbled in satisfaction. Papa took his first bite while Miguel crunched on his piece. As I devoured mine, I looked at the Okinos. Mama reached for her second piece. Then we all broke into laughter as Mr. Okino slapped his thigh and imitated Mama attempting to slurp the *nashi* juice that was rolling down her chin.

That was the last time I saw Mr. Okino. The year after college, I visited Mrs. Okino. She was frail, but remembered fondly our good-byes at the apartment.

\* \* \*

I counted the steps as I ran up the staircase to check out our new bedroom on the second floor. I remembered Tante Luise's insistence that a person should know by heart how many steps are in one's home. "After all," she would say, "you go up and down these stairs every day." I counted 13.

At the top of the staircase and just to the right was what would be Mama and Papa's room. Just ahead was a tiny hallway leading to what would become our playroom. It smelled musty, as if no one had lived there for a long time. But the scent of freshly installed straw mats also filled the room. Mama and Papa loved *tatami* so much, and as I walked on the mats,

I felt a little guilty knowing that ours would be the only rooms furnished with them.

Papa told us how this house had been the first one in our neighborhood and was designed during World War I by the father of our landlady. Mrs. Hashimoto cared for the property by herself. Her husband had died many years earlier. Before her father passed away, the family had lived for a while in Brooklyn, New York, so they had been relatively knowledgeable about Western styles and traditions. Their American experience showed in the architecture and interior design. The house was old but sturdy and well-kept. Nevertheless, I could hear Mrs. Hashimoto downstairs apologizing profusely for the terrible condition of the building.

I moved into the back room and looked out the window. From the 2-foot balcony I studied the backyard. At the periphery stood a whole hedge of 12-foot-high bamboo trees, a strange looking palm tree and two maple trees, making it look like a mini jungle with a green patch in the middle. Miguel appeared from behind one of the red-leafed maple trees, crouching in his usual insect–stalking pose. I thought about my favorite willow tree in our backyard in New York, with its long, delicate branches, like fingers caressing my head in the breeze.

Mama's call broke me out of my trance. I hurried down the stairs. Thirteen steps. I counted again, just to make sure. Mrs. Hashimoto was leaving to let us unpack and settle in. She smiled and laughed nervously as she continued to excuse the condition of the house, then welcomed us one last time. We stood as a family and watched as she stepped into her shoes in the *genkan*. Turning around in the tiny entrance, she bowed and we reciprocated. After Papa closed the door, he waited for a second and looked at Miguel and me. "Well, here we are ... what do you think, you two?"

"Did you see the praying mantis outside? It was huge!" Miguel exclaimed.

"Well, you two will have the honor of mowing the lawn and weeding. Consider yourselves lucky to have a backyard. You'll have to learn to take care of it. In fact, the grass looks like it hasn't been cut it in years. Next weekend, I want you two to buy a lawn mower."

Not having a clue as to how much work goes into caring for a yard, I was excited, and daydreamed of the weekends I would spend in the backyard. In New York I had watched Grandpa and his neighbors mow their lawns and I imagined myself steering a big gas-powered mower just like them.

In the afternoons when I came home from school, Mama was usually arranging furniture, pictures, and knick-knacks around the house. This was the first time she had so much welcome space. We had a huge hallway, a living room, separate dining room, a small kitchen and laundry room, three bedrooms, and not a lot of furniture to fill the rooms. The living and dining rooms had floor-to-ceiling sliding glass windows looking out on the backyard. There were wooden storm windows that retracted into the walls, readily accessible for the spring monsoon season. Most of the walls were covered with Papa's paintings, wood block prints, and lithographs. My piano was against a wall under an unfinished painting of Mama, Miguel, and I that Papa began late one night when we first moved to Mejiro and never had time to complete.

The stove, barely large enough to make a meal for a family of four, was made in the United States. "Welbilt?" Papa used to chuckle at the brand name. "What a testimony to the American education system. They should call it 'Badspelt.'" In the laundry room we had a normal-sized American washing machine. Early 1960s Japanese appliances were not known for their reliability or functionality, and the hand-cranked contraption Mama struggled with in Mejiro she gladly left behind.

The television sat in the living room on a cart next to the wooden chest that contained all the family photo albums and loose pictures. Sometimes Papa and Mama moved the cart to the dining room to watch our favorite Japanese comedy or music and variety shows while we ate supper at the large dining room table we had shipped from the United States.

Upstairs, Miguel and I had a bunk bed that fit just inside the alcove at the end of the bedroom. I had the top bunk and 3 feet of headroom. I liked sleeping on our *futon* on the floor, but I figured at least this way I would be further away from all those large cockroaches that one cannot escape and that I had come to despise in Tokyo. In our playroom we had our Fisher Price record player on which we would play our three LP records: the soundtrack to "Doctor Doolittle," "Alvin and the Chipmunk's Christmas Special," and the American Heritage's "This Land is Your Land" sing-along album.

Outside the house, next to the garbage cans, spider webs clung to the oil drum from which we would pump fuel for the stoves in all the rooms. It would be Miguel's job to pump out kerosene and fill the stoves a couple of times a week. It was my job to take out the garbage. Monday was non burnable garbage day and Tuesday and Thursday were burnable garbage days. Saturdays were for larger, disposable items like appliances.

The summer lingered as the humidity dulled my sense of time. Unlike our former place, the new house was built with a dark, lower leveled *genkan* at the entrance and a brighter, higher living room with large screen doors, which, when open, let in gentle breezes throughout the first floor. Mama urged us to go outside to play, and I got to know the neighborhood quickly. We didn't live in a traditional Japanese district. Most of the houses were considered mansions, hidden by high walls and metal gates. There were only a few kids our age near us. I was reminded of how long it took to make friends in Mejiro, and that only with patience could we expect to get accepted. Mama had explained that building a friendship, especially for grown-ups, was a long-term process in Japan. I had heard but had never seen the two boys our age that lived next door. I was wary of getting to know them because they tormented their caged, pet chimpanzee who screamed horribly unless he was placed by the window.

The corner variety store down the hill was reminiscent of the five-and-dime store where I used to purchase Papa's Sunday newspaper in Parkway Village. The wooden structure had living quarters upstairs and the store on the first floor. A sign outside read Mikado in *hiragana* and *romaji* (roman letters, phonetically Japanese). The owner, Fujisawa-san, was a gentle man whose smile was as welcoming as his candy displays. Once a week I picked up a loaf of white bread and other staples. Fujisawa-san would turn on the rotating blade, unwrap the bread and carve off the crust, slice the loaf into thin pieces, and return it to its package.

One day, as Fujisawa-san was slicing the bread, he asked me, "*Teja-kun, anoo ... America no onna no hito tachi, oppai wa ookiindesuyo nee....*"

I didn't fully grasp the question. He had asked something about American women, but I didn't understand one of the words. "*Eh? Nani ga ookiindesuka?*"

He stopped slicing the bread and stepped away from the machine. Then he cupped his hands over his chest and gradually created the image of two rapidly growing mounds becoming heavy, then hanging down to his belly. "*Chichi ... oppai wa dekkai daroo nee?*"

I started to laugh. He laughed along with me and resumed slicing the bread. "*Ookiindayo nee ... America jin no oppai wa ... Konna ookiindeska?*" He made the imaginative mounds even larger, seemingly hanging over the counter.

I laughed even harder. I had never studied the breasts of American women, let alone breasts in general. I had no interest in breasts. But obviously Fujisawa-san was getting a kick out of the notion that all American women had monster-sized mammary glands. I thought about Mama's breasts which, I guessed, were small, at least in comparison to the breasts of some of the women in Parkway Village. Wiping a tear from his face and sniggering, Fujisawa-san returned the sliced bread to its bag and handed it to me. Then he opened one of his glass containers, pulled out a strip of dried cuttlefish and handed it to me. I loved dried cuttlefish and tried to suppress a satisfied smile as I took a bite. Fujisawa-san started laughing again and repeated his impression of large-breasted American women. "*Kujira mitai na oppai nante ... hyaa ... ii desunee!*"

"Whale breasts?" I translated to myself. "Whales have breasts?"

I asked Miguel if whales had breasts, but he just laughed at me. I didn't tell Mama about Fujisawa-san's impression, but quickly learned in the following weeks that I would be rewarded with strips of dried cuttlefish each time I assured him that American women had ocean-creature-sized mammary glands.

Further down the street, past the dark, wooden liquor store and a row of stucco and wooden houses, was the butcher shop. The owner, Saijo-san, was also always happy to see me. He was convinced that my family consumed more meat than half his clients combined. He would stop everything when I entered, raise his blood-covered gloves and greet me with a loud commanding voice, *"Ah! Aruboleda, Teja-kun! Irrashaimase! Ogenki desuka? Guraundo beefu desunee! Hai wakarimashita!"*

Knowing exactly what I needed, he would swiftly wrap 300 grams of medium ground beef, 150 grams of bacon, and 8 chicken legs. After marking the price on the wrapper with a grease pencil, he would lean on the edge of the counter and ask about the family. The conversation always ended with a promise that he would expand the business in our honor. After all, what better customers could he have, but real, live, meat-eating Americans!

The local *soba* delivery men knew us as the foreign family who, oddly enough, ordered traditional Japanese meals. They grunted in awe when we ordered the likes of fried pork and eggs over rice, cold buckwheat noodles with mild soy sauce, and steaming noodles with baked soy slices and scallions. It was obviously strange to them to have foreigners living nearby, but *gaijin* who used chopsticks and ate soy products became good enough for gossip.

I admired and respected our delivery man. Endo-san braved every kind of weather on his three–speed bicycle, riding up and down the steep hills of Denenchofu, balancing with one hand more than 40 pounds of ceramic bowls filled with steaming food. I could always hear him coming closer as he jingled the bicycle bell while rounding each turn. Always with a smile, he would place the tray of bowls on the *genkan* while Mama fished out the correct change. Sometimes she would comment to us under her breath how happy she was not to have to figure out tips, as there are no tips in Japan. As Endo-san would bow and turn to leave, he would recite, *"Doozo, goyukkuri!"* We cherished this encouragement to take our time eating, especially on lazy summer weekend afternoons. Sometimes we forgot to clean the bowls for pickup, and Mama would hastily wash them in warm water as Endo-san joked with us at the front door. At this point, he usually produced some candy from his white apron and whispered to us not to tell Mama.

Months had passed since we moved, and everyone luckily seemed to have forgotten about the grass and weeds that had become knee-high. Papa was busy with work and Mama with college and teaching English at a kindergarten. Miguel and I played in the backyard everyday and didn't notice or care about the growth.

One Saturday morning during breakfast, Papa glanced out at the yard and noticed a group of 7-foot-high bamboo trees smack in the middle of the garden. "Oh my god! Where did those come from?" We all walked over to the screen doors and stared at the invaders. Papa turned to look at us. "I thought you boys were taking care of the backyard! I go to work every day of the week and stay late ... what the hell do you do all day anyway?"

Mama raised her eyebrows and started laughing. "Miguel, Teja, you guys spend all the time in the backyard. Didn't you see those things growing?"

Papa sighed and went back to his coffee on the table. "O.K., you two, today you're both going to buy a lawn mower. I want this backyard cleared by this afternoon."

There was only one place we knew of that even had lawn mowers: the combination supermarket and department store called Peacock, which was in Jiyugaoka, a district not too far from our house. As Miguel and I walked to our train station, we bickered over who would get to use the mower first. Miguel was worried about injuring our backyard insect friends, while I was concerned only with maneuvering it skillfully, like Uncle Gene did back in Grandpa's frontyard in New York.

Jiyugaoka wasn't at all like our old neighborhood market in Mejiro—it was much larger, louder, and flashier, almost American in its design. I pleaded with Miguel to walk around with me before heading to Peacock. As we browsed through a string of tiny markets connected by a narrow interior isle, I recognized the smells of fresh bamboo shoots, fried bean curd, freshly dyed cloth, and syrup–covered shaved ice. Clerks welcomed clients, yelling out greetings and prices as customers worked their way through the crowds. The umbrella store was the first unit, and, being at the exit, was a perfect location for customers caught in unexpected showers which were especially common during the rainy season in April. We passed a stationery store where the clerk dusted a proudly displayed rack of colored Bic pens. The small fish-market saleswoman hacked the head off a large silvery fish. We paused at the rice crackers and candy supplier, but Miguel decided it wasn't time for snacks yet. A woman whose back was severely hunched over straightened her apron and smiled at me, revealing her toothless gums. I quickly diverted my eyes when I realized she ran a women's lingerie store. I began to smell dark bean paste, garlic, teas, and magazines. At a smoked eel and squid counter, a vendor lured us into his booth to use us as bait for more customers. He yelled above the drone and commotion of the crowd. *"My eels are so tender and fresh, look, even foreigners love it!"* Some other clerks caught on and began to lure us, *"Welcome, foreign customers!"*

As we proceeded through the sea of people, we passed a wig shop that boldly displayed faded, outdated posters of White women with blond hair and blue eyes. I recognized a couple of the faces from some American movies I had seen. At the men's clothing store, a tall, White, blond mannequin stood deadpan in a suit. A cubicle selling toys vibrated with battery-powered yapping dogs; screaming, cymbal-crashing monkeys; and larger-than-life crawling, plastic Helmet Beetles. The music store blared the overexerted, cracking voice of the latest Japanese teenage pop singer idol. At the far end of the market sat an old woman on a bench outside her rice store. It didn't look as if she had much business. She quietly watched the crowds pass, as if her product, once the national pride of Japan, was no longer important.

We stopped at the nearest neighborhood police booth to ask for directions to the supermarket. We followed the officer's crude hand-drawn map through the narrow streets, passed a traditional *zori*–slippers and shoes shop, an electronics boutique, a *soba* restaurant, and some humble-looking office buildings. When we arrived at Peacock, we headed straight for the "greeting-woman." She wore a blue skirt suit with a tag around her arm to identify her as a customer relations personnel, white gloves, and a military-style hat with the department store logo on the front. She bowed and greeted all the incoming customers and then bowed and thanked everyone who was leaving.

*"Irrashaimase."* She began to welcome us, then realized we were foreigners. *"Ah ... hai ... anoo ...* Pureezu ... may I herrupu yuu?"

*"Shibakariki wa doko ni arundeshooka?"* I inquired, ashamed to ask in English where the lawn mowers were.

She looked puzzled. *"Shibakariki ... soo desunee ... shibakariki wa nai kamo shira nain dusukeredome."*

We couldn't believe that they didn't have at least one lawn mower. Miguel had been studying the floor directory; he nodded at me, indicating he had found something. I followed him upstairs to the second floor. After making our way through the lingerie department, we found the gardening section. A few tools, some bags of potting soil and a ladder rested against the mostly bare wall. A sales clerk approached us and smiled. *"Irrashai-mase."*

"*Shibakariki arimasuka?*" I asked, staring at the lingerie section, wondering how much lingerie could be sold in such a small neighborhood. Miguel imitated mowing the lawn.

"*Eh? Shabakariki?!*" His eyes widened, astonished. I was beginning to think lawn mowers were illegal or something. He bombarded us with questions as to how large the backyard was and what kind of grass we were dealing with. He made it clear we were lucky to need to cut grass, and that he hadn't sold a lawn mower in years. He climbed the ladder and pulled down a small manual mower with red blades and black wheels. With a cloth that had been hanging on the wall, he dusted the mower, making it shine. Then he wrapped the blades and wheels with newspaper and pink twine. As we left, he told us to be careful and let him know from time to time how our gardening went. On the train home, passengers looked at us with more than their usual curiosity. I became embarrassed, thinking it was wrong for us to show off something most people couldn't have.

I was lucky—I won at *jankenpoi* with my rock-shaped fist over Miguel's scissors-shaped hand, so I was the first to use the lawn mower. I pushed and tugged, pretending to drive a car around the yard, only this road was like the floor of a tangled jungle. Miguel ripped the bamboo shoots from the ground. In minutes I was drenched in sweat, and overheard Mama cursing the intense Tokyo heat and humidity from inside the house. Renegade blades of grass and weed stuck to my bare back, chest, and arms. In the shady spots, mosquitos nipped at my exposed skin, while hundreds of cicadas buzzed in the trees, mocking me. In less than 5 minutes, I realized that "lucky" was purely subjective.

*   *   *

As the weeks passed, I began to meet some of the neighbors. Most of the kids were a little older than Miguel and me and became increasingly bold in their curiosity about us. Mikiko, a 12-year-old girl who lived four houses up the hill, smiled excessively whenever she came to visit. Miguel always found an excuse to go catch more insects in the yard, a hobby that disgusted her. She was only interested in practicing English, so she would call for me from our driveway, armed with her English workbooks from school. After a brief, staggered comment in English about some new friends she made at school or a television program she watched the night before, she would jump right into having me look over her homework or correct her pronunciation. Sometimes her mother came by to make sure she was progressing well so that she would be properly prepared for the difficult college entrance examination. After I calculated that it would be

6 years before she entered college, I knew I had to escape her overdrawn smile and her pile of English homework, trapping me in a cage like a lion tamer.

Haruko, the 12-year-old-girl who lived at the bottom of the hill, was Miguel's secret desire. I caught him staring at her one weekend as she washed her parents' 1965 Volvo. Early one school day, Miguel leaned against the gate posts, chewing nervously on his nails, waiting for Haruko to emerge from her house. She always left earlier than we did to get to the train station. I watched him as he suddenly threw his bag over his shoulder and sped off down the street. He never told me what happened, but he was too shy to speak to her again for several years.

Around the corner from Haruko lived Minoru, a young teenage boy who always wore blue jeans and a white T-shirt, and who greased back his hair over his scalp. He looked like some of the characters in an American movie I had seen at school called *West Side Story*. On some afternoons his friends came over with their motorcycles and raced around the neighborhood, revving their engines and waving a flag with a picture of a skull on it.

Akiko, a gentle woman in her early 20s, lived directly across the street. She was the live-in maid for an aging former Cabinet minister, and was in constant preparation for a not-yet-arranged marriage. Occasionally, she came by to borrow pots and other kitchen utensils. Mama told us that this was Akiko's way of trying to get to know us and to help make us feel welcome as neighbors. Akiko always returned the pots and containers cleaned, dried, and filled with a small bag of rice, beans, or little cakes. Mama felt bad about Akiko's gifts, and explained to me that in Japan, newcomers to a community are supposed to offer gifts to the settled neighbors as a gesture of goodwill. She hadn't known about this custom until it was too late and now she didn't know how to make up for it. Papa told her not to worry because everyone had already formed this opinion of us as ignorant but well-meaning foreigners.

One Saturday morning while we were eating breakfast, a uniformed officer came to the front door. He introduced himself as Ohara-san, our neighborhood policeman. Papa invited him inside. As Ohara-san took his shoes off, I looked at Miguel, wondering if we had done something wrong. Mama went off to prepare some tea. Papa ushered Ohara-san to the living room where they sat down. I watched from the sliding doors. Ohara-san struggled to speak in broken English. "Berry nice house. I raiku jis house. Berry ordo house."

He spoke for a while in Japanese, but the cicadas had become unbearably loud, drowning out the sound of his voice and the oscillating fan that stood between the dining room and living room. Mama returned with tea and some cut fruit. Miguel joined me at the doorway. Ohara-san stood up, bowed low, and introduced himself to us, *"Ohara desu. Yoroshiku onegaishimasu."* We bowed in response and waited for him to straighten up. After Papa, Mama, and Ohara-san sat down, he began to speak again, officially welcoming us to the neighborhood and reminding us that he was always on duty.

After he took a sip of tea, he looked over at Miguel and I. *"Kawaii boya tachi desune! "*

I hated being called cute. I turned the subject around by asking him why he didn't have a gun. He laughed and pointed at me. "You raiku gun? *Ban! Ban!* Always American raiku gun, pistoru, raifuru. Berry dangerous. Crazy. In Japan, no need gun. Berry safe."

Papa must have been happy to hear Ohara-san tell us these things. He informed Ohara-san that guns and violence were one of the reasons he didn't want us to grow up in the United States.

As Ohara-san turned to leave, he invited us to stop by sometime for some tea and to meet his family.

I got to know Ohara-san well during the summer months. He lived with his family and worked out of a custom home police station. Their house was at the top of the hill overlooking the Tamagawa River and had a spectacular view of Mt. Fuji. During the days, Ohara-san made his rounds on his official white, three-speed bicycle, wearing his neatly pressed navy-blue police uniform and shiny black shoes. At his desk in the office, he would take off his shoes and socks and put on his beloved raised wooden clogs.

In the evenings, soon after it got dark, the fire marshal would walk the streets of the neighborhood, hitting two wooden sticks together rhythmically, in a ceremonial reminder to put out one's fireplaces. That would be our cue to finish our homework and practice our instruments.

\* \* \*

One morning when Miguel and I were washing our bicycles in the driveway, the two kids from next door climbed to the top of their fence and started yelling at us. *"Kono bakana yabanjin!"*

Miguel stood up in front of me and glared at them. They started laughing at us and continued to call us names. *"Bakayaro, kono yabanjin meh!"* As they called us "savages" and "strange foreigners" and ordered us to "go back to where we came from," they climbed back down to their side and started pelting us with rocks. One rock hit Miguel's bicycle. Miguel ran around the bushes and jumped over the gate into their frontyard. The two kids ran into their house. Miguel yelled at them in Japanese and English, calling them obscene names at the top of his lungs.

I could hear them laughing inside. Their caged chimpanzee began to scream hysterically. Then it was quiet again.

The next Saturday they resumed their name-calling and rock-throwing. They would have continued if not for Papa's reaction on learning that one of their rocks had broken a ceramic pot on our front steps. In a resounding, thunderous voice, Papa threatened to beat the living shit out of them. Although they didn't understand a word of his American slang, the message was clear enough. We never heard them or their chimpanzee again.

The summer persisted, and August rolled along in a haze of muggy afternoons and sticky, but perfect evenings. Sitting in my room, I imagined Tokyo from above, with its millions of lights shimmering through the haze hours after sunset. I listened to the trains arrive and leave Denenchofu station. The rhythmic crescendo and decrescendo of the metal wheels clicking over the tracks were comfortable and mesmerizing. Downstairs in the living room Papa and Mama listened to the U.S. Army-based Far East Network on the radio. Somehow the sounds of America seemed oddly appropriate.

# The Connection

September seemed to arrive late that year but I was more than ready for the fourth grade. The cover of my fat, used textbook entitled "World History" had a picture of the earth taken from an Apollo mission, showing North America bulging out through swirling clouds. Inside the book cover were the names of the previous owners who secured in this way, their own little piece of history: Liam Kim, Yeshwant Jain, Ono Hedeki, Dave "Rules!" McCully. As I carefully wrote my name in the next empty space, I thought of the countries Papa had traveled to for business.

I pretended I was Papa, studying my itinerary for my business travels. I flipped through the pages of the World History textbook and studied the pictures and captions, and imagined my destinations. Ancient Europe, Medieval Europe, Victorian Europe, recent Europe, the discovery of America, Pilgrims, the 13 original colonies, the Civil War, Abraham Lincoln, the Industrial Revolution, the 50 states. There were brief sections on Mesopotamia, Ancient China, and Japan, and no more than a half a page on slavery in America. When Papa returned from his extended business trips through Africa, Southeast Asia, and the Middle East, he told stories of his travels and discoveries. So I began to question why we weren't learning about some of these places in school. I verbalized my concerns in class, and stirred things up, sometimes at the mercy of the teacher. Papa, through his example, had taught me to stand up for my beliefs, so I brought up the topic of exclusion several times in class, only to get mocked and snickered at by some of the other kids who saw me as threat to their simplistic curriculum.

One afternoon while in the library, I came upon an enormous leather-bound book, resting on its own tiered, wooden bookstand. The book lay with the pages open to a color picture of a blond-haired, blue-eyed, White-skinned man and woman wearing nothing but a leaf in front of their genitals. Underneath the picture it read, "Adam and Eve, under the Tree of Knowledge." Eve's long, flowing hair just barely covered her nipples. She was handing a bright red apple to Adam who leaned against the tree. Above them, hanging from a branch was a snake with its forked tongue flicking. I thought about Fujisawa-san from the corner store, and how he would be disappointed with the picture because the woman obviously didn't have large breasts. I also thought about Miguel because he had been looking for garden snakes in the backyard all summer.

I turned the page quickly, suddenly realizing I shouldn't be looking at pictures of naked people. I had seen pictures of naked people before in some *National Geographic* magazines, but they were never White and blond-haired. Sometimes I had the nagging suspicion only Black people were comfortable being naked and that it was bad for White people to be seen fully unclothed. There were many brightly colored pictures of mostly men with long beards, White or pink-ish skin and blue and brown eyes, commanding large groups of people to do things like walk in the middle of what looked like two waterfalls, and who I recognized as Noah and his huge wooden ship that housed animals I had only seen in the Bronx Zoo in New York City.

I finally came on a picture of which I could make sense. A White-skinned, brown-haired mother and father smiled at a blond-haired, bright blue-eyed, White-skinned baby, who I presumed was Jesus. I read the caption that described the birth of God's son. A gold glow beamed from his head. Underneath him was a small, Black-haired, dark-skinned man who held open a little box of jewelry that also glowed. Two other small brown-skinned men just off to the right also held up objects that glowed. The caption under the picture read: "The Lord Jesus, Our King and Savior is Born."

I flipped through some more pages and found a picture of Jesus walking on the surface of a lake. The caption read: "The Lord Jesus Christ Walks Upon the Water." Several pages later there was a picture of Jesus commanding a dark-skinned man (the only one I had seen in the book and whom I presumed was Judas) to leave the group of apostles.

I felt bad that Judas was singled out as a darker skinned man, and wondered what Papa would say about these images. Now that we had been in Japan for a while, I thought maybe he might not be so concerned about being dark-skinned anymore. I also remembered how I used to complain to Mama about not having White skin myself. If Jesus, the son of God, was White, blond, and blue-eyed, then I wondered if our God was also White, blond and blue-eyed. These questions stayed with me as I observed the images of peoples, gods, and demons. To this day I have never seen a dark-skinned angel in a painting, nor have I ever seen Judas as a light-skinned man.

During lunch periods, I began to notice how the kids in the cafeteria divided themselves. A group of White kids, mostly U.S. citizens, Northern Europeans, and Australians sat at the table closest to the glass doors overlooking the central courtyard.

They were usually the loudest, throwing pasta at the ceiling to stick and commanding attention. At the table next to them sat the Japanese kids. Behind them sat the Korean and Chinese students, and against the wall sat the group of African kids. In the middle was a table filled with culturally and racially mixed boys, social outcasts, and newcomers. I usually sat at the latter, and rarely would I venture to another table to visit a classroom friend. But when I did, it was like some forbidden fruit, where knowledge of and connectedness with the "other" becomes an evil thing. I could feel myself getting smaller underneath my skin with each step I took into unfamiliar territory. A friend might wave hello, but the code of conduct was to confine socialization with "outsiders" to the hallways and the schoolyard.

I met Jeff LeFloch while I stood on the sidelines of the asphalt playground, observing some kids throwing rubber balls at each other. He was a shy, overweight kid, the son of French nationals. He was born in France, but grew up primarily in Japan and struggled, like I did, to be accepted as Japanese. We became friends instantly. In class we began to pass notes written on tiny pieces of paper rolled and stuffed into the barrels of dismantled ballpoint pens. With one good blow, the note-wad would soar across the room, mostly missing the mark, hitting unsuspecting classmates. We were sent to the principal's office on numerous occasions for our misdemeanors, but we always stuck together.

Sometimes, on weekends, we would sleep over at each other's houses. When I stayed with the LeFloch family, Mama always warned me not to waste my money on candy. I would get annoyed with her because I didn't think I had a real interest in sweet snacks, but as the months passed and Jeff got fatter, I inevitably began to gain weight as well. Jeff would lure me into candy stores where we bought Nestle's chocolate bars, Tootsie Rolls, and Wrigley's chewing gum. Riding our bicycles through the streets of Tokyo, we would stop at little parks and eat our treats while watching insects and tadpoles swimming just under the surface of murky, dark-green ponds. The longer we stared into the ponds, the more I recognized that his attention was focused more on the clouds and open sky reflected on the surface of the water. He would watch in silence as an airliner left its white tail streaked across the horizon.

Jeff's dream was to be an airplane pilot, and his obsession seemed to grow stronger by the month. His bedroom was filled with hanging plastic 747s and biplanes. His father continually taunted him by telling him he wouldn't be able to become a pilot because he was too fat and the plane would crash. About 6 months later his parents divorced and his father returned to France. Jeff started eating more candy and chocolate and gained so much weight that his mother had to take him to the doctor.

I hated to stand out. More than anything in the world, I wanted to look like what I thought was a normal person, better yet, a normal Japanese. By now I had gained enough weight and baby fat that I developed small breasts. This fact, combined with my thick, curly, bushy hair and my knock knees, I started to look like a little girl going through early puberty. I felt humiliated and didn't want to be seen in public. I was obsessed with losing the weight I had gained so quickly. I heard about jogging from my physical education coach in school, so I started with some early morning runs. I was under the impression that plastic helps increase sweating, so I taped two large garbage bags to my chest and stomach underneath my regular outdoor clothes. The first day, I rose early, before the sun came up, and took a route through the smaller streets to avoid being seen. While I ran, I almost collapsed, my body trying to breathe and cool off simultaneously. The few strangers I encountered stared at me with more bewilderment than usual: A foreign child running through the streets to the sound of wind-torn plastic sheets was weird, but then again appropriate for a *gaijin*.

One afternoon when I returned home from school I sat at my desk and pulled out an old color pencil box. I hadn't used this box since I had made an anniversary card for Mama and Papa several years back. I carefully outlined a face, hair, eyes, nose, and mouth. As the waxy colors stuck to the paper, the smell of the crayons brought back memories of my grade school in New York, and the days of busing, demonstrations, and snow storms.

I wasn't sure what I was doing, at least I didn't have any clear idea as to why I was even drawing this face. I made anatomical corrections and added the shadows. The strands of hair flowed straight down and the eyes were empty. The mouth was not smiling, nor was it angry—like the eyes, it showed no emotion. As I studied the image I felt something missing. I pulled out the White crayon and began to fill in the face. My hand gripped harder as I pressed the crayon to the face, digging in and dragging the white wax into every open spot. I ran over the face again, breaking off the smooth tip of the crayon. I grabbed the yellow crayon and made thick layers of hair pop out like a blinding sunrise, like the halo on Jesus in the picture bible. Then I took the light blue crayon and filled in the eyes. I felt myself smile as the name John Smith came to mind. Simple, normal and easy to pronounce. I took a red crayon and wrote the name on the bottom of the page. My hand continued to write, "This is what I want to look like." I walked to Mama and Papa's bedroom and placed the picture on their bed. As I walked downstairs to watch television, I felt oddly triumphant.

That afternoon when Mama returned from shopping, I watched her retreat to her room, and waited. When she emerged she called for me. In the hallway I stared at the dark brown hardwood floor and noticed how the areas with the most traffic were lighter, a medium tan. The color of my skin. "Why would you want to draw a picture like this of yourself?" She said. I felt her eyes sadden. When I looked up at her I thought she looked angry, then I saw a hint of a tear. "Teja, you should be perfectly glad with who you are!"

"Duh!" I responded. "Mom, you're always telling me you're jealous of the color of my skin, right? What do you do? You go outside and try to get a suntan. After 5 minutes what happens—you sizzle, you burn, and then you turn *red!* So why aren't you happy with the way *you* are?"

*   *   *

In geography class, we skimmed over a page that had a picture of some people who lived near Jesus' birthplace. They were fairly dark and had Black, curly hair. I thought of Jesus again. How could he have been so White, blond, and blue-eyed in the picture I had seen? When I finally posed this question to the class, a group of them drowned me in name-calling.

This had become the normal routine for me, dodging random insults for opinions I thought were honest and just. My viewpoints and imagination had somehow placed me between reality and fantasy. This was most apparent during the four hours allotted to the IOWA test, an intelligence ratings-based examination administered by the American education system. Well into the fourth hour I had only completed one third of the questions. I found myself struggling in particular with a situation where I was required to compare the size of an American quarter to a penny. Finally I gave up the whole test, nearly in tears, after I had struggled to solve a mathematical problem concerning the time it would take warring British settlers on horseback and Indians on foot, to reach a bridge from opposite sides. I was practically there, rooting for the Indians to reach the bridge first, to blow the settlers away and make all the rest of them go back to England or wherever they came from. I imagined the pain the Indians felt, having had to defend the sacred land they worshipped, watching their world succumb to the greed and demonic pride of the Europeans. What tribe, nation of Indians were they? Could they avoid the bloodshed? Did the Europeans have superior fire power? If the

Indians were killed off, would they be returned to their villages for proper burial? The minutes and the speed of travel posed in the test made my stomach turn hot with humiliation and shame. I hated the settlers, the pilgrims, the Mayflower, and Columbus. I thought of spitting on John Wayne, Bob Hope, Bugs Bunny, and all the rest of the characters that made the Indians look stupid and "less than."

Somewhere along the line, prayer before lunch had become an option. Some of the wealthy non-Christian parents put pressure on Brother Andrew and the administration. I could almost hear a great sigh of relief from the body of students in the cafeteria when this decision was first announced. Consequently, my group became much more religiously and culturally diverse.

This is when I started to lose my sense of belonging. Most of my friends would only be in Japan for a couple of years, then would return to their homelands. What seemed fair and secure to me slowly turned uncomfortable. A young boy's criticisms aren't taken seriously, after all, "experience is the true teacher." Yet experience is relative, and I knew that my perceptions were at least somewhat real. With that realization I became bold and even more outspoken. The color of my skin, my language, my talk, and walk, mattered. No longer did I just see myself as an outsider in Japan, rather, I became a floating object, a satellite. I was awkward, wrongfully designed, ill-fitted, and afraid of perpetual rejection.

I yearned deeply to be attached and grounded. My few friends offered me that solace freely. But most of all, we were still very young, and I secretly worried about growing old and spiteful like some of the bitter, old Jesuits who ran the school, or like the discarded, unfinished apple of Adam and Eve.

Papa's harsh carping behind the crease and crinkle of his *Asahi News* evening edition had become at least tolerable. He voiced his opinions, unsolicited, sliding from article to article as if all news was singular. "African nations have never had the support of the Western world. Rhodesia's civil war is an *international* crisis. On the other hand, the coup against Allende? You know what that means. It's not like the old-fashioned religious wars in Northern Ireland, Lebanon, Israel, the Arab world—you *know* are just going to continue. And this Nixon *joke*—that's what's on the front page? I come home to this!"

* * *

In the middle of growing up, memories are created, some of which come to us much later in sudden flashes. Of the many friends I had, and the ones with whom I became bonded for life, how could I ever imagine that our hands reaching across the oceans would symbolize so much? In our small world of school corridors and train platforms, we exchanged cultures like a dealer hands out cards, but held them close to our hearts like security blankets. Then, by either following in the footsteps of our parents or pioneering new territory, we remained independent of the cultural stereotypes that threatened us: Alvin Lin, Taiwanese, became a corporate investment trader in Manhattan; Jacky Spillum, whose yearbook quote read: "American by nationality, 'half' by looks, and Japanese by heart" is now a successful animation producer; Craig Yanagi, Japanese-American, lives in New Jersey, married a Japanese woman and works for Sony; Thierry Cohen, French, married a Japanese woman and is president of a trading company in Japan; David Griffith, half-Japanese, half-American, lives in California and is a graphic artist; Asaki Iimura, Canadian by citizenship, Japanese by heritage and college-educated in California, is currently a middle-manager in an international real-estate firm in Japan; Hiroshi Hara, Japanese citizen of Korean heritage, lives in Japan with his Japanese wife, and has taken over his father's restaurant business; Dan Watanabe, half-Jewish-American, half-Japanese, and became an executive in Hollywood; Christopher Due, British, married a Japanese woman and lives in England with their daughter Yuki-Teja; Paul Leake, Mexican-Canadian, son of a vice-president of Coca-Cola, is a lawyer now living in Manhattan; Salik Taufiq, Pakistani, became a doctor after attending medical school in Georgia.

# 12

# The Adjustable Pedestal

Deepika didn't tell me why her father must never know about us. I thought it was because she was in seventh grade, a year ahead of me. She attended Seisen International, an all-girls Catholic School, the sister school to St. Mary's. We dated for 3 years and I never met her family.

I never asked her about India and she never asked me about the United States. I guess we assumed we both would live in Japan for the rest of our lives, so maybe talking about our home countries was irrelevant. Together we decided that she would become a scientist and win a Nobel Peace Prize, and I would become an actor and win an Oscar. We exchanged notes many mornings through her classmate, Emiko, who traveled to St. Mary's in the morning for choir practice. These notes were filled with dreams, a simple joke, and sometimes a poem. Our friendship was simple and honest. We hardly gave a passing thought to her Indian culture and my mixed heritage. Yet it seemed that there was always something important she had to say to me that remained for the longest time on the tip of her tongue. I assured myself that secrets are sometimes silent thoughts wrapped in a package, and if the wrapping is beautiful, one would surely hesitate before opening.

For much of the world, tradition remains a necessary constant. The tradition itself may evolve, but its presence and function are paramount. But when one chooses to part from family expectations, especially when living in a culture separate from the homeland, the seeds of guilt or embarrassment can take form.

In Japan, where jeans and T-shirts had become a staple, Deepika and my public identity were nothing less than expected: Foreigners were usually seen holding hands and even kissing in public. We were only teenagers, but according to the world around us, we were far ahead of our time. By our example, in the midst of a growing inferiority complex among

Japanese youth, we became icons; no more, no less than Western in all its abundances and successes. Then to be condemned for the sins of nonconformity, our trust in keeping true to our identities was dashed and scattered. One moment riding high on the pedestal, the next moment, acknowledged only as "disruptive." How is a person supposed to immerse one's self into a culture that does not accept outsiders?

Years later, we met for lunch in Tokyo. We were both visiting Japan on our summer vacation from our respective colleges in the United States. She told me that during the years we were together, her father had been the vice ambassador from India, and that if he had ever found out about us, he would have promptly sent her back to India to marry her off. Now that she was studying in the United States at an all-womens school, her father, she claimed, was at least contented: He had secured her a husband who was waiting for her "return." Briefly, in India for an arranged rendezvous, Deepika met the gentlemen, a young doctor-to-be. "If only I could extend my stay another semester, maybe I could learn to like him," she confided, "or maybe he will find someone else." I remembered how she always smiled, no matter what she was feeling. "I am very unhappy at the college, and I don't like America. But I can never live in Japan either, so I must go back to India. Maybe if I succeed in medical school and became a doctor, at least I would have my work."

Not wanting to disrupt the family with its traditional values, Deepika had always kept her Indian identity in her mannerisms and her walk, but she also had Japanese traits. Maybe she always knew she would return to India, with hopes of living in Japan or the United States, a fading possibility.

At the time I felt deeply sorry for her. I thought of how I would probably have protested against my parents in defiance, to break from the expected. But something told me she didn't have that choice. Her ties to the family were rooted in deep-seated traditions, something I couldn't comprehend. I had learned that all cultures were sacred, and that as an outsider I was not empowered to criticize, interfere, or challenge, so I didn't say anything to her.

But then I thought about wars and injustices, rape and poverty. How could I, as a caring human being, be not touched by the lives of other humans, regardless of their heritage and nationality. Was I not also responsible for those outside my world? Could I not criticize those aspects of other cultures that seemed harsh and unfair? Should I then also ignore the newspaper and radio news? After all, why bother if I am not to be involved? And what *was* my culture? Did I have the right to criticize Japanese customs, or would I always merely be a casual spectator, a mere visitor in this country I had come to accept as my home? And Deepika, the woman I had once loved, in my puppy-love innocence—would we stay friends? And had she changed during her years in America, would I ever find out?

After lunch we walked to the train station in silence, said good-bye and have never seen each other again.

*   *   *

Mr. Glauche was very different from his wife, whom I still feared. In his sixth-grade homeroom, he encouraged a rigorous examination of different cultures, discussing them in detail, with interest and deep respect. So it was expected that no one would laugh when Salik demonstrated his prayer routine, on his carpet toward Mecca. Carl, the whining troublemaker, described how he would become a man after his bar mitzvah. Tim, the pickpocket, recited in prose, Simon and Garfunkel's "Bridge Over Troubled Waters," claiming its relevance to his beloved America, a country he hardly knew. But after each colorful, sometimes heart-felt demonstration of another culture presented by one of our classmates, there were always others who snickered and mocked them.

Mr. Glauche was hard of hearing and seemed almost ignorant to the teasing by my classmates. The moment I sat down after my presentation on Germany, the loud Australian wisecracker, Peter McDuffy leaned over at me from his desk.

"Nigger." His eyes danced but his mouth quivered.

I looked away to the blackboard, preparing for war. "What did you say?"

"You're a nigger," he whispered.

I shot up and flashed my eyes at him. "You called me a what!" Mr. Glauche peered over his glasses at me. I looked back at Peter, cupped my mouth in my hand and whispered back, "3 p.m. in the hallway next to the bathroom."

Peter pretended to read his textbook. "Nigger."

It was only 10:30 a.m. I was hoping he would apologize—I had no idea what I was going to do. I had challenged one of the most popular jocks in my class and I was doomed. The day continued like I was sitting in a vat of molasses. "Better wear a cup, you little shit," Peter's puppy dog cohorts warned me in the hallways. "Bring a friend or two—you're going out on a gurney."

School let out at 2:50 p.m. I had 10 minutes to run. My head spun with rage and fright, so I entered the bathroom to wash my face. Then I heard the door open. "Teja ... Peter wants you outside."

"They're early," I thought to myself. All I could think about were some of the stories Papa told me about how in the Philippines they were never in as much a rush as Westerners were. "At least in the Philippines they wouldn't be in such a rush," I answered back.

Peter stood with a friend to each side, Andy and Charles. Both of them were my friends. "Philippines? What are you talking about? I thought you were from Germany? Little shit! You don't even know where you're from!" He guffawed like a hyena, which prompted his posse to do the same. "Said you wanted to see me? It's 3 o'clock." He walked toward me. Miraculously, the concentration techniques I had learned in judo kicked in.

"What did you call me in class?" I said, steadying my voice, and breathed from my stomach. I remembered from horse riding that some animals can smell fear.

A smirk appeared at the edge of his mouth as he spread his legs. "Nigger, you stupid shit, did you forget already?"

I took two steps forward, landing my left foot in front, and launched my right fist through his face. I watched him curl back and snap, blood streaming from his nose. Andy and Charles were already halfway down the hall by the time Peter's body ceased sliding on the freshly waxed floor. I stood above him like a hunter with excess testosterone, like a hero in a Hollywood movie.

The next day he apologized in that minimal way that Westerners tend to, and we became friends. If this is what it took to gain respect from a Westerner, then so be it.

I felt awkward, however, like another animal was living inside of me. Why did I slug him? What a nasty, but satisfying feeling! I walked home slowly, smiling with my heart racing, replaying the scene in my head. During dinner I was quiet, then spent the rest of the evening in my room in a pool of trepidation and bliss. I had been reminded that Japanese society is based on nonconfrontation, and so I felt like a traitor. Were my actions purely a natural defense mechanism, or learned from those around me? Was I reliving stories of my father's childhood? I decided I had been wrong—it was too easy an action. Even though we ended up as friends, I should have allowed my feelings to dissipate and find reason for his actions. My Judo *sensei* had been quite clear about finding alternatives to violence: "*Opponent's offense is my defense*," he had taught us to recite, a credo that he hoped would stick. I had broken this promise to myself, and I worried that I could never become Japanese because of it.

* * *

It was a relatively calm, but muggy Saturday afternoon. Mama had been gone for several hours and Papa, Miguel, and I were dozing in the living room after having had a soba delivery. Even Endo-san seemed mellow that day. The doorbell rang. I pressed the intercom speaker button to listen.

"It's me! I got a surprise! Come to the door!" Mama sounded exceptionally excited.

We rushed to the *genkan*. Papa opened the door. A woman with a glowing blond, queen-sized afro stood in the doorway smiling like Mama. I thought again of Jesus in the manger. She also had Mama's nose and eyes, but something was terribly different. "So ... don't just stand there," the face and hair said. "What do you think? I had it done today."

*Mama!* She must have been thinking, "If we're not going back to America, then let America come to me!" Brave, bold, different, chic!

Papa's head popped forward and his legs bent out slightly for emergency balance. Miguel innocently jumped in. "That's an afro."

I started to laugh. "It's big."

Papa closed the door behind her and looked over at us, his eyes making orders to shut up and approve. "It's really nice. It's very you," he said. He knew if he didn't sound genuine it would backfire. I bit the inside of my cheek to keep from laughing again, now with the image of Papa with a matching hairdo.

"I figured something nice for next semester, you know, something so I can 'fit in.' But this is not at all what I had asked for at the parlor. I don't think they knew what they were doing. I wanted a perm, but the hairdresser obviously has never worked with curly hair like mine." Mama's fingers were lost in the depth of her hair, as she tossed it like an unruly but radiant bed of lettuce. "She must have put on too much conditioner or whatever."

"You're going back to school ... with *that*?" Miguel looked at me as if Mama was going to be sitting next to him in class. I took a step back as Papa's head fell to his chest. We were all well aware that Japanese had primarily two positions toward foreigners: outsiders to whom you can be rude, or enviable strangers to be placed on pedestals because of the wealth and ebullience they generally represented. We were agents of mixed blessings: jeans, T-shirts, The Beatles, peace signs. So, a blond afro would be no less worthy than front page news. Heads were sure to spin to catch a glimpse of the spectacular yellow lollipop-figured woman. I imagined the pedestal would be ordered two notches up if I were to be seen with her.

Mama smiled a very controlled smile. "And I expect all three of you to take care of your chores because I'm going to be very busy with classes again."

\* \* \*

Goto-san arrived on her three-speed bicycle and parked it under the tree. She bowed deeply in the doorway. *"I am Goto. I am here respectfully at your service."*

Mama took her bag while Goto-san removed her shoes and placed them neatly in the *genkan*. She then asked Goto-san to speak more slowly as Mama was still not up to speed with her Japanese. Goto-san apologized and obliged. *"I know this house—I have always admired it. My husband and I used to come up these hills for picnics. We would sit at the end of this road, looking out over Tamagawa River to admire the gentle slope of Mt. Fuji. Your house was one of only two in the neighborhood, the rest was grass and fields. That was a very long time ago."*

Goto-san's husband had died many years earlier so she took house-keeping jobs around Tokyo. She worked mostly for foreign families, so she was familiar with some of the habits and needs of Westerners. After they became acquainted over tea, Mama gave her a tour of the house. As they went from room to room I could hear Goto-san shower Mama with compliments. *"What a beautiful dining room."* And *"The stairs are classic European!"*

For the next 12 years, Goto-san would have her own can of green tea leaves, house keys, and her routine. She was a simple, earthy woman, but full of life and interest. It wasn't rare for her to ask us details about our daily routine and about life in America. She saw Miguel and I grow from skinny, disorderly children into young adults, then witnessed the unraveling of Papa and Mama's marriage. Never stepping in, but always present. She was a constant in our lives. Years later, during my summers home from college I watched her get older, sometimes finding her asleep in her favorite chair with the television on.

I don't know if Papa asked her to leave because she had become ineffective or if she left on her own, but it wasn't until after I graduated from university that I heard she had discontinued her services. She knew all the edges and cracks in the house, every floor board, every irregularity; she was in part of our lives even if only on the periphery. How could I say it was my house any more than hers? I began to realize that *home*, as a physical attachment or possession of property, does not necessarily guarantee a spiritual link. Goto-san had became part of the family, and maybe that was all she really wanted.

*   *   *

I had been in school plays since the fourth grade, so when I was asked by a prominent Tokyo-based agent if I would like to appear in a Big John Jeans ad, naturally I agreed. I was willing to do anything to be in front of the camera, and blind to the humiliation it would cause me as I continued in what I had on occasion fantasized as my career.

"*Try these on.*" The assistant handed me a pink pair of bellbottom jeans. It was my eighth pair that morning already and the director hadn't gotten what he wanted.

"*Don't smile so much, you don't have to smile.*" The director looked at me over his sunglasses and took a drag from his cigarette.

"*You don't want me to smile?*" I asked.

The assistant clicked his tongue. "*Don't argue with the director. Only your legs are in the camera. Go on, change.*"

I had spent the whole night before this shoot practicing poses and smiles, why would he want only my legs? I struggled into the pink jeans and returned to my post where the client walked up to me and tugged on my pants. His cigarette butt fell on my new shoes as he barked at the director. "*I only want his long legs, okay? No face. I don't want to see the face! We need an* American *face.*"

The assistant bowed and apologized. The director placed the megaphone on his lips. "Long *legs!*"

"*Dance, can you dance?*" The client clapped his hands in rhythm. The director ordered, "*Dance! You love Big John Jeans!*"

I recalled a Christmas party from a few years earlier when Papa showed me the "Monkey" and the "Swim," so I flailed my arms and performed a standing backstroke.

"*Cut! Cut! No good. Don't dance.*" The director bowed in apology toward his client. "*I'm sorry, this gaijin cannot dance.*"

The client's eyebrows edged upwards. "*How strange. Okay. No dancing. Just legs.*"

A couple of months later I saw the ad. It was a composite shot of legs and faces. My legs in pink jeans were on the lower left, overshadowed by the blond-haired blue-eyed smiling face of Mark, my classmate.

It wasn't long after that I found myself doing voice-overs for cheap Japanese movies. I read the lines of kids in trouble, like a stowaway on a pirate ship or the victim of fiery blasts between ground troops on the streets of a city under attack. It didn't matter if the voice didn't match the movement of the actor's mouth; as long as a recording was made, that was sufficient. And what English in the script! Certainly I wasn't there to second-guess my character's motivation, or worse, advise the director on correct English.

At one audition for an advertising firm, I was trapped by seven gray men and their cigarette smoke, as they mumbled and groaned, trying to decide if I was looking "American" enough. I knew I didn't get the job, and I had to ask if I could leave the room to get some fresh air.

On the way home I sat on the train and watched *Daikan Yama* train station flash by. Next was *Nakameguro* station. Five more stops and I would be home. The train was quite empty—not many people to stare back at, so I studied the advertisements. I counted four wedding service posters featuring blond, blue-eyed women in white gowns. In another ad, a muscular blond-haired man chewed on a power bar.

A schoolgirl sat next to me, reading one of the popular weekly cartoon anthologies. She sat bent over, scanning the pages, feverishly engrossed in that week's episode of a romance story between a blond, ultra long-legged, motorcyclist Frenchman and a red-haired, blue-eyed Japanese school girl wearing an ultra miniskirt that most traditional Japanese would have considered obscene. I imagined my train partner defying her parents for the sake of popularity and dying her hair like Mama's. Then I wondered if she also wanted blue eyes, long legs, and a French accent. Was she jealous, or in awe? Did she feel badly about her conservative uniform, her straight black hair, her legs, and the complexion of her skin? Did she hate her eyes?

At some point, Japanese students seemed to become bolder, even rude about approaching foreigners. I first encountered this while packed in a rush-hour train ride home from school. A few bodies away and to my left stood a group of teenage girls in school uniforms. They had been going through their English language workbook together, and had spotted me. As they wormed their way over to me, they took turns reading out loud the exercise questions. The loudest one nudged up against me and began to conjugate the verb "run." The rest of her gang mouthed along with her, frequently breaking up the rhythm with giggles and excited shouts.

"What ... kindo ... musikku ... do ... you ... raiku? I raiku ... Bay Shitti Roraas ando disco. I know! You raiku disco!" She gave me a demure look, then shoved her English study guide booklet in front of my face.

"*Lass mich in Ruhe,*" I said, hoping she wasn't a student of German as well. I closed my eyes and pretended to meditate. It didn't help.

"*Eh?*" She pointed to something in her booklet. "Do ... you ... eato ... fish? Za boy ... in za ... car ... wave herro! '*Haroo' datte, kawaii janaino!* Please ... to ... helpu me ... wis ... homewaaku."

As we pulled into Denenchofu station, I looked her straight in the eyes. "*Auf Wiedersehen!*" As I walked away from the train, I could hear her loud voice commenting on my odd use of English.

Mrs. Takanori, Mikiko's mother from up the street, seemed more panicked than ever. She brought Mikiko to ask me formally for my help with her daughter's English. Apparently Mikiko wasn't doing as well as her grandparents expected, and a low grade would certainly shame the whole family. Mrs. Takanori invited me over for chilled fermented milk and green bean paste cake, but the refreshments developed an after-taste when Mikiko commenced her pronunciation exercises. Over the abandoned crumbs on my plate, Mrs. Takanori grilled me on American culture and boasted of her plans to have Mikiko attend medical school in the United States. *"Maybe Harvard. That would be very nice."* I briefed her on the little I knew, which she took as my reluctance to cooperate. *"You have forsaken your culture,"* she said, practically scolding me. I got even more annoyed when I got home when Mama laughed at my predicament. The next day I walked over to Mikiko's house to follow up.

*"I am Japanese,"* I said to her.

*"That is impossible. You do not understand—you are a foreigner."*

She didn't get a valentine from me that year. Or ever again, especially when, a year later, she explained that in Japan valentine cards are only given by girls to boys. My heart dropped to my knees—I had already mailed 14 hand-made, *Old Spice* sprayed valentine cards to potential girlfriends. Love was lost in that foul-smelling air, and someone, maybe Mikiko, would have to pay. That is when I began my retaliation campaign. If I couldn't be Japanese, I would be exactly what they wanted me to be.

\* \* \*

Some said it was because I liked the attention. And they were right. I auditioned for every school play Brother Franks put on. This year he was casting *You Can't Take It With You.* It was 4:15 p.m. when I entered his homeroom where the auditions were being held. Brother Franks sat on the window sill, shifted his 455-pound body slowly and squinted at me.

"Well, well, if it isn't the smaller Arboleda." He checked his nails. "What can I do for you?"

"You told me to audition."

He wiped his brow and pulled his pants over the bulging fat on his middle. "Right. Who do you want to play?"

*"The main male character."*

"Oh ... ah ... well, we have Kimberly playing the main female character."

All the guys lusted after Kimberly, the voluptuous, blond girl from Sacred Heart, another Catholic all-girls school across town. Brother Franks liked her too, in a suspicious kind of way, so she always played the lead, and was invariably paired with a White guy. In the following years, Kimberly racked up the credits, including the role as a sexy Mary Magdalene, paired with Chris who was a blond, blue-eyed Christ. That was the same year Brother Franks dropped out of the ministry and became a civilian. I was deeply mistaken when I thought he would have relaxed, now that he was no longer tied to the church, because in the end I realized that as long as I was at St. Mary's, I would never have a lead role.

"Tell you what. Why don't you try out for *what's his name*, the Italian guy?"

I got the part—a minor role. And out of the nine characters, only one other role was filled by a non-White student: a walk-on police character with one line—four words. Then during the first day of rehearsal Brother Franks ordered me to play my character with an Indian accent. "Now, you see?" he said, checking his other actors' reactions for approval. "It's much more fitting, isn't it, everyone?"

\* \* \*

It was getting dark earlier, and the walk home after play rehearsals was usually quiet because we were exhausted. I took to walking by myself the long way to the train station, past the graveyard with the long, wooden *kanji*-inscripted stakes bunched together like a ripe cornfield. Down the steep and narrow winding streets, past the dark wooden stained stucco houses and over the moss-covered canal. The trees in Tokyo were thicker and greener than the ones I remembered from New York. They hung over the gutter-lined paths like old rice farmers hunched over from decades of field work. The crickets and frogs were already preparing their beds for winter, little shelters under leaves and rocks. Once in the park, I would hear no traffic, and few people ever passed through. Sometimes, before continuing to the train station, I would sit on the stone steps next to a little pond. I imagined myself as a boat, slipping through the cracks between the rocks that line the basin.

One evening in November, as I made my way down the hill and toward the park, I heard a voice from behind me. It got louder and closer. Through the voice I could hear rusty metal grinding on gears. A man shouted and the grinding got louder, quicker. "*Konoyaroo, Yankee goo hoome!*" I turned around to see an old man on a rickety bicycle coming straight for me. I jumped to the side to avoid collision. He didn't even look at me as he darted past. "*Kusottare! Stupid Yankee goo hoome.*" His squealing brakes hardly slowed him down as he headed like a bullet down the street, straight into on-coming traffic at the "T" where he was nearly run over by a Coca-Cola delivery truck.

I didn't even know what a Yankee was.

I bypassed my little stone step and pond and walked, dazed, into McDonald's. I sat at the end table and watched some American St. Mary's kids throwing pickles and yelling at each other. The Japanese patrons left them a wide margin only to observe them with disgust. I focused my eyes through the window and across the atrium. On the other side of the entrance to the train station, a Kentucky Fried Chicken employee soaped down a life-size statue of Colonel Sanders. I sipped my freezing-cold chocolate shake that went straight to my head. I hated America. I hated Colonel Sanders with his perpetual smile and inviting arms. I was embarrassed of my uniform and my face. I wanted to apologize to the old man on the bicycle for whatever was done to him. Maybe if he had looked into my eyes he might have seen that I was not the enemy.

I never went back to the park again. What was I supposed to say to my friends—that I no longer took my favorite route because someone called me a Yankee? No one could possibly understand my dilemma. Or better yet, I wouldn't let anyone understand it. This reaction, I learned years before from an older Japanese friend, was truly a Japanese trait. "*Wakette tamaru ka!*" I snapped at him. He laughed and put his hand on my shoulder. "*Teja, you might be Japanese after all!*" Then he placed his hand over his heart and nodded his head.

Years later I realized that at *that* moment, when I remembered that statement and the image of his hand on his chest, I had internalized Japanese culture. Maybe I was, like he said, Japanese after all.

# 13

# Hokkaido

*"Good afternoon, my name is Arboleda. I think it would be a good idea to hire me because you have many English-only speaking customers."* I bowed again to Kobayashi-san, the manager of Shell Gardens supermarket. *"Yoroshiku onegaishimasu."*

He looked around his store. Then he studied my face, and I could hear the engine in his mind gearing up. *"You like to work hard?"* he asked in Japanese.

*"Yes. I will work very hard."* I bowed once more.

*"Yes. We do need an English speaker. Hmmm ... 10 a.m. to 10 p.m. Six days, sometimes 7."* He lit up a cigarette. *"So, you speak English. That's good. The salespeople are lazy—their English is only so-so. My English is very good. How do you say, 'The bread is over there.'?"*

I switched to English. "The bread is in the bakery section at the end of Aisle 7."

He darted his eyes at me. I looked at the floor, embarrassed that I had the audacity to show off in front of an elder—a potential employer at that. Then he began to laugh. *"Very good! Very young too—you have guts. Okay, fill out these papers then I'll show you around. You start on Monday. I normally don't hire people so quickly, but we need an English speaker. You're lucky. Don't let it get to your head."*

Miguel and I had 2 months to save up for our month-long bicycle trip around the northern island of Hokkaido. Halfway through the trip, we would meet up with Miguel's Japanese-Filipino classmate, Alex Udujan, in the northern part of the island. Although we had traveled to Europe often, even alone, this was our first real independent trip. We had to plan everything ourselves. We had to buy bicycles, camping equipment, book the ferry passages, and secure campsite lots and youth hostel beds. The toughest part was convincing Mama that we could handle the trip.

108

One of the great things about living in Japan is the sense of safety. Even now, as I walk the streets of cities and towns across America, I still crave the freedom, a lack a danger I find inherent in the heart of Japan. The security in Japan allows growing up to be full of healthy exploration. That was in 1977, when the island of Hokkaido was still considered the "wild north" and had many road sections still unpaved, or no roads at all. Papa pretended to have confidence in us. "If this was the U.S., there is no way I would let them travel alone like that—you could forget it. They'll be fine here."

We worked hard that summer, and loaded down our older bikes with rocks and trained during lunch breaks and after dinner. Kobayashi-san had placed me as a packer and translator and nodded with approval when I went out of my way to help a customer. The other employees knew I was trying to stay in shape for the long trip, so when I finally opened the bottle of Cheese Whiz I had been salivating over, the manager snatched it from me and reprimanded me in front of the others. *"You must not eat this! It is American garbage food! Look, says 'cheese food!' What is 'cheese food'? Sell this only to American customers!"*

One month into the job, the impending reality of the long bicycle trip finally hit me, and I became nervous. I had learned from a fellow bagger that the resident butcher was also a palm reader. So I asked Takenori-san to read my palm for guidance. Without even taking my hand he bowed and apologized. *"I'm sorry. I cannot read American hands. The lines are different—different meaning, I'm sure."*

"But, I'm Filipino," I said. "Asian."

*"Different."*

During my last day on the job I worked especially hard. My last impression was going to be a good one, then I could say goodbye to my fellow workers with respect. At 10 p.m., after Saijo-san made store-closing announcements over the microphone, they all gathered around me to wish me a safe trip. One by one they bowed, gave me a present, and recited a little speech in my honor. Finally, I bowed low to Takanori-san. *"I'm sorry to have been such a tremendous burden to you. Please accept my humble apologies. And thank you for the opportunity to work for you—you have been a tremendous inspiration and mentor. Thank you very much. I will carry memories of all of you on my trip."*

Takanori-san bowed back. *"Teja has shown us hard work and humor. We should be thankful for his presence. He is practically Japanese! One day he will marry a Japanese, no?"* Our laughter carried through the store over the microphone that hadn't been turned off. Takanori-san handed me a jar of Cheese-Whiz. *"Take this with you on your trip—you will never have to refrigerate it."*

* * *

Papa and Mama stood silhouetted under a sulfur light on Tokyo Bay's
Dock 14. The ferry loomed over us like a fat, bobbing blue and white
skyscraper. A row of cars slowly crawled up the loading ramp into the
gymnasium-sized belly. I still remember Papa's proud but nervous smile
as he watched us go through our checklist.

Mama produced two brown paper bags. "Here's some food for the boat
trip." Don't forget to eat well, okay? And don't let yourselves get too wet
or cold when it rains. Be careful with those pocket knives, and don't forget
to keep in touch, send postcards at least, okay?"

"Okay, Mama." Miguel nodded. "Don't worry so much. Everything
will be fine." He stood straight and confident and put his arm around me.

The ferry departure horn sprang to life. We hugged, then walked our
bicycles up the ramp. I took in the evening air, heavy with an odor of
brine and oil, and watched Mama and Papa waving beside our orange
Honda Civic. Upstairs on the deck we waved good-bye again as we left
the dock, and watched a glittering Tokyo sink into the night and the
horizon of water.

Third-class passengers shared two large rooms padded with tatami. We
found a space for ourselves and unfolded our futon mats. The couple
preparing their beds beside me wore black leather jackets and had
motorcycle helmets placed next to their pillows. They both smiled and
nodded at us. *"Where will you be traveling?"* the young man asked.

I tried not to let my pride show. *"All around Hokkaido."*

*"We are also going around Hokkaido. It's faster by motorcycle, you know."*

The young woman punched his arm. *"Don't make fun. They're too young
to ride motorcycles."* She looked at me and leaned over. *"Where are you from?"*

I hated being young, especially to an attractive older girl. "America."

*"That's a long way on a bicycle."* The young man chuckled.

The woman moved in front of him. *"Don't listen to him. You're from
America? Someday I want to go to America and go to Marlboro Country. West
Coast, right?"*

The young man looked stern. *"Your father will never let you go to America.
He doesn't even know you're traveling with me!"*

* * *

We arrived at *Tomakomai* port two mornings later in the middle of a
torrential downpour. As we adjusted to the stable ground, we covered
ourselves with ponchos, then followed the main road north toward
Sapporo, the capital of the province. It would take us 3 days to reach the
city, and the weather forecasts were grim. We camped in the woods and
stopped at drive-ins for quick lunches of curried rice and hot green tea.

Heads turned to look at the two dark, skinny gaijin with their bright red touring bicycles. *"Where are you from?"* they would ask, and almost never, *"Where are you going?"*

With Miguel's lead, we arrived in Sapporo and stayed with my classmate Hideki, who was spending the summer with his uncle. From Sapporo we headed southwest to Lake *Toya*.

Three days later we found ourselves lost on a lonely country road, nightfall approaching and our destination nowhere in sight. Miguel had developed a bad fever by the time we rolled into what looked like a deserted old gas station.

*"Excuse me!"* I shouted, trying to be loud enough to be heard, but quiet enough not to agitate Miguel's fever.

Silence. No movement.

*"Excuse me! Is there anyone here?"* I looked around and watched the evening clouds blush. "Maybe there's no one here," I suggested.

Miguel shook his head like he always did when he was under stress. "Of course there is," he called out very loudly, almost angrily.

A few moments later a woman poked her head through the doorway. Her face was dark and weathered. She wore the traditional indigo-dyed farmer's clothes of baggy pants, black split-toe shoes, a heavy tunic, and a scarf around her head. She slipped out, smiling broadly, her eyes slits, her teeth gold with fillings.

*"Oh, I'm terribly, terribly sorry,"* she said. *"I didn't hear you."* She pointed to her ear. *"I have bad hearing. May I help you?"*

*"Yes,"* I said. *"We are lost, you see, and my brother is not feeling very well. We want to get to Toya Lake and settle down for the night. Could you tell us the way?"*

She nodded her head gravely. *"Yes ... I see. You have a long way to go."* She shook her head. *"And on those bicycles? Mmm...."*

Then she brightened up. *"But of course, I know a short cut!"* She pointed across the street to a tiny path that cut into the hillside and disappeared into the forest above. *"That's the way I always go."*

She detailed a series of directions which sounded easy enough. *"And don't forget to turn right at the fork in the path,"* she said. *"It should only take about half an hour."*

We thanked her and started up the path. The shadows were dispersing among the trees. Miguel lagged behind with his fever, cursing to himself. An hour later, we still hadn't arrived at the fork. At one point, as we trudged up a hill, pushing our bikes ahead of us, we were surrounded by a wide circle of small farm houses. The last brilliant light of the setting sun filled the sky. Miguel grabbed my arm and silenced me. "Look!" A family of foxes paused in the path ahead, watching us. Miguel began muttering something about wild brown grizzly related bears living in the wilder parts of Hokkaido. Right then we heard a low buzzing sound, like an power saw. We glanced behind us and saw a beam of light sweeping across the fields, and then it disappeared. The foxes were gone. The light appeared again moments later, closer, and the buzzing yet louder. Then suddenly a little man on a white delivery motorcycle came into view. He stopped when he saw us, astonished.

"*Good evening. Are you all right?*" he asked.

I explained about the fork in the road and Miguel's fever and Lake Toya camp ground. He raised his eyebrows. "*That's serious,*" he said. He gunned his tiny 50cc engine. "*You must follow me. I will bring you to my brother who owns an inn. I cannot let you camp when one of you has a fever.*"

We thanked him, mounted our bicycles and followed him over the bumpy rise and fall of the path. Ten minutes later we came to the fork in the road. We took a path down to a paved street and rode beside the dark expanse of Lake Toya. In the distance I could make out a faint hint of the towering dormant volcano, Mt. Shiribetsu. "*Moo chotto da!*" he yelled back, encouraging us.

We arrived in a little town and were told to leave our bags in the entrance hall to the inn. The old man herded us off to a noodle shop where he bought us two large bowls of piping hot miso ramen. "*The best miso noodle soup in Hokkaido,*" he boasted, then bowed humbly.

The old man waved aside any of our attempts to pay for the meal. "*Just remember: The Hokkaido people are a humble people. It is taken for granted to help travelers. That is our tradition.*" During the meal I thought about what he had said: The *Hokkaido* people are humble. Does this mean he doesn't consider himself Japanese? Is the tradition to help foreigners only a fact in Hokkaido? Or was he saying this to make us feel welcome all during our travels?

After the meal he took us back to the inn. He left us there to retire for the night. "*I must go home to my wife,*" he said. "*She made korokke and I don't want to miss that! Maybe she fried them a little longer than usual—the way I like it!*"

After a long stay in the hot spring bath, I tried to fall asleep to the sound of guests playing *mahjong* in the room next door. As they moved their pices over the wooden game board, I drifted off remembering how I used to watch Papa playing chess with Opa.

The next day we debated whether to stay for another night and pay our respects to the old man. We were told by the staff that he had gone to work, and that he wished us good travels. That afternoon when we were about 50 kilometers away, without warning, Mt. Shiribetsu erupted. There was severe damage to the town, and we never learned what happened to the inn.

"Last night the foxes warned us," Miguel said. "They know more than we ever will."

* * *

"*Everybody wake up! It's 6:30 a.m.,*" the P.A. system at the *Kogane Inn* blared throughout the youth hostel. "*First is group exercise, then breakfast! Please make sure the two gaijin have made their beds and cleaned up their mess!*" The manager then listed the exercise routines and the composition of the morning's meal. A young man who had slept in his jeans and peace-sign T-shirt leaned over to Miguel and reminded him that we had to make our beds.

By 6:45 a.m., more than 80 guests assembled in the frontyard for calisthenics. During breakfast the announcements continued. "*After breakfast please make sure the two gaijin have washed their dishes and thrown away their garbage. Have a good day and come back soon!*"

During the next few days we completed a loop around the "tail" of Hokkaido, then proceeded north again, circumventing the city of Sapporo. We pitched tents in the wilderness, cooked dinners over the portable kerosene stove, and hung garbage from trees to keep the bears away. With each passing turn and hill, the open sky and rolling grassy hills of Hokkaido made me feel increasingly intoxicated. The roads were relatively quiet, and we cycled further toward the northernmost tip of Japan to the town of Wakkanai. Cycling through its gentle streets, the idea of Japan harboring a massive city like Tokyo seemed impossible now. Heads turned and cars slowed as we passed through. We were formidable curiosities, almost shockingly so for farmers or store owners who claimed they had never met a foreigner. But we found there was a deep tenderness among the people, perhaps because of the relative isolation from the Western influences that dominated much of modern Japan. It would only be a matter of years before the streets would be lined with R. J. Reynolds billboards and littered with Coke cans. But for now, this island, which for centuries had been labeled as "wild" and "uninhabitable," was still pure and simple.

We reached Soya Misaki, the finger-shaped peninsula that pointed across the channel to Dalnyaya, the Russian-occupied outpost. The Japanese military had been conducting exercises off the coast, in demonstration against Soviet occupation of the island of Sakhalin since World War II. Two Soviet submarines floated in the near distance, mocking the demonstrations. How quaint it was to observe two world powers, both of whom were equally guilty of domination, occupation, and cultural rape, virtually stick their tongues out at each other like little children. Then I remembered that practically every country I had learned about was equally as guilty of subjugation and occupation. It became hard for me to see Japan as innocent, nor Russia or the United States for that matter.

Miguel and I turned south, through the heart of Hokkaido. Our gears cranking, we pumped our way up the highest elevation points. From the summits of Mt. Asahi and Mt. Tokachi we visually traced backward, amazed at the distance we had traveled. Then as we glided blissfully down the opposite sides of the mountains and hills we had conquered, we waved at other tourist bicyclists on their way up, only minutes later to be faced with another stiff 4-hour climb.

On our way to Akanko, we were picked up by a family who offered us hospitality in return for a quick English drill session with their daughter and son. We were fed well and spoke into the night about our travels, America, and life as a foreigner in Japan. The father was from Hiroshima and remembered well the hate he professed to have had for Americans, but now that his son and daughter wanted to study in Massachusetts, he had to learn to change his perceptions. *"Besides,"* he said, *"I cannot possibly hate Americans when there are people like you! I cannot hate forever. It's a waste of energy. Now we must forgive."*

We arrived in Akanko where Alex had been working for and living with an Ainu craftsman and his family. In the evening, the Ainu villagers gathered to perform their tribal dances, songs, and stories for tourists. They were the original inhabitants of the islands that are now Japan, and they look quite different from the Japanese. With their long hair and thick mustaches they were seen as savages; some anthropologists used to say they were Caucasian. They were pushed north by the newcomers to die in the long, harsh winters near Siberia, but they survived, building villages and keeping alive their heritage. Now all but extinct, the Ainu still cannot legally own land or gain Japanese citizenship. That night, as the Ainu dancers chanted and danced, a young Japanese couple next to me commented on how wild and animal-like the Ainu were. The next day I saw them tear onto the main street in a bright red Toyota with a bumper sticker that read, *"Beautiful Green Hokkaido."*

Alex, Miguel, and I traveled through the dirt roads of the eastern tip, setting up camp in the woods. We had averaged 85 kilometers a day between the towns of Nemuro and Hombetsu, peddling 60 kilos each up and down mountains. Sometimes between breaths, I cursed Japan's 85% mountain range.

Nevertheless, we were always welcomed graciously in the youth hostels. *"Yookoso!* Please, welcome! *We have been waiting for you."* The manager of The Red Bird Youth Hostel placed a check mark next to our names in the log book. *"You are just in time for dinner, please wash up!"*

We placed our bags in the room and introduced ourselves to our five roommates. After washing up we went to the dining room and joined the other 60 guests. When the manager introduced us to the group we stood and bowed. Then, as the food was brought out, each person served the one sitting next to them and eagerly poured them drinks. The more one served the other, or filled the cup of green tea, the deeper grew the communion. Not in contest, but as a gesture of giving; not taking or hoarding but sharing. And the pride and community spirit, respect and honor made sense—a sense of belonging, building up deep inside. Soon we nodded in response when someone spoke, allowing enough time for the statement to sink in. The older ones were most respected, and we listened intently, grunting and nodding quickly, as was the norm.

The hot rice, salted fish, and pickles were a relief from canned camp stove food, and I made sure Taka on my right was filling up. He had introduced himself to Alex, Miguel, and me with his nickname only, Taka, and refused to give his last name. In return, he asked us only for our first names. *"American tradition!"* he exclaimed.

Soon the room was buzzing with stories of travels and laughter. *"You are from America!"* one girl wearing a Bay City Rollers T-shirt announced. *"Hey, they are from America! They will sing for us later!"* Another girl placed a fish on my plate with its eyes staring at me. *"Wait until the 'penalty game'! The games at Red Bird Inn are really severe."* The room broke out in laughter.

*"What is 'penalty game'?"* Miguel asked.

A young man stood up and raised a glass of beer to the room. *"What is 'penalty game'? Oh, we are going to have a great evening tonight!"*

During bath time, as I dumped a bucket of water over my head to rinse out the soap, I became giddy thinking about the forthcoming games. While I scrubbed Miguel's back, a young man pulled his plastic stool toward me.

*"Please, let me wash your back!"* he asked, taking my washcloth.

*"Thank you,"* I answered.

He scrubbed hard. *"I am Yoshitake. You like Japanese girls. I know because you look at them. I think they also like you. So, tonight during the games, you might be lucky—if you play badly, they just might penalize you by making you kiss one of them. Good luck!"* He dumped water on my back to rinse it, then submerged himself in the deep spring bath. He let out a sigh of relief as the piping hot water permeated his body and relaxed his muscles. *"But first, you must prove yourself a man—get in!"*

The others, already in the large tub, turned to Alex, Miguel, and I and waited. I knew it was hotter than usual because one of the men who had just gotten out was red with steam rising from his skin. I couldn't lose face before the games; the girls would know I was chicken. I stuck my toe in the water and promptly pulled it out.

Miguel looked at me in his mirror. *"Just get in, Teja, or they will eat you alive tonight!"*

I braced myself, encased my privates with my cupped hands and lowered myself in. Within 10 seconds, every muscle and bone in my body drooped like a Dali painting. My head spun in defiance of the heat, but my fingers floated to the surface, relaxed. I was ready for the games.

After we all gathered in the activity room, dressed in our hostel-supplied yukata the manager and his wife called for quiet and gave the directions for the first game. The rule was if you lost, you or your team would have to do anything the others demanded. When my team lost the spoon and egg race, they chose me to take the brunt, to which I was ordered by the other team to attach 20 wooden clothes pins to my face. At the 12th pin, my eyes were tearing and the room cheered me on. Once I had all 20 pins attached, including one on each eye lid, I had to remain calm and sing "I'm on Top of the World" by the Carpenters.

Yoshitake leaned over to me. *"The one in the red shirt thinks you're very cute."*

As the evening progressed, my team managed to improve, thus lessening my chances of being hooked, or worse, married off. Miguel's bad luck was awarded with an instruction to drink a glass of Tabasco, cigarette butt, beer, cooking oil, soy sauce, and shreds of a paper napkin. The girl in red began to look at Miguel more favorably.

After the games we settled down for storytelling and music. Miguel, Alex, and I were given the responsibility to lead group sing-alongs to American folk music. Given that we didn't know any of the lyrics, the group was more embarrassed for us than we were.

*"We will teach you American songs. Here are some lyric sheets."* The manager tuned his guitar and the whole room, chorus and all produced a version of "This Land is Your Land." Most of the guests knew all of the songs. *"Since you don't know these songs, the three of you must be penalized,"* the manager explained. We had to kiss one waiting girl each on the cheek. *"Aren't Japanese women the best?"* someone cheered.

The next day on our way to breakfast, we passed the three girls. *"Good morning,"* I said. They giggled and bowed and sat at their table. Breakfast was quiet, and as we served each other and ate, we talked of our destination for that day, and recounted the excitement from the night before. Then, as if we had become friends for life, we bowed, then rode away from the hostel. The remaining few guests, the manager and his wife waved goodbye and wished us a speedy return.

The last few days in Hokkaido were solemn. We rode in silence, prepared to end the excitement and adventure of bicycling through a countryside so beautiful, so perfect, for a return to the megapolis of Tokyo. One month had passed since we were last in Tomakomai Bay at the "belly" of Hokkaido. When we saw in the distance our ship already docked, Miguel looked at Alex and me and nodded his head. "Well, I guess that's it." We raised our water canteens and cried. Our last night was spent in a dilapidated bus station, with a tin roof we didn't even know was rusty and broken until it started raining.

*　*　*

It was pouring the night we docked in Tokyo. We switched on our handlebar flashlights and mounted out bikes. Our lights barely broke through the sheets of rain coming down. Far in the distance, the lights of downtown Tokyo shimmered through the downpour, only to disappear again.

"We should have stayed in Akanko. I hate this place." Miguel shook the water off his poncho hood. "I don't even know how to get back."

"Let's call Papa and ask him to pick us up," I said.

Miguel's eyebrows were pressed together. "No. We came this far, we have to get home by ourselves."

At that moment an old man on a delivery motorcycle stopped next to us and spoke in broken English. "Where you go? I help you, yes?"

We followed the old man to the outskirts of Otaku, two kilometers from our house. When we asked him how we could thank him, he said, "*You can return the favor by helping someone else someday.*"

We separated from Alex a little while later near his house and rode the rest of the way home in silence along the *Tama* River. After what seemed like an eternity, I realized we were just minutes from our house. I was homesick for Hokkaido already, but also, I was home.

Grandpa, approx. 1933.

Grandma, approx. 1933.

Arboleda family, 1942. Uncle Freddy, Aunt Soli, Grandma, Papa, Grandpa. Aunt Connie was not yet born.

Opa and Oma, approx. 1959.

Teja's father, biologist, Germany, 1958.

Teja's parents, Teja and Miguel, approx. 1966.

118

Teja and Miguel in their "yukata," Tokyo, Japan, 1969.

The Arboleda family on their back porch, Tokyo, Japan, 1978.

Still from Teja's one-man show, *Ethnic Man!,* approx. 1994.

Miguel and Yumi, Japan, 1996.

Barbara and Teja, 1998.

Asaki, David, and Teja, Tokyo, Japan, 1985.

119

# Two Steps Back

I applied for a job at a new English language school near St. Mary's as a "conversation motivator." My purpose, I gathered only after Papa deciphered it for me, was to lure young local school girls into paying tuition. It was a perfect marketing plan: an endless supply of students from a foreign boys' school and an abundance of eager Japanese girls.

The textbooks provided for them were mostly irrelevant, as the classes were inevitably transformed into excited conversations about America and rock stars. Although I couldn't offer much in the way of cultural details, I did, naturally have a young boy's burgeoning sense of sexual identity. But I felt awkward and didn't have a clue as to how to impress these girls. They all looked extraordinarily cute or pretty. I had so much to prove, and in an uninhibited, embarrassing way, succeeded in providing evidence that I had not been raised by the same kind of parents they were. No, I was undoubtedly raised by savages.

This is where I learned to be the American *they* wanted, and as I was beginning to think, the person *I* always wanted to be. It was obvious that although I had become Japanese, the Western humor and wit shot through like a needle in a tatami mat.

One afternoon, a group of girls chimed in chorus, as if rehearsed, "You aah soh American, Teja, because you aah craji and kookoo … and you lukku like Michael Jackson!" Within 3 months the registered student population had doubled.

This is where I met Chieko. Her mother was a designer and her father an industrialist. She had a genuine interest in the United States and had dreams of becoming a movie star. I liked her enthusiasm for theater and her warped sense of humor. She was different from most of the girls I had gotten to know. She was open, direct, introspective, and strong. After college, she abandoned the traditional marriage-and-children track and made her way to Los Angeles to try Hollywood. She returned to Japan, discouraged but not broken. These were probably the qualities that helped propel her into stardom in Japan, but ultimately the same ones that isolated her from most of her friends, and left her, to her desperation, husbandless. She had become a successful Japanese television icon, playing despondent, sometimes evil characters—roles that would only reflect, in the eyes of Japan, a woman who is not worthy of marriage.

But stuck in our high school innocence, we were full of optimism. Chieko liked me because unlike what she would expect from a Japanese boyfriend, I didn't count on her to walk three steps behind me, serve my food, or do any of those things Papa and Mama thought were sexist or unfair. She dyed her hair in streaks and wore clothes that simulated the surfer culture of southern California. We hopped from one café to another and went on double and triple dates with our friends, to the movies, the ocean, and through the thick glob of Tokyo's shopping centers.

*  *  *

At home, there were arguments about whether or not we should return to the United States. Through the walls we heard Papa argue that Japan was better for us, that it would be too difficult now to move back to the United States. Mama argued that she couldn't live anymore in a world were she felt desperately isolated, always an outsider. She wanted more out of life—a degree in a field she liked, a job she liked, respect, and most of all, acceptance. Their arguments turned in to shouting matches. Eventually, Mama and Papa's differences jarred through the walls; I learned to tune them out until I couldn't hear the words anymore. For us there was never any discussion or explanation. Dinner was usually quiet and on weekends we all seemed to have our own little projects.

I found that I could easily shut down my emotions, and I looked for something to disregard early signs of discourse or pain. I took up motorcycle racing with Chris and eight guys from the bike shop. On Saturdays, before dawn, we shot west on the highway, using the drag pocket behind trucks to accelerate like popped corks and wedge through a convoy. By 6:30 a.m., we would be on the mountain roads, hugging corners with the engines screaming. I was alive and immortal, aware of every seam and rock in the road, every corner and opportunity. Racing and traffic weaving were more than a game. Without concentration, death was assured.

*  *  *

I think Miguel applied to colleges late because he wanted to stay in Japan, but it was predetermined—he would return to the United States. There really wasn't a choice. It would have been virtually impossible for him to enter a Japanese university, and if he did, there would not be any opportunities for him in a Japanese company. He was angry and scared, knowing that everything he had come to love would be yanked away for the pure purpose of making a career. It was Miguel's dilemma, but it scared me too.

I was determined to stay put. If I planned early enough, then maybe, just maybe I would never have to move again. I would marry a Japanese woman, and live and die in Japan. All I would have to do is become a Japanese citizen, graduate, and get a job.

I was walking to the train station with Akira, Hiro, and Katsu when I told them of my plan.

"Teja, *that's impossible*, you know, *I don't think* you can *become a Japanese*," Akira said. "*Third generation* Korean and Chinese *cannot even* get *Japanese* passports *dayo*."

Hiro looked at me funny. "*Soo dayo*, but why would *you want to* become Japanese, anyway? *Don't you* want to *go back to* America?"

"*No*. I don't *want to go back to* America," I said. "*I want to stay in Japan*."

"*You are* American, *right?*" Katsu asked.

I wanted to say "no," that I was Japanese like they were. "*Right*."

"Okay." Hiro still seemed confused. "*But you know, you can never get into a* Japanese company. *You cannot get into* Japanese university *dayo!*"

"But Teja, we know you will *marry a Japanese!*" Akira joked. "*You must* marry a Japanese!"

*  *  *

Miguel packed his suitcase as if he was about to go camping. By the promotional brochures, the University of Oregon seemed mystical, surrounded by rolling green hills, wildlife, and the roaring ocean below spectacular cliffs. The university seemed to offer everything Miguel wanted. Everything he needed he would take and the rest would follow by ship. What do you take with you when it's not a trip? If you know you're leaving for good, do you take a framed picture of the family or little trinkets for valued memories?

"If you take everything, you won't come back," I suggested, hoping for a vague hesitation on his part.

Miguel sat on the suitcase and indicated for me to close the latches. "Of course I'll be back, stupid. I promise. But of course, you're next."

"I'm not going to go. I'm staying."

"That's what I thought. Anyway, it'll probably be fine. Did you see the brochures?" He smiled and looked out the window. The moon was caught on the *ginko* tree branch in the backyard. "I'll miss you, little brother. I won't have anyone to pick on."

"When will you be back?" I asked.

"Well, I really don't want to be leaving anyway, so, soon, hopefully."

Soon he distanced himself more and more from us and his friends, spending much of his time alone. By the middle of the summer he was harder to reach than ever. Then at the end of July he was gone. Suddenly the dinner table seemed awkward. Although we moved the chairs closer together, we couldn't seem to fill the space.

\* \* \*

"Teja, could you come down please?" Papa's voice quivered over the intercom. When I got to the dining room, Mama and Papa were sitting together on the opposite side of the table. I forced a smile, and wondered what I had done wrong.

"Hi! What's up!" I said.

Papa face was stiff. "Teja, sit down, please." He straightened his glasses. "Mama and I have been doing a lot of talking … we've been having a lot of fights lately, and, well, Mama has decided to go back to America just for a while to see how things go."

I looked at Mama whose hands were folded tightly. Her hands were naturally pale, but her knuckles were almost purely white. "What are you talking about?"

Papa continued, "We're getting a separation. A temporary separation. And we felt it would be better that Mama go back to the U.S. for a while."

"Well, why can't you work it out? You always tell Miguel and I to stop fighting."

"Well, it's not that easy." Mama's voice cracked. "This is the way we have to work this out. We want to make sure you understand that it has nothing to do with you."

Papa leaned closer to me. "She's just going for a year … but we thought it would only be fair if we asked you—would you want to stay with me in Japan, or go with Mama to America?"

"I don't know," I said, suddenly scrambling for a rational thought. Nothing logical came to mind, only random thoughts about homework, my old pet hamster that died several years earlier, and the permanent coffee stain on the table that Mama hated.

"Well, you don't have to make your decision right away," Papa said. "Take your time."

Mama reached out and held my hand. "We just want you to know that we both love you very much, and that whatever decision you make, it will be fine with us. Papa won't be hurt if you decide to come with me, and I won't be hurt if you stay here."

"Okay." I stood up and headed for the door. "I gotta finish some homework."

I sprinted up the stairs. I had left my radio on, and Wolfman Jack was introducing an "oldie" love ballad on the Armed Forces Radio. I wondered why so many songs were about love when it seemed to me that love obviously didn't work.

* * *

The McDonald's at Futako-Tamagawa train station had expanded again. The voracious appetites of St. Mary's students afforded the franchise to increase its seating capacity to lure more Japanese clients. A McDonald's with faithful foreign customers was perfect marketing strategy for a Western capitalist icon in Tokyo. From the news I had learned that only several months earlier, Tokyo had become the city with the most McDonald's in the world.

Chieko and I sat below a poster of the new fish sandwich, at the far end near the door with my classmates Carl Chao and Ed Perron. I was waiting for my fries when a tall, lanky senior, Steve Minami, came in and stood above Carl.

"*Oi, kimi,* come here, *sempai ga* wants to see you, *dayo. Hayaku shiro.*" Steve waited for Carl to stand.

Carl walked outside. Steve looked at Ed and I, then followed Carl behind the building.

"*No one talks to Carl like that,*" I said. "*Who does Steve think he is?*"

Ed didn't look up. "*Don't mess with Steve. He's Carl's sempai*—his senior, *dayo,* it's not your business anyway."

"How could Steve be Carl's *sempai*? Neither of them is *Japanese,*" I said.

"*Steve is half. He's half but he's Japanese,*" Ed explained.

"*So, you're half,*" I said.

Ed looked at me. "So are you."

Carl returned, his face white and his hands trembling. He sat down and finished his Coke. The cashier placed my order of fries on the table when Steve returned.

"*You, next.* Get up!" He grabbed my arm.

"*Take your hands off me,*" I warned.

"*Mark wants to see you, so you better come.*"

I pulled my arm away from him. Mark could not be my sempai—I didn't even know his family name. The *sempai-koohi* system, like the arrangement in Philippines, was reserved for a formal relationship between an elder and a respectful younger follower. I so desperately wanted to *become*—to *be* Japanese, but I wasn't going to stoop to a bastardized dictator's version of the system. The arrangement called for respect through understanding and healthy examples, not brute physical force. Sometimes cultural rules are twisted for control and someone gets hurt. Besides, if my face was going to get rearranged I would rather it look more Japanese.

"*I'm not Japanese!*" I yelled at him. "*The system doesn't apply to me. So you can go tell Mark to* fuck off!"

Steve winced and went back outside. Chieko sat quietly looking frightened. Ed stared at the table and said, "*You should just go, Teja, it would be better. Just pretend you accept being his koohai, and he'll forgive you.*"

Steve returned with Mark and another Japanese-American, Paul. The three of them pulled me out of my chair and dragged me outside and dropped me next to the McDonald's dumpster. Then, Mark and Paul pinned me against the outside wall. When Steve cracked my left cheek with his fist, my arms tensed up, but I didn't let out a sound.

"*Nanda kono taido wa eh?* I'm senpai *nandazoo!* You have no respect for your elders! You listen to me! *Yatchimae!*" Steve drew his arm back again. As I tilted my head up, his fist barely missed my right eye, but popped my jaw. Then another embedded in my stomach. I doubled over, but they propped me up again.

Steve's spit landed in my eye. "*Kussottare!* You think you're so smart! *You are my koohai and don't forget it! That means you do what I tell you!*"

"You are not my *sempai!*"

He grabbed my throat. "*Well, are you Japanese or American? Decide now!*"

My voice broke under his grip. "I *am both. Just like you*, you idiot!"

"*Kono baka yaroo! Don't play games with me!*"

He slapped my face. "*Traitor!*"

Everything I had learned in Judo was ready at my fingertips. "*You are a coward. You have no koohai, and you are weak like a worm! I'll take you on, but one on one!*"

Steve coiled back his arm and launched it through my chin. My head snapped back and I dropped. Blood from my mouth and nose mixed in with the overflow of McDonald's garbage on the ground.

"*Kiss my feet you* piece of shit!" Steve pressed his foot on my head.

I couldn't see an end to this, and there would be no way to rationalize with this moron.

I submitted. "Okay, okay, you are my sempai. Okay?"

"*You are a liar! Get on your knees and bow!*"

I braced myself as pain shot from my neck to my stomach. I propped myself up on my knees, then bowed with my head to the ground. When I finally looked up, they were gone. I spit on the ground where Steve last stood. I managed to stand and worked my way back to the door. Before I entered I straightened my tie and noticed my right blazer arm had been ripped off, and my shirt was soaked in blood. I returned to my seat and looked at the others one by one. Chieko wet her napkin in her cup of Sprite and rubbed the blood off my face. I looked outside and watched a white limousine pass by with a large sticker on the side that read *Rock and Roll Forever!*

"*Let's go,*" I said.

\* \* \*

Mama packed her college papers and other important things in silence. I had heard her crying, but I didn't want to embarrass her, so I waited until she stopped. I wanted to ask her if she needed help packing, or if she was going to finish college in America, but what I really wanted to know was when she was planning to come back. I kept quiet and watched as she crossed off our address on the used cardboard boxes and replaced it with the address of her best friend, Waltraud, who, after 9 years in Tokyo, had recently left to live in Boston with her husband.

I wondered about America, sometimes with interest, but mostly with trepidation. It seemed a totally alien place. I worried for Mama, and wondered how she planned on dodging all the bullets, pickpockets, and gangsters I'd seen in the movies. At least she would be able to speak English again, and make friends in a culture she understood better. She would be accepted outside of the home and she wouldn't have the stares and the doubtful looks on strangers' faces. I could understand, now that I was a little older, how she had become so lonely in Japan, even humiliated by the rampant sexism and sexual harassment.

A few days earlier, Papa's first boss, Mr. Minowa, called Mama to say goodbye. "I thought you would adapt the best of all the foreign women I know."

Mama was scared to leave and be alone, but she couldn't stay either. Papa couldn't make up his mind whether he should marry someone else and Mama couldn't wait in Japan for him to decide. All she could look forward to was the prospect of moving back to a culture she understood better.

\* \* \*

The conversation in the car on the way to the airport was trivial. I watched Tokyo rush by. Gray apartments and office buildings stood sandwiched together and butted up next to the concrete guards on the shoulder of the highway. Hanging laundry flapped in the wind that ventured between the structures and neon signs blinked on roofs, competing with each other for space and attention.

"Wow, look, two more buildings have gone up since we dropped Miguel off at the airport!" Papa tried to keep the conversation light.

Mama turned on the air conditioner. I recognized a noodle restaurant below the highway where Hiroshi and Hisato and I used to get cheap lunches on weekends. "Well, I'll just be glad I'll be away from these awful summers! And a white Christmas, that will be a nice change!"

"Teja, have you thought about what you'd like to do?" Papa asked.

Mama cut in. "Not now, give him some more time."

As we passed the neighborhood where Hiroshi lived, it was all suddenly very simple. "Well, I'm going to stay in Japan."

Mama looked out the window. "Oh."

"Are you sure?" Papa asked, looking at me in the rearview mirror.

"Yeah. Then when I graduate I have to leave anyway, like everyone else, so I'll leave."

Papa took a deep breath. "Oh."

The concrete jungle of the city slowly dispersed, making way to rice paddies and farm houses. In the distance, a man on a bicycle pulled a cart filled with lumber and watermelons.

Mama opted for a Japanese lunch at the airport terminal, imagining it would be her last real Japanese meal. After lunch, we watched her pass through customs and then through security. We exchanged waves one last time as she disappeared on her way to the gate.

Papa and I drove home, engaged only in small talk, watching the lights of Tokyo grow closer.

"Well, I guess it's just you and me for now," Papa said as he pulled into the driveway.

*   *   *

I bought a larger motorcycle. And to pay for gas and upkeep, I needed a job, so I signed up with a temporary agency for foreigners. Within a week I was placed as a product spokesperson for a supermarket. I arrived at the store with a summer cold, but ready.

The manager took one look at me, then turned to his colleague. "*Not quite American, but what can we do? It's too late to call the agency.*"

*"He can use your wife's blond wig!"* the second one said. They both looked at me and laughed.

The manager handed me a white apron and lead me to a 12-foot high Coca-Cola can pyramid. He positioned me in front of a large cooler that housed the samples I was supposed to give away to customers. It was under an air conditioner that blew air directly on my head.

*"Do you speak Japanese? Speak only English. Pour customers a sample. If they like it, give them a can. And smile! Look like American surfer boy!"*

He walked away shaking his head. I sneezed and a customer approached.

I took a deep breath. *"Irrashaimase! Doozo, sampuru ikagadesuka?* Coca-Cola *totemo oishii* summer drink! *Ikagadesuka?"* She took a sample and walked off.

Then I realized I had already broken the no-Japanese rule. I looked behind me at the big stack of Coca-Cola bottles and sneezed again and I began to get dizzy. I waited almost 10 minutes for the next customer. My forehead was burning and my hands became numb. I hated Coca-Cola and everything it represented. At least if I was blond, I might have attracted more customers. An old lady approached me. *"May I please have a sample?"*

*"Sure, please. Here, let me."* I took two arm-fulls of cans and placed them in her basket. *"Thank you very much, please bring your family!"* Then I took off my apron, hung it over the cooler and walked out of the store.

\* \* \*

Papa and I both came home late everyday, and usually ate dinner while watching television and continued to watch television until it was time for bed. We shared in the cooking and cleaning and occasionally we went out to a restaurant. We rarely spoke about Miguel or Mama; the house had lost so much of its spirit and had become in many ways purely functional. At school, Mr. Braun, the guidance counselor, offered me his services, but I couldn't talk about it because I didn't want to think about it. The absence of Miguel and Mama was too emotional. And if I had learned anything in Japan, an emotion is representative of an opinion, a judgment. Thus sadness and happiness and loneliness could be controlled and pass as quickly as a thought.

\* \* \*

"How would you like to visit Mama for Christmas?" Papa asked. Mama's birthday (in October) and Miguel's (in November) had already passed. I had avoided thinking about Christmas and had become resolved to having a rather lonely winter. "Miguel will be there too. I just spoke with him."

Christmas in America. The idea of something seemingly so normal and apropos had turned into an alien ideal. Christmas in Japan was plastic and ethereal, with skinny Santas and a rash of misguided, misinterpreted colloquialisms. Not that we were Christian, but the history and meaning behind the holidays went relatively unnoticed. Except, of course, for St. Mary's, where non-Christians were ambushed with grim reminders of our duties, like attending mass. Blinding displays of Santa, Jesus, Virgin Mary, and reindeer lined the hallways, prompting random holiday greetings. The Jews, Muslims, and nonbelievers felt the pressure to fall in line, afraid of the consequences.

I used to like Christmas. Even in Japan, at home in our living room with our abbreviated Tannenbaum, authentic tinsel, gingerbread cookies, and Stollen. When I was younger, my heart would race through the night in anticipation of opening my presents. Now in high school and eager to be mature, I could think only of returning to the United States, and hope for a chance to surround myself, maybe for the last time, in the tender, warm glow of family and candlelight.

We packed our suitcases and headed to the new Narita International Airport in Chiba. In the car, I braced myself with my hands under my thighs, clutching the fabric of the seat. Maybe this trip would finally give me direction as to where I would end up.

We arrived at Logan Airport in Boston on the evening of December 22. In the city, frozen skyscrapers reached for the sky like the last attempt of a drowning victim. Pedestrians hunched over in puffy winter coats, navigating around the mounds of snow bulldozed onto the sidewalks. Cars passed in silence over the white carpeted streets and broke through wisps of steam rising from manhole covers.

"Hiahppy fuckin' nyu yieeah!" a passerby yelled at another.

"Hiahppy fuckin' nyu yieeah?" Papa whispered to me and raised his left eyebrow. "You think Mama's picked up the Boston accent yet?"

I watched a mounted policeman stop to let his horse defecate on the sidewalk. "Yeah, that combined with her German accent would make a real killer, huh?"

*   *   *

Miguel and Mama had already eaten some of the Stollen while waiting for us. The studio apartment smelled like almost every Christmas I had known. In the corner, next to Mama's futon bed, was a mini Christmas tree with presents gathered at its trunk. Mama kept busy with the cooking and baking. She didn't seem different at all; in fact, it seemed as if there was no reason for her departure.

As the evening progressed, she enthusiastically told us of her jogging routine, her newfound graphic artist friend Edwina, and the freedom she felt in Boston. Then Waltraud and her husband Stefan, who lived in the next building, came over to reminisce about old times in Tokyo and entertain us with exaggerated stories of Mama's recent escapades. We shared memories deep into the night with the Boston skyline shimmering through Mama's 14th-floor window. I watched her face as her eyes searched the sky, and I realized that for many years Mama tried to cover up her loneliness with laugher and smiles. I knew that I also denied her this sadness because I was too scared to believe it could be true that she was so vulnerable and human.

Miguel was radiant and in great shape. My brother! I didn't realize how much I missed him until the old jokes and innuendos filtered into our conversation. Oregon was good for him, with its abundance of woods and wildlife. For once he had close friends and time to himself. Maybe, I thought, America wasn't so bad after all.

For the next few days we compared Japan to America incessantly, and in conclusion, as patterns emerged, we conceived that neither was better. All we knew was when we were in one place, we missed the other. From Miguel and Mama's stories, I began to doubt Japan was the right place for me. Only 2 days from Tokyo, and I missed the city and my friends already, but out on the streets in Boston, I never got the feeling people were staring at me. I felt somehow lighter, even less significant; a nonperson at times. I wasn't different, I just *wasn't*. Had Mama and Miguel found what they were looking for or were they both temporarily hopeful?

The day after Christmas we went to see *The Goodbye Girl*. The streets were empty as we walked to the theater along Atlantic Avenue. It was -18°F with the windchill and we braced ourselves, leaning forward into the wind with out eyes tearing. The narrow, cobble streets and black sidewalk lanterns were like something out of a movie that took place in London, not America. Brick buildings with black shutters and a tiny graveyard were laced with frozen snow and icicles dripped from strained tree branches as if in pause mode. Mama laughed and hung onto Papa; a curious, but encouraging image. If only for one moment, they were together again, here, halfway around the planet. It was as if memories and distances could never exist as one.

Miguel left for Oregon. This time I was prepared for it. The next day Mama took Papa and I to the airport. As they kissed good-bye briefly, I had an uncomfortable feeling that they would never be together again.

# 15

# The Official Proxy

Hideki peared at me from behind the glass counter. *"This time I want my car to look like a* California Highway Police Patrol Car."

I crawled around from the back of the store and through the narrow isles to hear him better. *"You mean from the TV show* CHiPs, the California Highway Police Patrol?"

"Yeah. *It's very* excite!" He cranked up his Buddy Holly tape and howled.

*"You mean, it's very 'cool.'"*

*"So so so, soonanda. Teja you are so lucky, you can speak* English. *Iiinaa, shaberitainaa!"*

Hideki managed Bunka Zakkatten, an American cultural junk store. Old Coca-Cola bottles, retired G.I. Joe dolls, James Dean posters, and tired copies of *Playboy* and *T.V. Guide*, among other odd items, were packed into every centimeter of the shop. I picked up a Popeye Pez dispenser and Hideki instantly mimicked Popeye's laugh. I flashed him a Flash Gordon postcard—he whistled the theme tune. I rolled out an autographed poster of Farrah Fawcett—he pretended to drool.

He was not a very attractive young man, but he did wear the right clothes. With his pressed jeans rolled up over his hightops, he showed me the basic moves of "The Twist." "Beri cuuuru!" he insisted, egging me on to copy him. He knew more about American paraphrenalia than any Westerner I had known. The plastic, metal, and paper knickknacks were veritable landfill refugees that he had saved, enshrined, and finally worshipped. Inevitably, however, I thought he would probably never know the America from which these objects came.

Hideki was Korean. His father and mother, both from Korea, had legally changed their family names, just as the millions of other Koreans and Chinese did following Japan's occupation of the Far East. The government-sanctioned employment discrimination made it virtually impossible for non-Japanese Asians to obtain jobs. So, along with many other survivors who had some money, Hideki's parents opened a Korean restaurant. Now, living in the wealthiest suburban neighborhood in Tokyo, Hideki and his family chose the illusion of relinquishing their Korean heritage for a life of well-deserved comfort. Still, in a rare moment of reflection, Hideki spoke of his true heritage and the pain his fore-bearers suffered for him. Like many young Asian men, Hideki, the oldest child, was expected to take over his father's restaurant business. For now, however, he had his college years to let loose before settling down.

It was in the bars and coffee shops where I began to see the disintegration of the Japanese image I thought I had absorbed. Of course, because I had chosen not to consume alcohol, I was already out of the loop. In his favorite bars and cafés, Hideki would order a beer for himself and an iced coffee for me. After lighting a cigarette, he would take a deep drag, sigh, then introduce me to the other patrons who were obviously regulars.

"Jimmy," the bartender and owner at California Suite, liked to keep the lights low. "Laiku American bar saloon!" He was proud of his authentic reconditioned early-1950s jukebox at the far side of the counter. It was close enough to his counter so that he could reach over and punch in a requested song. Hideki's entrance was always greeted with reverence. He was clearly the neighborhood expert; a Robin Hood of Western pop culture. Without prompting, Jimmy would cut short a song in process to play "The Wanderer" in honor of Hideki.

"*This is* Teja. *He's my* American *friend. I like him because he's very* crazy and cookoo! *And he looks like* Michael Jackson!" A small crowd would gather, or wave and observe me, wondering what kind of crazy and "cookoo" things I was going to do. I was Tonto to Hideki, and he was sending me to town.

"Teja *is from* Brukkurin Nuu Yooku! Zatsu kuuru, *desho*? Hey! Fuckingu assuhohru! Get me a Cohku!"

Jimmy seemed to forget I didn't know much about the States, and his questions were always undoubtedly out of my league. "*In* Phoenix, *do they have* hippies?"

"*Of course*," I said. I always gave him what he wanted in fear of risking my status.

"*American women are very easy, no?*" another interested patron asked.

Not only was I naive when it came to matters beyond kissing, but my version of American women was born virtually from television and a 15-year-old *Playboy* magazine Rob Sullivan once brought to school.

"*Of course*," I offered.

The other patrons lifted their glasses and cups, tipped their heads lightly, and in unison, toasted to long-haired, peace-sign waving easy women from Phoenix. *"Kampai!"*

\* \* \*

Hideki and I worked on his converted Nissan Crown Classic for 2 months, giving it a new life as a Tokyo-born California Highway Police Patrol car; light blue and white with decals on the sides and a makeshift siren on the top. On weekends we would hop into "Chips," roll down the windows and cruise down the narrow alleyways of Jiyugaoka cranking 1950s rock-and-roll songs. "Sha la la la la la la la, happi bahsuday soweeto shiksteen!" We howled at the top of our lungs, flashing peace signs and waving at on-lookers. Hideki would slow down and urge me to woo some females. "Hey, baby!" I would yell, not knowing what I'd do if they ever were to respond favorably. "You wanna go for some coffee?" Sometimes I would add a little John Wayne to my English just to add some intrigue. After my catcalls, I nonetheless felt ugly, stupid, and as Papa would add, "low." Inevitably, I would sheepishly slink below the dashboard.

Hideki would park Chips in front of coffee shops with names like "American Pit Stop" and "Hot, Fresh USA!" He liked when I ordered in English so he could look around and smile at the other guests. While he practiced the few English phrases he knew, we would sip what tasted and looked like brown, tepid water that the menus typically referred to as "American-style coffee."

*"One day I will go to California to become a used-car salesman,"* Hideki mused. As I could tell, he envisioned considerable romance in this idea. I nodded in approval. I offered to hook him up with my uncle Gene who had a used-car lot in the Bronx, New York, but Hideki had seen *Escape From New York* and didn't want to chance it.

Three years later, during my sophomore year in college, I received a letter from Los Angeles. Hideki had found an apartment and an Italian girlfriend and was working as an assistant at a used luxury and sports car lot. He found it amusing that most people thought he was Mexican. He boasted about his meager diet of stale donuts and bad coffee and his run-in with some Los Angeles police who mistook him for a drug dealer. He had 1 year to live it up. After that, he would be expected to start his training to take over his father's restaurant back in Japan and marry a Japanese woman.

\* \* \*

My St. Mary's friends and I stuck closer together than ever—our last year was reminding us of the inevitable parting. Somehow, we all had become oddly serious. We spoke of the future and the past more than the present, and our mood swings left us confused and anxious. We laughed less and contemplated more and talked of things that were still alien to us, like marriage, children, money, and careers. The familiar trees that surrounded the edges of the school grounds had matured with us, each year reaching higher and spreading out. We compared ourselves to the natural order of things, cycles, and adjustments, as if these analogies would ease our trepidations. We were men, now, and in Japan men were not discouraged from crying. So we shed our tears sometimes, sharing our feelings in the cool breezes of our last fall in Japan. America, the mysterious, all-encompassing idea, drew us in without description or preparation. Our hearts grew tight with sadness, knowing that our close-knit life with family and friends would be shattered forever. As foreigners in our own country we questioned the essence of belonging. We would never be home again.

"*Even if* I go to America for *college*, I will *come back to Japan*," Asaki promised. The others were equally emphatic. "*I will come back to marry a Japanese woman.*" "*My mother and father* are making me go, *but* I don't care, *I'll go a couple of years* and that's all."

We gathered regularly at McDonald's to weigh our futures. The United States had become more than just an option for most of us. I was completing my International Baccalaureate program and was accepted to Suffolk in England, McGill in Montreal, Canada, and the University of Hannover in Germany, but in the end I knew I was going to end up in America.

I scanned the billboard outside of the guidance counselor's office for ideas on U.S. colleges. I removed the thumbtack from the postcard-sized color ad from Clark University. It read, "Small, excellent private college in beautiful Worcester, Massachusetts—only a hop, skip, and a jump from Boston." Boston! I could be near Mama! I found the Clark brochure in the guidance office and flipped through it. Bright, vivid, glossy images depicting vibrant students in classrooms, pensive in thought one minute, then outside throwing Frisbees the next. Green pastures, streets lined with bright gold and striking red leaves, quaint neighborhoods, and smiling students. They even smiled at the food in the cafeteria! Suddenly America became a desirable possibility, and I grew more anxious to graduate from high school.

\* \* \*

On my birthday, April 11, Papa handed me a thick envelope addressed to me: I had been accepted to Clark. It was a sign, but I was tempted to debate it.

"Mama would be very happy to have some family near her," Papa said, giving me a smile I hadn't seen in a long time.

The last few weeks before graduation I was hysterical. Faced with the impending consequence of relocation and displacement, I chose to consume as much of Japan as I could. I desperately attempted to limit my friends, food, and television to only Japanese influences.

At Mikado, the corner store, Fujisawa-san pushed me a family-sized bag of cuttlefish. *"Teja, you are practically Japanese. One day you will be back and you will marry a Japanese woman. Now, promise to send me pictures of American woman?"* He cupped his hands under his chest and smiled. His long-term obsession had become childish to me, so I didn't laugh, but I assured him I would return and start a family.

*"Irrashaimase!"* Hashikawa-san said. Her gentle face and smile had remained honest and welcome throughout the 12 years we frequented her family's pharmacy. The distinct smell of homeopathic herbs in odd-shaped bottles mixed with Johnson & Johnson packages was pleasantly familiar. She had confided in me about her husband's death and now her mother's ailing health, and she remained solid, managing the only remaining wooden commercial structure in Denenchofu. The family business had survived three generations, and for the first time she realized it may be time to close shop.

*"In America you must keep healthy, they don't eat well, and they are very fat. Take ginseng and ginger and stay away from hamburgers! I have been responsible for your health since you were this high, now don't disappoint me!"* She laughed encouragingly and bowed. I slid open the wooden door and listened to the familiar sound of the ball bearings rolling on their tracks. A blast of humidity overwhelmed me in the entrance, but before I closed the door, I bowed low and thanked her for her wisdom and advice. She bowed back and smiled. One year later, when I returned during summer a break from college, the building had been replaced with a metal and glass coffee shop.

* * *

*"Friends forever,"* Asaki said, holding his hand out and placing it on top of mine.

Hiroshi put his hand above Asaki's. *"Always friends."*

"Forever," Arthur said, and placed his hand above Asaki's.

David, Jacky, and Alvin placed their hands over ours. We all looked at each other and nodded. The seven of us had been together since the fourth grade, two of us since the first. We poured each other glasses of beer and pieced together the history of our friendship with photographs and stories. Within 1 month we would be dispersed across the United States, and the validity of our ties with Japan and each other would be tested.

* * *

Realizing he didn't have much time left with me, Hideki convinced himself that he would succeed in initiating me correctly. It had become his mission to condition me appropriately for the United States. The weeks before I would leave he dragged me to his family's weekend house overlooking Yamanakako Lake which lay at the foot Mount Fuji. He brought a case of beer and a box of 1950s and 1960s rock-and-roll audiocassettes.

*"This is all we will need to prepare you for good. You will now be tested!"*

We drank into the night and sang as loud as we could, trying to out-do the volume of the boombox.

"Fukku yuu!" he said, nudging me to recite with him.

The room began to float. "Fuck you!" I yelled.

"Berri guddo. Now, say: You assuhohru!"

"You asshole!"

"Okay! Now: Checku itsu outoh!"

"Check it out, man!"

"Hey baby, wanna comu tsu my purehsu?"

"Hey baby, what'chu say you come on back to my place?"

"Is zat a rokku in yoah pokketto oah ah yu happi tsu see me?"

"Is that a what?" I hung onto the table and closed my eyes.

Hedeki howled. "I'm justo ah lohnly man!"

I remember vomiting at least twice. The next morning I cursed the lake and Mount Fuji for looking so calm and undisturbed. A flood of emotions raced through me, adding insult to my nausea. Hideki had been my mentor, my sempai, my guide, and despite his meek Westernization skills, I had reached a comfortable point of connectedness with my adopted home. My sense of *giri*, my determination and guts; my obedience; humiliation; respect; my *gaman*, patience; and my debts of honor and shame. I lay in full mockery of the sacred volcano that loomed over the hills, blue with pride, with a white cap, like the foamy head in the beer glass from the night before. I now understood Papa's pride in the Philippines, and his stories came back to me in rapid succession. I wanted Hideki for once to accept me as a Japanese, as he expected others to consider him.

"Now yu ah ready foah America!" Hideki yelled. *"Bring bak a souvenir!"*

My mind went through a list of things I could return with but I realized that somewhere in the nooks and crannies of his store, he probably already had one of each.

# 16

# "You're From China, Right?"

Papa sat with me in the middle of Narita International Airport's main terminal. The last time we had both been here together was 3 years earlier to see Mama off to the United States. Now it was my turn to fly away, far from Papa, my friends, and Japan.

At first, Papa braved my leaving well. Good-byes to family members had become a routine in his life, and he pretended to become stronger with each parting. I could tell, however, that this time he felt more isolated and alone than ever, away from all the people that gave his life purpose. He was never complete when he was alone, and I had the feeling that I wouldn't be either.

The departure times and flight numbers flipped rapidly on the large schedule board that hung above us. An old, sour feeling in my stomach shot back memories of leaving, the way cafeteria food reminds me of school days. My plane was now boarding and Papa put his hand on my shoulder and cleared his throat, "Promise me one thing."

"Yeah?" I looked at him as he pushed his glasses up the bridge of his nose.

"Just ... be careful." He cleared his throat again and shifted his weight to the other leg. "You know, drinking is one thing. You'll be in a college setting, and a little drinking is okay, but remember, America is quite a different place. There are a lot of things you've got to be careful of. So, just be careful. OK?"

I knew what he meant. Some of the kids at school, especially the Americans, had gotten in trouble for dealing and using drugs. One kid even was jailed for being caught with a pouch of marijuana. The American parents protested, but the judge told them if they didn't like the law, they should go back to America where their children could continue their drug abuses. I smirked. "Papa, I've never touched drugs and I never will. I promise. Don't worry about that. I hardly even drink."

"OK. I worry, you know." He pretended to scratch an itch as he curled his lips to hold back his tears. "Now, you got your passport?"

"Yeah." I checked my pocket. "And my plane ticket."

"When you get to Kennedy Airport, watch your stuff carefully. If someone offers to carry your bags, just refuse him. And watch your wallet, too. You have to remember, New York is not like Tokyo." He raised an eyebrow sarcastically. "You'll be glad you didn't grow up in America."

"Gee, thanks, Papa. I feel much better now."

"So, ah … say hello to Mama, give her my love. Tell her I'll be sending her birthday present early this year. And tell her that I, ah … well, just give her a big hug. She'll be glad to have you close by."

"OK." I broke into a little soft-shoe jig to break the tension. Papa leaned over and wrapped his arms around me. His glasses pressed against my ear as he choked, crying. I held him tight and began to cry as well. The smell of his neck reminded me of how he held me as a baby, patting my back to get me to burp. Home was never really far away, I thought. I didn't remember ever hugging him like this before, so it felt a little awkward, but the more we held each other, the better it felt.

When we broke the hug, Papa looked back up at the schedule. My flight boarding light was flashing. He handed me my carry-on bags and I headed down the stairs for the passport check stations. As I hurried down the hall toward the x-ray booth, I looked up and saw Papa waving to me. I stopped and put one of my bags down to wave back. Seeing him from below reminded me of how I pictured him on the deck of the steamer, waving good-bye to his wife, new baby, and in-laws in Germany back in the winter of 1961.

\* \* \*

The Manhattan skyline wavered in the exhaust of the left-wing engine. I turned my watch back 13 hours and realized that we were arriving at Kennedy Airport in New York 10 minutes before we had left Japan. As we descended, my ears began to hurt. I swallowed hard and opened wide my jaw to unplug my ear canals. Within minutes, the steady humming of the airplane engines became muffled and I could barely hear the flight attendant's announcements.

Waiting in the baggage claim area for my suitcase, I was suspicious of everybody. When I spotted my bag, I lunged for it, tripping over a mound of duffel bags. A woman yelled at me. "Hey, ya fuckin' joik! Watch where ya goin!" I passed her again on the way to customs. She and a man next to her both sneered at me.

I bowed apologetically out of instinct. "Sorry, I just ... "

"Just watch where ya fuckin' goin, huh?!" The woman checked her pockets and looked away. The man turned to another guy next to him and they started to laugh.

As I worked my way toward customs, I tried again to clear my ears. A customs officer, standing straight with his legs wide apart and his belly bulging over his belt, pointed at me, and then to my left. "That way."

I could hardly hear him. "Excuse me?"

"You're over there." He pointed again toward a large group of people at the end of the hall. I didn't realize where he had directed me to until I saw a sign that said "Aliens." More than 100 people waited in three lines, some of them filling out immigration papers. It took a few minutes for me to make the connection—I was no longer in Japan, so I was not a foreigner. I left the line and found the officer who sent me there.

"What, what?" He folded his arms and peered down at me.

I produced my passport. "I'm a U.S. citizen."

He grabbed my passport. As he studied the photograph and compared it to my face he snorted and looked away as he handed it back to me.

I dragged my stuff over to the "U.S. citizens only" lines. The booth officer was chatting with the people in line before me, so I didn't think I would have any more problems. I helped the woman in front of me lift her suitcases onto the counter. As she joked with the officer, I stared at her long, flowing golden hair, wanting to touch it. After he checked her passport, he let her go without opening her luggage.

I hoisted my suitcase and bags onto the counter and smiled at the officer. "Hi."

"What do you got?" he asked, motioning for me to hurry up in handing him my passport.

His voice was muted, so I stuck a finger in my ear and wiggled it while I forced a yawn. "I'm sorry, I can't hear you very well. The plane ... "

"What are you, deaf? He face turned stone-cold. "I said what do you *got*?!"

"I'm going to college," I responded. Hoping I was answering the right question.

"What, don't you speak *Anglaise*? Where's your passport? *PASS-PORT!*" He chuckled to himself as I handed him my passport. "OK, wise guy. I don't care if it takes all day! You got a whole line a people back there waiting for you, so open your bags. C'mon, let's go! I want EVERYTHING OUT!" He leaned back in his chair. "Sorry, folks, this is going to take a while!"

I unzipped my suitcase and two bags. The officer leaned over the counter and started poking through my clothes, toiletry kit, and underwear, dumping some the items on the counter in the process. He proceeded to take all the cameras out of my camera bag, removing the lenses to check the insides. After he had completely emptied everything out of the bags, he raised his eyebrows. "You can pack your stuff now. And hurry up, 'cuz these folks behind you don't look too happy." Then he tossed my passport on the counter.

Hastily, I stuffed everything back in my bags and struggled to zip the suitcase closed. I was so angry and humiliated I almost forgot my passport on the counter. As I left the booth I turned to the officer. I figured the only way to rationalize with Americans was to be frank, and use their language. "Fuck you, you fucking asshole!" I flipped him the bird and headed out to the street.

I asked a porter where I should catch the shuttle to Boston. He looked at me and shrugged his shoulders. I asked another who mumbled something and walked away. A taxi driver yelled out of his window. "Hey where ya goin', son?"

"Boston." I could barely hear him.

The taxi driver howled, "Boston! Don't you think you should take the shuttle!"

A passerby laughed. "Don't listen to him, he's fuckin' crazy."

I went back inside and found the information desk. There were three women behind the counter. One was eating a sandwich, one was making a personal phone call and the third was slumped in her chair looking lethargic.

"Excuse me." I looked at the one sitting down. She looked away. The woman eating the sandwich left the booth. The one on the phone finally hung up, and smiled at me. "Yeah?"

"I need to catch a plane to Boston." I showed her my ticket.

"Over there. A shuttle that leaves every 10 minutes can take you to the terminal."

I thanked her and headed back outside. Fifteen minutes passed and no shuttle. I went back inside to the information booth. Only the woman on the chair remained. I approached her. "The shuttle never came."

As she sat up slowly, I noticed how her huge thighs hung over the edge of the chair. "Mary gave you the wrong one. You gotta catch it over there." She pointed to an unmarked berth where a group of people were standing.

I thanked her, wondering why she didn't tell me before, and ran to the platform. To double-check, I asked the man in front of me if I was in the right place to get the shuttle.

He looked at me and smiled. "I'm not really sure. There are no signs or anything, and I've been given the run-around. I don't know, let's just hope for the best."

A van came around the bend and let some people off. As the head of our line proceeded to board, the driver stood up to make an announcement. "Sorry, no more passengers. We're out of service, got a couple of vans down and this one's in for repair, too. You'll have to find some other way."

"What do you mean you're out of service?" asked the man in front.

"Exactly what I said: OUT OF SERVICE." He closed the door and sped off.

One woman threw her bags down. "Shit! I hate this fucking airport!"

I looked at my watch. I had 20 minutes to get to the other terminal. "Anybody going to Boston?"

"Yeah." A guy in a business suit came over to me. "You going to Boston?"

"We can share a taxi to the terminal," I suggested as I started heading to the taxi stand. He followed me. I watched a few taxis fly by, already carrying passengers.

"You gotta flag 'em down." He smiled. "Not from New York, are ya?"

"Actually, I was born in Brooklyn," I answered, trying to figure out what he meant by "flagging."

"Brooklyn, huh?"

I mimicked him as he tried to flag down a taxi, but they all passed by, loaded with passengers.

"They're getting the cabs back over there!" The guy pointed at a group of people in the distance, standing in line for taxis.

"Let's go!" I picked up my bags and started sprinting in that direction, leaving the other guy behind. The sidewalk was closed due to a construction site that looked long abandoned. I negotiated the debris and garbage that emptied out onto the street. There were piles of broken concrete, dirt, and faded orange caution streamers that had come loose and trailed in the wind, getting tangled in a makeshift wire fence. Dust and grit flew about, getting caught in my mouth and under my eyelids.

At the taxi stand, I waited in line, discussing fare sharing. I teamed up with a woman and a man, both of whom were also flying to Boston. We arrived at the terminal, sped to the check-in desk, and ran to the gate.

When we got to the gate, a flight attendant announced that our flight was delayed. The seats in the waiting area were all taken, so I pulled my stuff over to a pillar, leaned against it, and began to curse in Japanese.

\* \* \*

At Logan Airport in Boston, I retrieved my luggage from baggage claim and looked for Mama in the crowd. When I found her, she somehow

looked younger and more vibrant than I remembered. "Mama!" I ran to
her and we hugged. "The plane was delayed—wait long?"

"It's OK." She examined the fabric of my new shirt. "How was your
trip?"

"I'll tell you about it later. Boy, Kennedy Airport is a real mess."

"Yeah ... but it's not just New York. Sometimes I wonder how this
country functions at all. Nothing works."

"They were really rude to me in New York."

"Things have changed since we lived here ... *there* in New York."

We got into a cab and Mama continued talking about trying to get
used to the general disorganization. I was embarrassed for the taxi driver,
thinking he might take it personally. Then I noticed the thick Plexiglass
that separated us from the front of the car. He couldn't even hear us. The
plastic seats were ripped, revealing their spongy inner foam. The driver
was unshaven and drove with one arm hanging out of his window, rolling
a cigarette back and forth between his thumb and index finger.

As we traveled through a two-lane tunnel, I studied the cars we passed.
Many had big dents, rust spots, lopsided license plates, dragging mufflers,
and doors tied shut with twine and duct tape.

When we reached the end of the tunnel, I noticed that most of the tiles
on the roof of the tunnel had fallen off, leaving large patches of bare iron
grating.

As we sped south on Interstate 93, I was transfixed: The highway was
four lanes wide, trucks were huge, and billboards were bigger than life.
There was garbage all along the shoulder, a stripped-down car, an abandoned shopping cart, and boarded-up buildings.

We arrived at Mama's place, a spacious attic apartment in a two-family
building in a small suburban town called Braintree, just south of Boston. She
had decorated it in a bohemian style with a slight Japanese flavor in the form
of masks and framed prints, and with an eclectic collection of African and
Native American art. There was a black-and-white photograph of Miguel
and I as babies on the wall between the bathroom and kitchen.

Mama opened the refrigerator. "I wanted to make you your favorite
dish, lasagna, tonight but I've been so busy. Are you hungry?"

"Yeah. Real hungry. It's 8 a.m. right now for me."

"You want breakfast?"

"No! Of course not. Whatever you want."

"Well, let's see." She looked again in the refrigerator. "I didn't go
shopping either. Damn!"

"That's OK. I can go to the store. What do you need?"

As she wrote down a list, she hummed a German song as she often did
when she was working in the kitchen.

"Here's the list and some money. It should be enough. Stop & Shop is just … "

"Stop and Shop?"

"It's a supermarket. It's right down the street. Oh, and why don't you go to Jerry's across from the parking lot and pick up some pizza? Why don't you get some pizza for dinner?"

Pizza was rarely an option in Japan, and was practically a drug for the American ex-patriots living in Tokyo. The high school counselor once paid me 500 yen for the four small slices of cold pizza Mama had packed for me.

I headed toward the supermarket down the street, making the turns according to Mama's directions. It was getting dark, and when I turned the last corner, a big, bright red neon sign beamed out into the night sky from the other side of the parking lot: STOP & SHOP. As I approached the store, I braced myself. "Okay, I'm stopping; now I'm shopping."

The automatic doors opened; I gasped at the size of the interior. The rows were wide and packed with colorful boxes, containers, and bottles. The produce section alone spanned the depth of the building. I shook my head and focused on the list Mama had given me. I looked up at the aisle signs and realized they weren't numbered, but had names like Beef Boulevard, Artichoke Alley, Swordfish Street. Nibbles Nook was an aisle totally dedicated to dog and cat food.

After wandering around for some time in complete amazement, I finally gathered most of the items on the list and brought them to the cashier. She didn't even acknowledge me as she chewed her gum, ringing everything up.

"$27.76." She held out her hand.

"$27.76. Twenty-seven dollars and seventy-five cents. Right." I suddenly realized I didn't know how to count change in U.S. currency. I didn't remember which one was the nickel and which one was the dime or how much they were. Unfortunately, Mama had given me handful of change along with some bills.

I tried counting what I had but couldn't get it straight. Finally, I scooped up all the coins and bills in my pocket and emptied them onto the counter. "Ah … here you go."

The cashier stopped chewing, looked at the pile of money and then at me. She extracted the proper combination of bills and coins and cautiously pushed the rest back toward me.

"Thank you. I, ah … " I wanted to tell her that I had just arrived in America, but then realized that because I didn't have an accent, she would think that either *I* was a fool, or I was trying to make a fool of *her*.

It started to rain as I walked across the parking lot to Jerry's Pizza. By the time I got inside, my shopping bag was wet and my hair was dripping. I placed the groceries on the table next to a cigarette vending machine. There were no other customers in the store so I went right up to the counter. A large man wearing a white apron looked up at me as he continued to slice green peppers. His name "Jerry" was stitched onto the breast pocket of his white shirt.

I studied the menu on the board behind his head and realized how hungry I was. I was sure Mama was too. I remembered the tiny portions of pizza we used to get at Shakey's Pizza in downtown Tokyo. But I wanted pizza, and America was the place to get it. "Hi. Ah ... I'll take ... four pizzas."

"Youwananytinonnat?" He stopped chopping and raised his eyebrows.

"Ah ... excuse me?"

"Youwanpepperonigreenpeppasshroomsextracheeseonionsanchovies, youwananextracoffeedonutwiddat?" He leaned down on the counter and rested his hands on the chopped green peppers.

"Ah ... what are ... anchovies? Never mind. Ah ... everything."

"F'teenminutes."

I turned around to look outside. It was pouring and the windows began to fog up. I felt like I was supposed to make conversation. In the airport, and then in Stop & Shop, I had seen men standing together, legs spread wide apart, scratching their crotches, or folding their arms. I spread my legs apart, cleared my throat and cocked my head. "So, ah ... it's rainin' out there, eh?"

Jerry remained silent, slashing away at everything that would comprise that night's dinner.

"It's rainin' cats and ... cats and do ... do ... donuts out there. Heh." I scratched my thigh, hoping he would notice my hip attitude. Jerry pretended he didn't even hear me.

I sat down at the table where the shopping bag was and leaned back against the chair. I picked up an old issue of *TV Guide* that was among a pile of magazines on the window sill. As I scanned it I noticed that my favorite American television show *CHiPs* was playing in reruns in the evening. I used to watch it at 1 a.m. in Tokyo, but I had always wanted to see it in English. Then I recognized a few more shows I had never seen in their original language: *The Love Boat*; *Colombo*; *Scooby Doo*; *Charlie's Angels*.

"You'reallsetat'llbe $32.90." Jerry placed four gigantic boxes on the counter. I slowly got up and walked over.

"Are those mine?" I laughed out of nervousness. "Why are they so *big*? How am I gonna carry them home—it's raining outside … I've got my shopping bag … Nevermind."

I gave him $40 and waited for the change. Then I picked up the pizza boxes and put two under each arm, sideways. I grabbed my shopping bag with my right hand and pushed the door open with my shoulder. "See ya, Jerry."

Within seconds I was drenched. The paper shopping bag looked like it had aged 60 years, and I was sure the groceries would spill out through the bottom any second.

All of a sudden my left hand started to burn. I looked down and noticed that the pizza cheese was drooping down onto my hand. I tried flinging the scorching cheese drips off my fingers and ran as fast as I could, losing a can of tuna fish on the way.

I rang the doorbell with my elbow. When Mama opened the door she saw the sagging boxes of pizza. "Ahhhh! What did you get *four* … you must be joking! We'll be eating pizza for the next 4 days!"

$$* \quad * \quad *$$

As the bus rolled west on the Massachusetts Turnpike, I watched the city of Boston dissolve into trees and hills. It looked just like the brochure had promised: green pastures, rolling hills, even some cows. I listened to Simon and Garfunkel on my Walkman, and fell asleep thinking of all the hiking and Frisbee I would enjoy in the hills of Worcester.

I woke up suddenly, because everyone was getting off the bus. I rubbed my eyes and looked outside. It looked like we were back in Boston. Short gray buildings and broken windows. I noticed a man lying, seemingly dead, in the alcove of a boarded up storefront. People walked by, passing him without taking notice. I guessed he was drunk. Looking further down the street, I saw another man lying in the alcove of another storefront. "This can't be Worcester," I thought to myself, as I watched the last person exit the bus.

The driver climbed back into the bus and saw me. "Last stop, Wustah!"

My heart fell to the sticky aisle next to my seat. I picked up my carry-on bag, left the bus, and retrieved my suitcase that was waiting on the sidewalk. A taxi pulled up right next to me. The driver got out and pointed at me. "Claaahk?"

"Huh?" I looked at him, then looked behind me to see if anybody else was there.

"Claaahk University?"

"Uh … yeah. Yeah. How did you know?"

"I went to Claaak. Get in!" He opened the trunk, threw my suitcase in among some oily rags, a pair of muddy rubber boots, a garbage bag full of leaves, then slammed the trunk shut.

I waited for the door to open, forgetting that in America the passenger is supposed to open the door manually. In Japan the driver opens the door with the same kind of lever found in school buses.

"Get in already! What dorm ya goin' to?"

"I'm going to the dormitory Wright Hall."

"Oh yeah. Ha! It's called The Zoo." He studied me in his rearview mirror.

"Ah ... no. The dormitory Wright Hall at Clark University?"

"Yeah. Yeah, I know. It's called The Zoo. Donworry'boutathing. I went to Claaahk."

Five minutes later we arrived at the campus. The fee was $3.60. I was going to give him a $5 bill and realized I was supposed to tip him. "Ah ... how much am I supposed to ... tip ... ah ... in Japan we don't tip, so I don't know what, how much I should ... "

"Hey, tip whatever you want, kid. You know, I gotta eat too, right?"

Several weeks later I figured out I had tipped him more than 200%.

I walked toward The Zoo, and suddenly I felt like I was walking on air. The campus was filled with people, but no one was staring at me or pointing at me. As I approached the steps to the dormitory, a young man stopped to greet me. "Hi, how are you! Where you from?"

"Japan," I replied, not yet thinking in terms of states.

"Oh, wow! That's far out! Welcome to the U.S.! The name's Mike. Who are you?

"Teja-José Manuel Arboleda."

His eyebrows closed in on each other. "Sorry?"

"Ah ... Teja Arboleda."

He raised only his left eyebrow, so I knew he was still confused.

"Just call me Teja," I said, watching his face wrinkle as I continued to pronounce my name. "Teja ... Teeeyaaa ... Teh ... ya ... Never mind. I'm an American."

A woman sat to the side of the main entrance door handing out T-shirts. She had large breasts and wasn't wearing a bra so her nipples seemed to poke through the fabric of her tank top. I thought of Fujisawa-san and his fetish with large-breasted American women.

"Welcome to Wright Hall. And who would you be?" The woman stood up, and her breasts bounced and wiggled.

I broke out of my trance. "Teja."

"Is that your last name?" She smiled and tossed her hair back.

"Sorry. Arboleda."

"That's an interesting sounding name." She checked her clipboard. "Oh, here you are. Great! Well, welcome to Wright Hall.
Here's your Wright Hall T-shirt. You're in room ... 206. That's up
that way. Bye!"

I turned the knob, opened the door and was immediately bombarded
by scores of piercing guitar solos and booming drums. It seemed like
there were heavy metal rock wars coming from every nook and cranny
of the dormitory. I climbed to the second floor where it was even louder.
A half-naked guy swung down the water pipe that hung from the ceiling
and came straight at me. A blond-haired, blue-eyed guy stood to the
side, guzzling a beer and cheering the monkey man on, "Go, Ethan
Hausman, go, Ethan Hausman!" There was a woman behind me with
wet hair. She had only a tiny towel around her torso and was smoking
a joint. I heard a couple having sex against a door to my right. There
were Playboy posters plastered down the wall on my left. Doors on
each side of the hallway were wide open with boomboxes facing
outward, each blaring different music. I dodged the monkey man and
ran to my room. I slammed the door shut, sat on the striped gray and
pale-blue plastic, stained mattress and took a deep breath. I chanted
to myself, "I'll be OK I'm in America now. All I gotta do is just blend
in with the rest of them ... how hard could that be?"

A blond-haired, blue-eyed White guy came crashing into the room.
"Heeey! Hey T.J., how are ya?" His booming voice echoed against the
bare concrete-walled room. "I'm Rob! Rob Petrie, your new roommate?
Hey, I thought you'd be sittin' on the floor eating Ramen noodles or
something like that! Hey, where's all your stuff? Don't worry 'bout a
thing—I got a great stereo, 100 watt/100 watt both channels. Dad?"

His father came in carrying a full-rack stereo system. Another guy
came in who I suspected was his brother, carrying two large speakers.
They placed the equipment on the floor and left for another load. Chris
went about connecting his stereo components. "So what do you like?
Jimi Hendrix? The Doors? The Who?"

I was still in shock from the noise in the hallway. "The who? The
who what?"

"Tell you what." He rummaged through one of his boxes and pulled
out an album. "I'm gonna start you off with some Jimi Hendrix." He
skillfully cleaned the vinyl album with a special brush, then placed it
on the record player. He turned the volume knob up to 10. Then I
watched his hand as he carefully placed the needle on the record.

The room exploded into a fog of screaming guitars.

*   *   *

Two weeks after I placed a request to move to a quieter dormitory, I was given a room in Bullock Hall. It was tame compared to The Zoo. Within the first week, however, my visitor's message pad was ripped off my door; several people tried to offer me marijuana, hashish, Twinkies, and cheap beer; a kid from the second floor had been arrested; the Falkland Islands were in jeopardy; someone carved "Oedipus was a mother-fucker" on my door; and I had a fight with someone who had to explain to me that when he called a woman a "JAP" he meant "Jewish American Princess." My roommate, Bob, whose every possession, clean or dirty, was shoved under his bed, finally took a shower, and the couple in the next room had already ritualized their noisy sex to three times a day.

One day after I returned from taking a shower, a tall red-headed freckled guy barged into my room followed by a big, heavy-set White guy clutching a beer can. I had only a towel around my waist, and the open door let in some cool air. My roommate Bob woke up from his nap as the first guy approached me.

"Hey, T.J.! My name's Mark. Welcome to America! Hey look, your nipples are erect!" He reached over and tweaked my nipples so hard my eyes filled up with tears. "Sorry 'bout that! But when they're erect it can only mean two things!" Then he waved good-bye and left, slamming the door behind him.

The second guy stood in front of me snickering. "You're from China, right?"

"No, actually I'm from Japan."

"Yeah, whatever." He took a swig from his beer can. "You do any of that martial arts stuff?"

"Well, I did study judo for 7 years."

"Whoa! Not gonna touch *you*! You know all those Oriental guys!" He broke into a frenzied karate hand chopping demonstration. "Hai ya! Hai ya! Hai yayayayayaya! Wachoiii *yah*!"

I playfully positioned myself for combat and flexed my chest muscles. His eyes bugged, he threw the door open and disappeared around the corner.

Later that afternoon I made a sign that read: "Watch out! I'm studying American slang!" As I nailed it to my door, a guy approached me, wearing thick glasses and his pants so that the waist of the pants nearly met his chest. He spoke through his nasal passage and kept poking his glasses back up the bridge of his nose. "Mr. T.J. You're from Japan, right? Tell me something—is it true that the Japanese still ride horses and carry swords and stuff? See I was watching this movie somewhere … *Shogun*? Yeah."

Feeling suddenly confident, I put my arm around his shoulders. "Sure the Japanese still ride horses and carry swords. Of course they do. You see, they just *make* cars. They can't drive the cars because they're too short, can't see over the dashboard?" I rubbed the top of his head with my knuckles. "Tell me something. Where can I find a great shoot-out, you know, a sheriff-outlaw kinda John Wayne–Indian deal ... *bang! bang!*, you know what I mean?"

When I realized what I had said, I felt a rush of adrenaline. Then, a tall, lanky guy I got to know as "Just-Plain-Adam" passed behind me. "Teja, where exactly 'djya learn how ta talk English so good, huh? Wonderful stuff. Wonderful stuff!"

Sometimes I sat alone in an alcove of the library, staring at the rolling hills and trees, and noticed how different they were from the trees in Japan. Frequently I lost myself on the winding paths that fed the dormitories and campus buildings, wondering how many of my new friends inside were genuine. I missed my companionships in Japan. I had never experienced homesickness to this degree before, and somehow I knew that this would be permanent as it was for many of my family members—the Arboleda legacy. But I also remembered the humiliation of having to show my I.D., and finger-printing in Japan. *A guest of the host country.* I had so often wanted to rip my green card into shreds. And now in America, I missed every corner, every smell of Japan.

As the weeks passed I settled in and often found myself overcompensating in gestures and language in order to adapt. I did feel peaceful at times, at ease, free from the stares and finger-pointing with which I had lived for 13 years in Japan. As I passed the crowds of the mostly White faces on campus, part of me felt empty, and I longed for the familiar. I feared that when or if I returned to live in Japan, I would have become yet further from the harmony of the group—the defining essence of Japanese culture. Knowing I would never be accepted into Japanese society, I decided to adjust, compensate and become the American behind the picture in my U.S. passport.

America, I had learned so many times from textbooks to guidance counselors, was a melting pot—everyone was the same, everyone fit in. I began to realize that this was propaganda like any other.

I refrained from boasting my Japanese language ability—the less they knew about me, the less they had to decipher. I dressed like my peers, in ripped jeans and loose-hanging, oversized shirts. I learned quickly to *talk different versions of English*. I became a social butterfly, hovering from table to table in the cafeteria, quickly adopting friends by making them laugh. I found that I could adapt my knack for humor to an American style and milked Americans' need for comedy in everything. I entertained during meals and classes, in the hallways, at the movies and became a mediator between lovers.

Because meat was not an option in Japan, and because I was overly energetic, an abundance of red, juicy meat seemed the perfect American cultural directive. I spent more than an hour at lunch and dinner, helping myself to an average of three servings of the main course, several passes by the salad bar, yogurt, two desserts, four glasses of milk, two glasses of water, and two cups of coffee. With each pass I would venture to another table, quickly join in conversations and then leave.

I blended in better than I thought I could. Certainly better than I ever could in Japan, and within such a short time! Very rarely did people ask me where I was from, but I did wonder what they assumed I was. Because I didn't have an accent, no one suspected I wasn't from the United States. The only thing that gave away my identity was when I had to ask someone to explain a phrase, colloquialism, or slang. For the most part, however, I pretended to understand, nodding my head and laughing along with the others.

One evening during a "Special Dinner," through a raffle I won 100 Twinkies and Mellow Yellows. For the next 2 days, total strangers pretending to know me stopped by to say a quick hello and to pick up a take-home snack from my supply.

I soon discovered, however, that as quickly as I made friends, I lost them. Relationships in America seemed opaque and unassuming, merely temporary. People I had never met before would call me "buddy." A bookstore manager awarded me a discount with a "because I like you—you're smart." Women flirted with me and then a minute later they would make a pass at someone else. Classmates offered friendship with an "I'll give you a call," or an "I'll stop by your room," but never followed up. Neighbors would confide in me with deep, personal stories and a week later they wouldn't remember who I was. Kim, an attractive woman who about boasted her career as a face model, introduced herself to me by showing me how she had lost an inch from her thighs. "I'll be a full-fledged model, as soon as I get my thighs down 6 more inches. But maybe I'm not tall enough. Anyway, thighs first!" She showcased me as her "lover" around campus for a week, then bluntly discarded me when she was sure her three *real* lovers were still under her spell.

I felt like the campus yahoo. The sheer whirlwind energy needed to keep up with my self-imposed itinerary was taking a toll on me, and I was beginning to lose sight of what little direction I had. The act of becoming an American was eluding me, driving me into a frenzy. It had become increasingly difficult for me to reconcile my real, former self and the new, adjusted character I had embodied. In the middle of clowning around with a group of friends, I often found myself coming into a strange sense of altered reality where I could see myself from the outside. I frequently didn't like what I saw and secretly wished I was brave enough to be the Teja I was only months ago. It was difficult enough to find close friends, and I was too scared to lose the ones I had made.

My anxiety finally was exposed one afternoon during lunch. I had joined a group that usually hung out in my dormitory. As they planned their next keg party, I pretended to listen, actually bored by their concerns about the *kind* of beer and who could get away with buying it. Bill looked over at me. "Hey guys, did you know Teja's got a Japanese driver's license? Tej, show 'em your drivers license."

I hated when he called me *Tej*. I pulled out my wallet and produced my license.

"Look at that, guys! Isn't that messed up?" Bill took my license and showed it to the others. "'Cuz it's written in Japanese, no one will ever know the difference! How old are you Tej?"

"Nineteen," I replied, not knowing what he was getting at.

"Tej, here's what we're gonna do. We'll take you to the package store where you'll ... "

"What's a package store?"

"Oh boy." Marta slapped her hand to her forehead. "This'll be just *great*."

"A liquor store." Bill handed me back my license. "You have to be 21. Used to be 18, but they changed that—would rather have us go to war, sober. Now we gotta buy alcohol in New Hampshire."

"How far is New Hampshire?" I had been told that in some areas in America people drive for 2 hours to say hello to a neighbor.

"Just forget it, Bill." Marta threw her fork to her plate. "He obviously doesn't want to do this."

Bill took his fork and shoved it straight down the middle of his steaming rice pilaf. "You wanna let him make his own decisions?"

I gasped, staring at his fork sticking straight up. Marta threw a dirty napkin at Bill. "See, you stupid jerk! You scared the shit out of him. What's the matter Tej?"

My astonishment turned to pure anger. I stood up and pushed my chair back. "Don't ever, *ever* do that again!"

Bill raised his eyebrows. "Shit, Tej, what the hell are you talking about?"

"Where I come from, you *never* stick chopsticks, or whatever into your rice like that—it means death! It means someone's going to die!"

"It's just a freakin' *fork*, man."

I reached for my own fork, ready to stab my double-patty, extra cheese with red onions hamburger, and glared at Bill. Bill looked over at Marta and the others. Marta stood up with her tray in her hand and walked away.

"What the hell is wrong with him?" Bill yelled out toward Marta.

I got up from my chair, took my hamburger, and walked out of the cafeteria, fuming.

Marta was waiting for me at the door. "What was that all about? Are you OK?"

"Never mind. You wouldn't understand." I looked at my hamburger and threw it in the garbage. I returned to my room where I cooked up some instant Ramen in a hot pot.

\* \* \*

One evening when I was feeling sorry for myself, I confided in my friend Mary that Mama was traveling to Germany around Thanksgiving to visit her parents, and that I was going to be alone. Mary wouldn't hear of me spending the holidays alone, so she demanded that I join her and our friend Vonni at her home in Vermont. I was extremely apprehensive at first, not wanting to impose. I knew I shouldn't have said anything, and realized that a part of my Japanese-self had shed as fast as the leaves outside. I wouldn't have said anything back home in Tokyo, because when one indicates a wish for something, it is usually fulfilled promptly, leaving the receiver embarrassed. But even more so, the idea of being with such a cohesive-sounding family was already too overwhelming for me. I didn't want sympathy, I didn't want temporary companionship, and I didn't want to see, hear, or feel the love of others. If her parents were divorced, maybe I could handle it. But how could I survive being surrounded by the beauty of what I could never have again? Nevertheless, I didn't have anywhere else to go, so I braced myself.

I watched the scenery pass by and looked in the windows of homes, imagining families coming together, celebrating, eating, and laughing. Vonni sat with Mary in the front of the car where they joked and told stories of their childhood together in Vermont. Vonni had come to the United States from Micronesia as a high school exchange student, and had decided to stay with her adopted parents who lived down the street from Mary's family. Four thousand miles from the warm island she had once called home, she settled in the northern-most region of New England, just below Canada, a Black girl in the Whitest state of the union. She and Mary met in school and had been best friends from the first day. As I listened to their stories and their laughter, it was clear to me that their friendship would last.

Their voices grew dim as I began to drift back to the days when my own family came together for Thanksgiving in New York. Everything changed once we left for Japan. With family all over the world, Papa's traveling, and then the separation, I could never again have the comforts of nearby family. I leaned my head against the edge of the back seat and watched the sky turn dark blue and finally black. I cried silently and vowed that one day things would be different. I would get married and have the perfect family, and we would never move.

Mary's family welcomed me warmly that evening, and I felt strangely comfortable, like I did when I would visit our cousins in Germany. Mary's mother was a generous cook, and although it was the day before Thanksgiving, we ate unhealthy amounts of food while we laughed and mockingly railed each other.

I wanted to tell them how happy I was to be there, and also how jealous I was. The pictures of family on the walls; the glowing candles; the little knickknacks each family member placed under the rails, on the stairs, or on the bathroom vanity for no explicable reason. The old kettle on the stove and the crackling fireplace—all these things seemed intangible to me, as if they never existed at all. But I imagined the years behind every footstep on the floor boards, the handprints on the doorknobs, the rounded edges of the door jambs—every nuance was a testimony to all that was precious and important.

This feeling of timeless paradise ended abruptly when her father discussed his plans to renovate their massive farm land into a lodge and hiking area. He complained jokingly, that when tearing down the decrepit farm buildings and barns, they might have to chase "some niggers" out of the henhouses with sticks.

*Nigger. That word again.* The good food I had just gorged on became sour.

That night I cried under the covers in the guestroom. Vonni came to the room and sat at the foot of the bed. She understood my anger and humiliation perfectly and remained quietly with me for a long time. When she finally spoke, she tried to assure me that Mary's folks didn't really mean what they said and probably wouldn't even remember it in the morning. I couldn't help wonder how much pain she had lived with in this rural outpost, thousands of miles away from her family. I never asked her why she decided to stay, and I wondered if I, too, would be able to see past the ignorance of my company and strangers, and accept them despite their prejudices.

* * *

Back in Worcester I started jogging around the neighborhood in the evenings. It got dark early, so on my route I could look into the warm glow of living rooms and kitchens. I looked for people hugging, eating, and playing with kids. I imagined large, sumptuous dinners and desserts.

Each house was perfect to me and each home was blessed with the security of family.

But soon I became angry at not having a home to return to and eventually began to hate looking into the houses as I passed them. I felt like I was dying every time I saw even the hint of a silhouette move past a lighted window. I learned to hide my pain well. I tried hard to become the happy-go-lucky American I thought everyone expected me to be, and accumulated "friends" whose names I could never remember. Ultimately, I spent so much of my time trying to be accepted by everyone that I often neglected my studies.

The evening before Christmas vacation, I packed my bags to stay with Mama who had returned from Germany. Several of my dormitory acquaintances stumbled into my room in a mass drunken stupor. Mark, balancing himself against the doorpost, held up a family-sized bottle of Jack Daniels. "Teja, hey, tonight's the night we're gonna get you smashed."

"Yeah, man!" Paul gulped from a plastic cup of beer. "Susan tells me you don't drink. What, don't they drink in China or something?"

I wanted to tell them I hated the taste of alcohol. "Well, I just don't ... "

"Well, that's the way it's done here in America." Mark placed his beer bottle on my desk and proceeded to open the bottle of Jack Daniels. "How come you're just sittin' in your room alone? It's Christmas, man! Party time!"

I tried to imagine Jesus slugging down a gin and tonic with his disciples. Is this what Christianity had come to? "And then what," I smirked at Mark, "tomorrow we go to church to repent at Christmas morning mass?"

"Yeah, well," Mark said. "God wouldn't have created alcohol if it wasn't meant to be drunk. Besides, at mass they give you wine."

Paul looked at me curiously. "Come on, Teja, you gotta party with us just this once, right?"

Ian barged his way into the room and spoke as he let out a king-sized burp. "Oooookaaaay! Teej, here's what we're gonna do." He grabbed me and nudged me all the way down the hall to his room. The rest of the guys followed.

Ian pushed me through the crowd that had gathered in his room and presented me to the makeshift bar he built out of plywood and milk crates. Lined along the top were bottles of all shapes and sizes and a stack of plastic cups. The crowd had obviously been prepared for my initiation. Some of them cheered me on. Someone cranked up the song in progress—"Louie, Louie!"

Ian leaned against the bar. "So, everybody! What should we start Mr. Adobl ... Abrobel ... Mr. Japan with? Any suggestions?"

"A Sloe Screw!" yelled out one woman, eyeing me and tossing her hair.

"Black Russian!" suggested another woman.

*Black Russian? I wondered how that would have played out in one those James Bond movies. Surely James Bond's Russian nemesis would never be Black.*

"No, a *White* Russian!" heckled a guy from behind me.

"No, he's from Japan. Give him a Kamikaze!" suggested a voice that sounded familiar.

"Hiroshima! Give him a fuckin' Hiroshima! Bomb the mother fucker into oblivion! He'll never know what fuckin' hit him!"

"A Hiroshima it is!" Ian began to measure and pour from several different bottles.

Susan came up from behind me, put her hand around my waist and whispered into my ear. "You are gonna *love* it." She pinched my behind and drifted toward the door. As I watched her leave, Ian shoved a red plastic cup in my hand.

"OK, let's go. One gulp." Ian raised his cup. "Banzai, everyone, banzai!"

*Banzai? That's what suicide bombers yelled on the way to their death.*

A chorus formed, chanting, "Banzai! Banzai! Banzai!"

I took a sip and swished it around my mouth. It wasn't bad. In fact it was quite tasty. I took another sip.

Ian tilted up my cup and nearly choked me as I inhaled the contents. The room burst into cheer.

"What do you want next?" Ian asked as he headed back for the bar.

I wiped my face and chest of the aftermath of my Hiroshima. I didn't feel drunk or tipsy at all. I nodded to Ian. "Whatever you think."

During the next hour Ian served me introductory portions of beer from a bottle, beer from a can, beer from a keg, straight vodka, red wine, white wine, Jack Daniels, a Slippery Nipple, and a Screw Driver.

I remember first feeling elated. I joked with strangers, I hugged every woman I saw. I hugged men. I was under the impression people liked me. I ventured out into the hallway and into other peoples' rooms. In my neighbor Tom's room, I nabbed a large bottle of Kahlua and poured it all over his bed. Susan found me licking the neck of the bottle and hurried me out of the room, and into mine. She sat me down on my bed and I became strangely sad. As she spoke, all of which was unintelligible to me, I became angry. I stood up and marched to the hallway.

"OK all you little shits! Anybody wanna fight me?" My words seemed to take shape long after I spoke them. "I want you all to speak Japanese with me. If you don't speak Japanese I'll do a judo flip on you!"

Ruth, who had been sleeping with Peter the week before, was now shoving her tongue down Sam's throat. She looked over at me and laughed.

I staggered over to Karl and demanded he speak Japanese. For some reason I thought that because he was from Denmark he should be able to speak Japanese. I grabbed his shirt collar. "Speak Japanese or else!"

"Ahh! Ah … *Konnichiwa!*" He pried my hands loose and moved away.

I turned around and found my new roommate, Jeff, standing next to me. He turned me toward my room. "Teja, I think you've had enough. Let me take you to the room, OK?"

"You're not speaking Japanese! You're not speaking Japanese!" I grabbed his shirt. "I can recite the Communist Manifesto in Japanese, wanna hear it? *Wanna hear it?*"

Jeff tried to push me away. "No, Teja. Come on, you're gonna be sick tomorrow. You should go to bed."

"Doesn't sound like Japanese to me!" In one swift, instinctual move, I grabbed his right sleeve with my left, braced my right fist and elbow on his chest, turned and bent my body under his belly and threw him over my head. His glasses flew off and shattered as he crash-landed next to the girls' bathroom.

* * *

The next morning I woke up covered in my own vomit. When I tried to move, my head exploded. Except for my underpants, I was naked. I tried to pull the cover over me but my body wouldn't budge. When I finally managed to roll onto my side, my friend Kevin came in, and laughed. "Teja, you sick son-of-a-gun, you! Had a good night I can see! Boy, were you a trip last night! We're all real proud of you, you know that? I hope you don't mind, but I've packed almost all your stuff in my car because I'm taking you to your mom's place. I figured since she lives about 5 minutes from my folks in Quincy, why the hell not. We're gonna have to leave soon because there's a blizzard out there. So get up slow and go take a shower."

I tried to thank him but all I could do was wink at him. It took me almost 10 minutes to sit up, all the while grimacing in pain as my head made a left turn to reality.

Ron from next door came into the room and gave me a standing ovation. I had to close my eyes and whisper, "No. Please."

"Teja, if you're not using your shampoo, I've run out … I take that as a yes." He began rummaging through my toiletry kit. "Hey what the hell is this?" He held up a bottle of Prell Shampoo. "I thought Japanese didn't use this American shit. I'm ashamed, man. Do you know what's in this crap? I thought you'd be more Japanese-like. Green tea shampoo and stuff—I saw it in a Zen magazine. Prell! Well, I'll just use my soap, thank you very much."

\* \* \*

As Kevin drove down the Massachusetts Turnpike toward Boston, he told me stories about his own drinking adventures. He was proud of having survived countless parties and hangovers and gave me advice on how to regain my strength for the next round. But with each bump in the road, an excruciating pain shot through my head. I granted victory to the Kamikaze and White Russian warring in my bowels and I vowed never to drink again.

When we arrived at Mama's house, all she could do was laugh. She laughed for 3 days.

# 17
# The Awakening

The point at which a true friendship develops is a mystery. There were usually about seven of us, and we gathered every morning for breakfast at the third round table next to the window in Jefferson Hall. On weekends, we lasted sometimes 3 hours over brunch, competing for attention, challenging one joke with another, and occasionally out-philosophizing each other.

It was an eclectic group; relatively casual, but even more importantly, each brought to the table individual ideas and passions that seemed to defy what I had come to learn in Japan as the general concept of group consensus. Conversations could switch with the touch of a button, spin into an argument or a sidetracked ad-lib skit, only to come full circle again. Words and ideas popped out, flew in circles, evolved and piled up with everyone contributing to this phenomenon. I found a voice there, a real casual social vocabulary that felt, on occasion, natural.

I adapted quickly; my language, posture, even my priorities. And for the first time in my life I realized I was okay on my own. Along with this came a satisfying sense of freedom—a tangible place, void of curious questions and demands for serious conformity. America had become an opportunity beyond what I imagined.

However, my attention was hyper—comparing, adjusting, weighing, and evaluating every word, gesture, and role play. Japan, now thin in my blood, but nonetheless apparent to others, would suddenly surface. I would get annoyed that certain basic values didn't come naturally to so many of my colleagues. The sense of sharing, for example, was not as apparent as it would have been in Japan. Rather, the sharing was more of an expression of one's self—the strong "me" in the context of "others." In this way, individuality in its purist form, in a country that promotes "rugged individualism," generated a series of complexities that in the end could tear apart the fabric that keeps this country together.

Like a child learning to reason, I committed faux pas that were no less than bizarre to my friends. Filling another's glass with water from a pitcher or dumping a second serving on another's plate without asking was enough to cause a discussion to skid to a halt. "What *are* you *doing*, Teja! You know, you really are weird."

It seemed like they rarely considered my perspectives on things and just generally spoke without thinking. "In Japan ... ," I would begin.

"We're not *in* Japan," one of them might challenge.

"When you're in Rome, do as the Romans do," someone else once added.

"We're not in Rome," I retorted, trying desperately to turn the table on them.

"Yeah, but this is the God Fearin' 'merica, man!" Steve mocked, raising his fist, "home of the red, white, and blue!"

Anne was always the smart one. "Do you even know what those colors mean?"

"Blood, purity and something!" Steve charged.

I raised my left eyebrow like Papa used to. "Which one's purity?"

"White! You know, pure as white ... no stain ... starched ... like our friend Anne, here."

* * *

I didn't really notice that most of my closest friends were women until Kevin asked me if I was gay.

"Gay?" I asked. I hadn't even thought of the word.

He spread his legs, placed his fists on his hips and spoke briskly. "You know, prefer men over women ... "

"Actually, I prefer women to men. At least here I do."

"What do you mean—you swing both ways? Boys in China, or wherever you said you're from, and then girls here? That's messed up."

"I guess I get along with woman better here." I was about to explain that most American men were too bent on confirming their testosterone levels, and that in Japan, I could cry with another man and talk about feelings, but I caught myself. Somehow I knew Kevin wouldn't understand.

Kevin scratched his beer belly. "You know, I saw a documentary about Japanese baseball players—when they lose, they cry. What the hell is that? Pretty faggish, don't you think?"

"No. Crying is a human emotion. By the way, why do American football players always pat each other on the behind?"

* * *

"Are you sure you're not gay, Teja?" Kathy sat next to me on my dorm bed and began to unbutton her blouse.

"Why does everyone think I'm gay?"

"Well, you're not really, you know, like a *guy*."

"I'm not a guy?" I tried to ignore her casual stripping.

"No, no, that's not what I meant. I mean, you know, the booze, the walk, the belching, and you're real nicelike. Maybe it's just that you're from Korea." She unpinned her hair.

"No, I'm not gay. And I'm from Japan."

"You spend a lot of time with me and you don't have a lot of guy friends. Wow, it's really hot in here!" She pulled her blouse off and tossed her hair. Her breasts bulged out of her bra as she arched backward.

"Ah … yeah, it is kind of hot in here you're a great friend and I feel I can talk to you about anything hey your shirt is off aren't you cold maybe it's cold wow! okay well let's just not tell anyone and say this didn't happen no I'm definitely not gay but I gotta go because I'm hungry thanks for the mac and cheese talk to you later bye!"

"Teja, wait, it's okay if you're gay! Some of my friends are gay!"

* * *

"The Freudian element in Scene 12 is pervasive and quite didactically colorful, then continues in various forms throughout each primary character and, except for a few shots like where the antagonist is reflecting on his father figure's relationship to him, the subjective elements converge, lending themselves naturally to that Freudian force which dominates." Professor Seth Freiburg's thick unruly beard rippled with his triple chin as he spoke. He nursed it with rhythmic strokes as he released his version of the content of some obscure experimental French film. I had chosen to become a filmmaker when I was 14 but never did I suspect that "penis envy," according to Seth, would be a theme running rampant in so many domestic and foreign movies.

Seth dissected scores of films from some obscure, experimental 40-minute, fixed-camera observation of a silhouetted man getting a haircut, to Orson Welles' *Citizen Kane*, tearing them apart, then reconstructing the pieces. I was fascinated with every element of film biology. I even took a job as a projectionist, so that between my communications classes and work, I saw no less than 9 movies a week. Soon, the concept of making my own films became a quest, an addiction. I learned to analyze every element, idea, and hidden agenda. I often disagreed with Seth's psychological rationales of plot and story lines and even gained his respect by proving my own theories in my papers.

But I was unfulfilled. The abundance of stories, messages, and art I was studying was lacking something and I couldn't place my finger on it. My curiosity revealed that even beyond consuming film history and the mechanics that give the art form life, I discovered a serious dearth of positive images of non-White people. Naturally, the focus was predominantly on Western media except for the occasional analysis of a Yasujiro Ozu or a Godard film. Gradually, deep into the course of mass media studies, the concern became only more pronounced. The study of shows like *Father Knows Best* was understandably condemned as sexist and unrealistic, yet never was there a concern for the lack of healthy minority representation—as if the whole world revolved around White Americans. When a character with dark skin (*All In The Family*), thinner eyes (*Charlie Chan*), or a heavy accent did appear, it was usually to their default, out of range of the critical eyes of my educators. It wasn't until 10 years later, when I was working for PBS, that I saw D. W. Griffith's *A Birth of a Nation* again. The civil war, as usual, was treated as an idealistic, romantic conflict between the north and the south when, in fact, much of Griffith's profits from the film was awarded to the KKK for their support.

It became increasingly difficult for me to concentrate on the contexts and analyses I had been presented with in all my classes. I wanted more and had to find it on my own. I began to formulate an idea for a healthier course of study, and drew up plans for a self-designed major. The lack of non-White ownership of American historical and popular culture was as a constant, nagging sore spot, and as a result of this, I managed to upset otherwise streamlined classes.

"I'd like to suggest a Soseki Natsume novel for next semester?" I probed during an English literature class.

"Who's that?" a woman asked while chewing on her pencil.

"He's a Japanese author," I offered.

"Well, this is an American lit class, duh!" The woman rolled her eyes.

"You mean 'English.' So, Shakespeare was American, huh? No, I just thought a Natsume novel as a comparative view of language. It's translated, you know."

"Teja, why are you always trying to make things complicated?"

"What about a Black author. One who writes in English?"

"Teja, shut up and sit down."

* * *

In all of life's hidden ironies, there were sometimes beautiful surprises. In the hallways of classroom buildings and dormitories and on the grassy campus grounds, I came to understand that the concept of a coherent society and the idea of "normality" was quite simply not an American fact or virtue. The media had tricked us all, and I had been the fool. Just in my own little circle, I was surrounded by Jews dating Christians, Jews dating Muslims, Jamaicans dating French-Canadians, dark-skinned women dating light-skinned men, men dating men, women dating women, a blind woman dating a seeing man. The small community of Clark emerged as an experiment far more complex than a Jean Luc-Godard film. How could America, Hollywood, or Disney, in their self-proclaimed "innocence," manage to elude that truth for so long, and how long could the charade last? I concentrated wholly on a yet-undefined mission. I grasped for answers, often not knowing the questions. And perhaps my pensiveness reflected outward, sometimes prompting others to seek my advice.

* * *

I am still not aware of where empathy and sympathy begins or ends, but in the eyes of some friends, my bedside manner was like a key that unlocked their tormented lives.

"Teja, Alan wants to see other girls," Karen confided in me once.

"Wow," I remember saying with false confidence. "Simply, love is a two-way street. If clearly he is unattached, then get off the road."

My general answers, born of complete ignorance of human romantic bonds, had somehow become directives etched into some moral marble. In the end, I may have unwittingly destroyed a number of otherwise mendable relationships.

Perhaps I could have used the ignorance of my own advice. I knew I had steered myself wrong when Papa and Mama announced they would officially get a divorce. It had been 3 years since the separation and I had learned to draw pictures of them apart and separate in my mind.

Their legal paperwork was to take place in Japan. Leaving the apartment for a long trip was good for Mama—she was depressed and had never liked living in Boston. She wanted to find another place where she could feel more at home. After Japan she planned to look around, so she left her belongings in my apartment.

For Mama, returning to Tokyo was unbearable. She was scared to go and sad to arrive. There was nothing for her there anymore, and she wondered where the years went and what she had done with her life. She desperately wanted to avoid landing in Tokyo and seeing the old neighborhood, so on the way there Mama decided to briefly stop off in Germany to spend some time with her parents. She called to tell me she was packing to leave and asked me if I wanted anything from Japan or Germany. A wash of tangible items and memories flooded my head, but my answer came up empty. There were so many times I wanted nothing but to return home to dinner with Miguel across from me, Mama to my left, and Papa to my right.

Two days after arriving in Hannover, Mama's purse was stolen and with it her money, German passport, and her green card to the United States. For the next 4 months she was stuck in Germany, staying with her parents and Tante Luise waiting for the German and U.S. governments to sort out the bureaucratic mess.

Then, on a whim, Mama diverted her plans. With her new passport and visa, she decided to travel to India. With only the contents in a black duffel bag, she traveled to Bombay where she stayed with the Ram family, who we knew from Japan. She continued on to Delhi, Rajnesh, Peryar, Puna, Madras, and the former Portugese colony, Gia. In her seventh week, she traveled by camel across the deserts of Jodhpur and Jaisalmer in Rajasthan near the border of Pakistan. When the unbearably hot Indian summer started, she decided to leave and face the divorce.

*　*　*

"Tomorrow is your birthday?" Mark yelped. "Whoa! We gotta get you tanked again, man!"

No one was going to ruin my 20th birthday by filling me up with Tequila shots and "Kahlua Orgasms." I had been planning secretly something I could really be remembered for, a proclaimed ritual. Turning 20 was, after all, not to be taken lightly. "Just wait," I thought to myself, "my coming-of-age initiation would be remembered by many." The next morning I was to wake up at 4:45 a.m. to face my biggest fear.

*　*　*

"Teja, get up! Me and Angie are waiting in the van!" Carl yelled flicked on the light. My roommate groaned and covered his head with his blanket.

As I struggled to get on all my clothes at once, I reminded myself of the purpose of this day's mission. I had thought about turning 20 often, and wanted to make a significant statement to myself, and to everyone around me, that I was indeed an adult. A man. Papa had told me of his own coming-of-age ritual—at the age of 13, so I felt I was late already—he completed with his father in the Philippines. It was the first time they had a real conversation. Advice was shared and guidance was given to initiate the respect that comes with adulthood. I often wished that Papa and I could have continued that legacy. I was certainly sure I wasn't going to get any serious support from my dormitory mates so I had to invent my own initiation.

I jumped into the van half-dressed. Angie laughed as she watched me pull on my pants over my long johns. It was pitch black outside, and as we turned onto the highway, the headlights raced across pine trees still wet from yesterday's melting snow. Angie's voice quivered. "Shit, I'm already freaking out!"

By the time we reached the site at Pepperell, we volleyed for the restroom.

"First time?" a man with deep wrinkles asked me.

"Ah ... yeah," I said.

"Well, don't forget to flush!"

My knees were shaking violently. "Oh, I will. I will!"

Angie emerged from the bathroom and I jumped in. As I sat on the toilet I stared at a curled poster of a young Arnold Schwarzenegger flexing his muscles so that he looked like an angry rottweiler.

The classes and physical training took 5 hours, during which I communed with Arnold 5 times. At 2 p.m., I was to become a man.

We piled in, joining the instructor and a pilot named Cracker. I was placed next to the only door that the instructor opened a few minutes later for a better view.

"Beautiful, huh?" he asked. "If things don't work out, we owe you a six-pack."

"Thirty-two hundred, boss," Cracker confirmed.

I watched earth float away.

"You!" The coach touched my shoulder and stuck his finger in my face. "Out!"

"Remember, left foot on the step. Arch back, count to 10. Don't let the cable get between your legs. If nothing, then pull the cord! Now go be a man!"

*Go be a man.*

Jim cut the engine to minimum cruising speed. I placed my left foot on the step. I stared at the planet and forgot my mission.

"You! Go or I'll kick you!"

I released my hands but I forgot to arch or count. The cable snapped tight between my legs and I flipped over backward. Schwarzenegger laughed. My scream disappeared in the clouds as my feet appeared between me and the tail of the plane. All I could think of was how odd the concept of skydiving was—that dogs don't skydive, neither do cats or turtles.

Suddenly I felt a tug and then silence. I looked up and saw the chute fully expanded. I checked the chute and the toggles. The ugly glass skin of Boston's Hancock tower 70 miles away shimmered in the afternoon sun. I was not a man, I decided, but I *was* alive. If I came back here to do it again, *then* I would know I was a man.

By the time I got back to my dormitory, most of the lights were out and it was unnaturally quiet. There was a knock on my door, and when I opened it, Pacita stood at the entrance with a cake.

"It's 1 a.m. Where have you been all day?" she asked.

"Ah … skydiving."

She tilted her head. "Yeah, okay, and so pigs *can* fly." My roommate sighed loudly and pressed his face in his pillow. "We had a surprise birthday party for you. Now, of course, everyone's gone to sleep, stupid! By the way, apparently you have a package from your dad."

"Sorry, I didn't know. I did jump out of an airplane, though."

"Sure. You just didn't wanna be with friends. They don't like surprise cakes in Taiwan?"

Sleep was not going to come early that night, if at all. I was still flushed with adrenaline, trying to replay the event of the day frequently enough to dull it. Thoughts of bravery and stupidity spiralled out of control.

I sat in the lounge with a can of Mellow Yellow and the package. As I unwrapped the box, the faint smell of Papa's cologne, our living room, and bamboo quelled my anxiety. The package contained dried squid and cuttlefish, a pad of vertically lined Japanese writing paper, a recent edition of the *Jump* cartoon anthology, and a manila envelope that had a thick stapled stack of paper and a card paper clipped to the front.

"Happy birthday! You are now a man, an adult, and I'm very proud to be your father. I know I have not been a good father, but maybe you'll see that I was at least adequate. I wish I could be there to celebrate your coming of age as I did with my father. Here is a copy of a diary I have written about your life since your birth. Miguel got a copy of his diary when he turned 20—now I would like you to have yours. Love, Papa."

*A diary about my life? So, Miguel got a copy 2 years ago—why didn't he ever tell me about it?* I flipped through the pages cautiously, stopping only briefly to read passages. Papa's handwriting had changed in 20 years from calligraphic to rushed to almost incomprehensible. At the end of the stack I found the last passage, dated April 6, 1982. I could tell by his writing that he must have been filled with anticipation.

*"Now that you are old enough … the one thing I have never discussed with you that I must mention, is race … I'm sure you have always suspected, but were never quite sure of what I am about to reveal. I am also part Negro … What you have is probably the most vibrant combination of heritage that could possible be given to*

*a human; from Africa to Asia, from Europe to America ... why have I kept this from you? It was my feeling, right or wrong, that since you are not Negro, at a time when Negroes were so disadvantaged, there was no need to make you confused about your heritage."*

The Mellow Yellow aftertaste coated the inside of my mouth like an old rug. It was as if after 20 years I hadn't yet discovered the simplicity and beauty of plain, pure, drinkable water. I opened the bag of dried seafood and cuttlefish and stuffed my mouth with a handful, hoping this would offer solace. I returned the diary to its envelope. It would be another 8 years before I would have the courage to read it from the beginning.

As I leaned my head against the back of the dusty, dark green lounge sofa, I closed my eyes and felt them twitch with exhaustion. With each bite of the cuttlefish, I smelled the sweet potato vendor down the street calling out, *"Yakiimoo! Yakiimoo, oishii yakiimoo ikagadesuga?"* Hundreds of cicadas buzzed in a steady, rhythmic drone, the older ones clinging to the maple trees, the younger ones pushing up next to the bamboo shoots. The neighborhood was alive with *Omatsuri* summer dances and the summer evening set with the drama of a sun that gave the country its name, The Land of the Rising Sun. The gentle aroma of wood-framed paper doors comforted me like an old friend. I was home again.

# 18

# This Land is Your Land

"Dat happens to my wife all da time, donworryaboudit." Our landlord wiped more mice droppings from the cabinet. "Get some rat poison and take it off the rent."

My housemates Carl and Todd had bad feelings about Mr. Tudor ever since he urged us not to bother reading the lease before signing. I had spent the summer by myself in the apartment while interning at a video production company. I lived on a 10-pound pack of someone's donated government surplus cheddar cheese and 3-day-old bread from the supermarket. I became a master at virtual cheese disguise—turning grilled cheese on white bread into a hamburger, chicken Kiev, and even sushi.

Now, already 1 month into my junior year, I barely knew my neighbors. There were five other units in the building, and I thought maybe one of them had invited in the mice. I ruled out Ms. Giardella, however. She lived in the apartment next to us and could not have been guilty. Although she had advanced arthritis and other ailments, she managed to keep her apartment spotless. She stayed in touch with the outside world only through her six yapping Chihuahuas and three wide-eyed cats whose ears were perched perpetually backward. She spent the days keeping her house spotless and calling radio stations to win gift coupons to restaurants and tickets to concerts she could never use.

If Todd, Carl, and I had been scientists, our apartment would have been host to grave experiments. By early October, our toilet experienced nauseating back-up problems. A couple of weeks later the lights started to flicker and dim. In early November the refrigerator got frequent hot spells. Then finally, the electric base heater in Todd's room died. To all this, Tudor calmly answered, "Donworryaboutit ... It happens to my wife all da time!"

It was so cold in Todd's room, we removed our perishables from the dying fridge and dumped them there. Then, if we needed milk, juice, or cold cuts, all we had to do was retrieve it from the room and defrost it on a working radiator in the living room.

"That's it guys!" Todd was furious. "From now on we don't pay rent until Tudor fixes this shit. And I don't care if this has happened to his wife or not!"

Carl, the intellectual, nodded. "Right. All we have to do is open an escrow account and dump our money there. He'll never fix this place up, and then we'll all be rich!"

I couldn't help smiling at Tudor's misfortune. *America—what a country!*

Tudor never came around, nor did he ask for his checks. Finally, in April, he did come by, wondering how many months of rent we owed him. Carl simply pointed at the refrigerator that was now being used as a closet. Tudor tilted it back and dragged it across the kitchen floor, tearing the linoleum.

"You want any help?" Todd asked, taking a few steps back.

"Naw, used ta be a linebackah, ya know." I thought of the only two American football players I knew: O. J. Simpson and some Namath guy. Tudor's eyes popped and his face turned beat read as he lifted the fridge from the bottom and slid it up on its back against the railing on the balcony. He let out an impressive primal yalp as he heaved it into the air and into the backyard. I suddenly imagined the downstairs kids playing out back. In a thundering crash, the Maytag exploded into metal and plastic shrapnels. "Well, that's that." Tudor wheezed, "Don worry, it happens to my wife all da time."

*   *   *

Three weeks before Carl and Todd graduated, we collected more than $1,000 each from the escrow account. Todd and I decided to drive across the country, so we bought a used Oldsmobile Cutlass Supreme we aptly named "Boat." I was convinced that in the embrace of a car large enough to float, I was going to find a place to settle down after I graduated. We had to be in Oregon in 4 weeks to visit Miguel who was getting his master's degree in architecture. Then on to California where we would sell the car and I would return to Japan one last time. My two trips back to Japan had left me with the sinking feeling that I had to stay in America. If I was going to stay, I would never move again.

For the next 4 weeks we would sleep in the car at rest stops or camp in the woods. We traveled along the winding roads of upstate New York on the border of Canada, then south over the rolling hills and factory towns of Pennsylvania. I remember Pittsburgh was much like Boston, with its glass-plated high rises and crumbling downtown. It was the first of the major cities I had considered.

At each turn, America seemed to transform abruptly, and at the same time it felt as if we never moved a mile. I could still smell the exhaust fumes of a truck we had passed in Pennsylvania by the time we arrived at the foot of the Blue Ridge Mountains of West Virginia. We cruised through hidden valleys and villages and bought our groceries in local markets. We headed back north into Ohio by way of West Virginia.

We dressed up and crashed catered receptions in ritzy hotels, then dressed down and joined barbecues and showered on college campuses. At the Sheraton Hotel in Columbus, we changed into our formal set of clothes, shaved, and joined a wine and cheese reception at a dentists' convention. We picked up lingo and mixed in with the crowd. Later on in the day, boozed and exhausted, we passed a three-block-long line of people waiting to enter the city unemployment office. I noticed that most of them were Black, and recalled that all of the guests at the convention were White. I felt decadent and privileged, and couldn't wait to change back into my jeans.

One dark night in Kentucky, we thought we had pitched our tent in a safe, hidden path off a small street. The next morning we woke up to a thunderstorm, only to find ourselves staked out in the backyard of a man with a rifle and a German shepherd snapping its teeth. "What the hell areyadoinhere, boah!" His mouth said one thing but his eyes looked forgiving. Either that or he thought we were stupid.

We continued south and arrived in Nashville, Tennessee, on a Sunday. No people on the streets, no stores open and no music. "Not exactly the music capital I was told about," I said.

"It's Sunday, stupid," said Todd.

The only place open was a bar with four Harley-Davidson motorcyles parked in front. "Well, either we eat or we're eaten." Todd said as he pushed open the door. A waft of cigarette smoke wrapped around my face and I choked. A group of White faces turned in the dark and peered at us through the fog of nicotine. The country song that was blasting from the jukebox faded, then ended in a down note with lyrics eluding to an arrest for drunk driving and incest. I was even skinnier then, and I felt all 12 eyeballs in the room checking out my bony legs. The two men at the pool table straightened up. The one under the fluorescent Budweiser light casually flexed his right bicep to reveal multiple tattoos. The bartender, eyes wide, paused in the middle of serving her other two patrons at the counter. They must have thought we were aliens or something, or maybe it was just me they were not sure about because I realized they were not really looking at Todd. Maybe they thought I was Mexican or Puerto Rican, especially now that I had gotten much darker since we left New England. I thought of the *Sesame Street* song—"One of these things just doesn't belong here, one of these things just isn't the same."

"Ah, Teja, I think it's time to go," Todd whispered to me.

I smiled and nodded my head at the man furthest away at the pool table.

"Hi," I said. His eyebrows shifted. "Todd, I think we just have to get to know them. Hang out, so to speak." I waved to the bartender. "Yeah, hello!" I continued. "Glad you guys are open today, here in Nashville. Uh, a couple of Buds, please!" I thought of how proud Mark from Clark would have been of me now. The two men at the counter slowly swung around to get a better look at me.

"We don't ... ," the bartender began, and then looked over at the guys at the pool table, " ... have Bud."

"Oh, that's okay. Miller would be just fine."

"We don't have Miller."

"Haben Sie Dünkel Bier, bitte?"

Todd cleared his throat. "Teja ... "

"Okay, fine. Anything," I sighed. "We're from Massachusetts, and we're really thirsty. Water, milk, orange juice?"

One of the men at the counter stood up. My eyes met his chest, and I could smell what could have been last week's chilly dog wafting out from under his arm pits.

"Max, forget it." The bartender leaned over the counter. "They're from Miami." She poured two deep glasses of a dark beer.

I had forgotten I didn't really drink beer. "Thank you, ma'am!" I said, and swallowed the beer in three gulps. I tugged at Todd who was enraptured with a faded poster of Farrah Fawcet. He finished his beer and we went back outside into the blaring midday sun.

In Missouri, we traveled along the Mississippi River north to St. Louis. By the time we hit Kansas City and Topeka, our rations had waned, so we crashed more hotel receptions and campus barbecues. As the land became flat, the plains fluctuated from dark green to brown and cracked. Near Lincoln, on Route 70, I took a time-lapse movie of an approaching storm by placing the camera one quarter of a mile from the highway and programming it to shoot one frame every 10 seconds. Within 5 minutes the empty blistering blue sky turned dark, then heavy with a shower of hail. When I retrieved the embattled camera, I imagined the clouds that had passed were the same ones we left back in Massachusetts. For a moment, the millions of square miles surrounding me were all connected by the simple elements of water and wind. I thought of the rivers that run and the water I drank. It would only be a matter of time, like the blood that runs inside of me, before it would all come full circle. Even in the vastness of this country, I could drink that water and it would be a part of me again. Shouldn't this alone define my place, my final destination or would I continue to search and weave, leaving a trail of veritable bread crumbs like the clouds?

The seemingly infinite stretch of highway lingered on through Kansas. Neither of us was interested in country music, but we discovered the minute we exited New England, the choices on the radio became more limited the further we headed into the heart of the country. Our handful of cassette tapes had worn out and we both couldn't sing, so we sat quietly and watched the monotonous horizon repeat itself. We set the cruise control at 54 miles per hour exactly. Whenever a police cruiser would pass, my muscles locked and the sweet taste of adrenaline charged my tongue. Although I rehearsed how I would explain my expired international Japanese driver's license, I knew that with the wrong cop at the wrong moment, I would be spending the night in the slammer.

By the middle of Kansas, my hay fever, which had remained dormant up until this point, erupted violently. We got off the highway and followed signs to a local motel. It was dark by the time we saw a flashing neon sign in the distance: Halley's Truck Stop and Motel. Between the motel and us was a sea of idling 18-wheelers, towering over us as we passed below them like a child in a toy superstore. We parked the car in front of the main building and walked in. Again, my skinny legs and Todd's white socks with black sneakers drew all the attention. The sound of a fiddle, a washboard, and a singer's twangy voice was muffled by the heavy haze of cigarette smoke that lingered at eye level. A couple walked by me, looked down at us, then exited the building. Todd sniggered nervously. I heard the couple laughing outside when I realized that everyone in the dance room had to be at least 6½ feet tall and about 150 pounds heavier than us. I was watching a wave of cowboy hats and boots move to the rhythm of the band, when a 7-foot-tall man with rhinestones covering half his shirt approached us. *My skin. He's looking at my skin! Fuck you!*

"Howdy there, boys." He spoke slowly and pushed up his hat with his finger. "What can we do for you?"

"Ah ... howdy," I said. "We just want a hotel room for the night."

Two men passing by overheard, stopped, and squinted their eyes.

"Just the two of you, huh? Hey, Mellissa, get over here and arrange for these two fine young men a room!"

A row of heads turned and I wanted to tell Todd that my hay fever had cleared up and that we could be on our way. Then I sneezed again and my eyes began to fill up with moisture. *He must think I'm on drugs or something. A druggy Mexican, that's what he must be thinking!*

"Don't make too much noise, and we don't have breakfast." With that, the manager ushered us out. The next morning as we drove off, I saw a sign at the entrance to the main building a sign that read, "Breakfast served daily."

We drove steadily up a gradual incline westward on Interstate 70 in Colorado. At the crest, the clouds seemed to rise as we began a slow descent. Then, suddenly, a wall of mountains appeared like a string of giants with white hair and brown and green chiseled robes. At the foot of the Rocky Mountains, firmly nestled like a baby in a mother's arms, lay the city of Denver. "I could live there," I said to Todd.

Denver was experiencing an economic boom, so the dichotomy of the old and the chic was as apparent as the rich and the poor. The downtown district was buzzing with yuppies eating frozen yogurt and a steady drone of panhandlers. Dark-skinned homeless men held out their crumpled paper cups to light-skinned businessmen who flashed by in sunglasses and pressed suits. "What is it about America?" I said to Todd. "From afar, the mountains, the lakes, the forests, even the city skylines are magnificent. I always think, 'this time, things will be different.'"

Then we skimmed over the top of Mt. Evans at 14,250 feet and began the long descent toward Grand Junction. We blew a tire on a deserted mountain detour without a clue as to how to fix a flat.

"I'll go and find a phone," I offered.

"No, I should go," Todd said, for once serious. "You don't look like you're from these parts and there's no telling what someone will think when you appear at their door."

"You mean there are not a lot of unshaven Mexicans roaming the back hills of the Colorado mountains?" I said, smirking. I was angry that I was a prisoner in my own country and an "unshaven Mexican" was probably exactly the stereotype they would have of me. Here in the middle of America, I was still living on the fringes, just like in Japan, but at least I felt safe in Japan. I remembered the bicycle trip through Hokkaido, at 13 and 14, Miguel and I exploring the northern wilderness of Japan. But here, in America, I had to be careful. A stranger in someone's backyard could be shot out of self-defense, and a foreign-looking stranger, or a dark one, could be shot twice.

One hour later Todd returned, having placed a call with the American Automobile Association (AAA). Another hour later, a leather-clad, bearded man arrived on a Harley-Davidson motorcycle. Tools bulged from his jacket pockets and his forearm tattoos rippled as he powered down the bike. "I'm supposed to be on vacation," he droned. "You're lucky, otherwise you'd be out here for a quite a long time. Where are you from?" he asked me.

"Massachusetts," I said.

"Yeah, okay, I knew you looked like a foreigner."

We continued through the spectacular, ever-changing terrain of Utah. From desert to green, and back again, through microvillages and outposts. We arrived at Salt Lake City late in the evening on a Sunday night. No stores were open except for a pizza joint. It was empty and we called out for the counter service. A young woman appeared with a mop. "Oh, hi! We're already closed, but I can probably get you something."

"Just a pizza and could you tell us where we can find a package store?" Todd asked.

"A what?" she asked.

"A package store. Liquor store. Beer, wine, booze."

Her eyes bulged. "Ah, you guys are from out of town, right?"

"Massachusetts. Why?"

"This is Salt Lake City. Utah. Dry. Mormons."

I looked at Todd. "What are Mormons?"

Todd looked at me and laughed. "Don't mind him, he's from Japan, actually."

"You mean to say that all of Utah doesn't drink alcohol?" I asked.

She giggled and placed the slices of pizza in the oven. "No, not all of Utah, just around here."

I smiled. "Oh ... I get it. So we gotta go up the street or something."

Todd snapped his fingers. "Well, no, actually, it's Sunday. Blue laws, I guess, like in Massachusetts."

"Separation of church and state?" I said facetiously.

The next day, on the banks of The Great Salt Lake, we parked next to a red and purple Volkswagen bus. A woman in a tie-dyed shirt and ripped jeans opened the sliding door and jumped out. "Hi there! Hey, you guys are also from Massachusetts! You here for the show, huh? Because we need a miracle."

Behind her in the bus, I noticed a topless woman smoking a joint. "A miracle?"

"Oh ... you're not on tour with the Dead," she said. "Oh well! Hey, we're going for a dip, you guys wanna come?"

"Ah, no thanks. Water's too salty."

Todd's eyes followed her to the beach. I broke his trance. "Dead?"

"Dead *Heads*, stupid," he said. "*Look* at them. Haven't you heard of *the Grateful Dead*?"

"You mean, they're fans of *The Dead*?"

"You know, Teja, for someone's who traveled as much as you, you're really not with it, are you? She's cute, she seems nice, and you just blew it. Tell me, have you learned *anything* during the last 2,500 miles?"

Continuing north, we drove through eastern Idaho, then on to Yellow Stone National Park in northwest Wyoming. We sneaked into lodges where we relaxed in saunas and joined hotel patrons in front of large atrium fireplaces. At night, with the temperature below freezing, we slept in the car, bundled in our sleeping bags. During the 4 days in the park, I reached a creative, primal frenzy only a photographer could understand. The dramatic and sudden changes of light, weather, and moisture combined with the wealth of natural beauty was overwhelming. With my three cameras and four lenses, I climbed over precarious ledges under hail, ventured near buffalo basking in the summer heat, and trudged through the fringes of sulfur lakes in the snow. By the time we left I had all but depleted my case of chilled 35mm stock. On the last day, Todd and I sat still for 3 hours, just staring, mesmerized by the majestic messages written in stone and rock by the glaciers and the earth's breathing, rising from the canyon thousands of feet below.

Days later, in a frail town tucked in the middle of Idaho, I wondered how people ever decided to stay in one particular place. I felt out of touch with the concept of daily living. I watched two men walk casually along the main street, discussing something, probably their work, their house, a car that wouldn't start that morning, the news of the day. The corner store, with its limited supplies, struggled to remain open for business in the shadow of superstores only several miles away. Why, how, when do people settle, call it home, grow old and pass on their wisdom to the next generation? Here, in the outback of the midwest, a culture formed, and with it, pride and heritage, history and future.

Just past the barber shop, where a gentleman waited patiently for his turn to share the news and gossip of the day with the barber, was a travel agency. *Travel agency?* In a town of 3,000? A poster taped to the window promised 4 nights of heaven in the Bahamas. I thought of how so many Americans want to escape the United States to go on vacation in Europe or get lost in Bermuda, but they don't want to explore their own backyard. In the past couple of weeks I had experienced breathtaking physical beauty, more than I had in many other places in the world, and for once, the United States held promise for me.

We traveled west through Idaho and the deserts of eastern Oregon. At a rest stop on Route 30, an older man wearing a bandanna and a confederate flag T-shirt studied me as I washed my face.

"Where are you goin', son?" he asked.

"Oregon. Eugene."

"Got hay fever?"

"Yeah, a little, why?"

"Don't go to Eugene. Whatever you do, stay away from Eugene."

"You have hay fever?"

"Ragweed nearly killed me. Twenty-seven years in Oregon, and I finally can breathe, now that I'm away. I think Oregon means 'Land of Diseases' in some Indian language. So I'm moving to Texas. Like my boots?"

"It's that bad there, huh?"

"Hospitalized seven times. Good luck, and don't put your car fan on when you get near Eugene."

I imagined Oregon, with who knows how many of its citizens dying from simple pollen, the giver of life, beauty, and sustenance, might be bobbing in a sea of denial, just ahead.

The air conditioner in the car had died in St. Louis, so Todd turned on the vent to "external." Folks in cars passing us cheered and waved as we approached the Pacific Ocean. At first I was sure the people on the west coast were overly friendly, then I realized our Massachusetts license plate had given our origins away. As I waved back, my vision started to dull. Then I started sneezing. We passed a big green highway sign that was too fuzzy for me to read. "Hey, look, Eugene!" Todd said. I sneezed at least 20 times before I had a chance to catch my breath. I poked Todd on the shoulder. "Turd ob da bent."

Todd's face dropped when he looked at me. "Oh, Jesus! Your face!"

I grabbed the rearview mirror and bent it toward me. My face had puffed out and my eyes looked like a toad's.

* * *

By the time we arrived at Miguel's place in Eugene, I had gone through half a box of tissues and my head was buzzing. Mama, who had been visiting Miguel already for a couple of days, was horrified when she saw my bloated face and raw, red eyes. The next day we helped Miguel move to a new apartment. Todd abruptly decided to return to the east coast, and we dropped him off at the Greyhound bus station.

Miguel, Mama, and I hadn't been together in 3 years. It was the kind of separation we had come to know well, during which so much had been held back, undiscussed, and hidden. Under the enchantment of an Oregon evening, with its clear summer skies and forest green leaves, we discussed the divorce. We let our tears run freely, and all our frustrations rose to the surface. We were homeless, in a world full of homes, detached from a place and purpose. We cried, and our tears fell to the ground that was only temporarily ours. Japan had forsaken us and the United States, in its vastness, had left us isolated.

After we hugged and wiped our eyes, we thought of our predicament. "Well, at least you two got to grow up in Japan," Mama said. "You'd be very different if you had grown up in New York."

Then we compared Japan to America, trading politics for sociology, laughing about the hypocrisies of American cultural idealism and Japanese isolationist Westernizing practice. We claimed our shifting preferences as simply as raising a flag. It was clear there could never be the perfect spot for any of us and yet, we continued to search.

A few days later Mama left for the east coast.

\* \* \*

In a band of light, streaming in from the living room window, I saw a fog of pollen, floating precociously toward my nose. We rushed out to buy a dust mask.

The supermarket was a mirror of every other supermarket in America. Some things were consistent in a country as diverse as this one.

"Hello there! How are you today! Did you find everything you need?" The cashier looked me straight in the eyes and her smile expanded into an advertisement for teeth.

Miguel slapped me on the shoulder. "She said hello, Teja!" He turned to her. "You'll have to forgive him—he's from Massachusetts."

"Oh, I'm sorry, I thought he had special needs, with the mask and all." The cashier looked at me like a nurse who confronts the family of a deceased.

"Teja, say hello!" Miguel spoke through his teeth.

"Oh, sorry ... hi."

Miguel rolled his eyes and paid for the groceries. "In Massachusetts apparently no one says hello. In fact they never wave. Well, actually, they do wave, they just wave with one finger. But we won't ask him to wave good-bye."

Five days later we picked up Miguel's friend Poi Chin and we began our trip south to San Diego. Poi was an exciting addition to our tour; she was good-natured, funny, and patient with our constant sibling bickering. Side by side in the front, the three of us cruised down the coast on Route 1. Unlike the entangled commercial and elitist estates on the east coast-line, there were no billboards and private properties here. The beaches were completely accessible, uncluttered and stunning. At night, nestled in the folds of quiet sand dunes with the backdrop of the stars, we listened to the ocean breathing and told stories of our childhoods from other worlds.

Miguel was at his best, here, in the elements and without the demands of strict social life. For him, Japan and the United States had sold out, left him cold and disconnected. But now, at the edge of the country with his brother and a friend, he was inspired and content. "See the seagulls using the heat rising from the rock formation to gain altitude? Isn't that amazing how they know that? And people just sit around trying to figure out whether to put the peanut butter on top or the jelly."

We continued south, through Red Woods National Forest, then onto San Francisco. I expected the Bay Area to be like most of the other metropolitan areas I had been through. That was until The Golden Gate Bridge appeared before us, with the city snug in a blanket of fog on the other side. As we entered the city, the three of us became quietly anxious. I felt oddly secure and in a way, doubtful, when we emerged from the car. We took buses and street cars, and walked through Presidio, Golden Gate Park, the Pan Handle, Twin Peaks, and the Piers. I saw mixed couples, gay couples, young couples, old couples. No one stared at us or asked us where we were from. My stomach tingled at the thought of living here. We got tipsy that night, in a four-star restaurant on Fisherman's Wharf, and although my head was filled with drunken nuisance, I knew, for the first time in my life, where I was going to live. "Next year this time … ," I raised my wine glass to Poi and Miguel, "I will be living here, at the heart of San Francisco."

When we left San Francisco several days later, a strange, overwhelming sensation convinced me I would never be able to live anywhere else. With this odd but newfound confidence, like the painful process of losing a friend, Japan became less significant.

Over the next 3 days we toured the artist community of Carmel, and camped with a leather-clad biker group in Big Sur. I remembered the glare the bikers gave me at the bar in Nashville, yet felt strangely comfortable with these characters. I thought if the biker culture could be so diverse, then any group could be.

By this point, Miguel and I hadn't shaved in more than a week and we were five shades darker. "They'll think we're Mexican, you know," Miguel said, scratching his stubble. "In Oregon they think I'm Middle Eastern. In California they think I'm Chicano."

"We'll get arrested or something stupid like that," I joked. "Let's just not shave anyway, just to see what people say."

The Boat was by now plastered with 5,000 miles of bugs and highway grit. The further south we traveled, the less surprised I was as to what people thought of us. "This grainy wholesome loaf of bread will last you all the way back to Mexico!" A cashier in a San Simeon bakery offered, "Thank you for visiting!" I couldn't help thinking that, with a town name like San Simeon, who really was the intruder?

We knew we had arrived in Los Angeles when we saw ahead of us a 5-mile traffic jam. A thick, brown haze hung like gravy over the interstate and enveloped the top third of the downtown district. My chest tightened up and I began to wheeze. I tried the air conditioner again, to filter the air, then remembered it didn't work. We had to keep the windows open, so we got off the highway and spent the next 2 hours winding through the bowel of the city to drop off Poi at her sister's house in some fancy neighborhood on the outskirts.

The next day Miguel and I went to drop off one of Poi's bags that she had forgotten. I studied the decadent architecture of the surrounding mansions while Miguel went to ring the bell. The Boat sputtered and belched and I checked my stubby beard in the mirror. No one answered the door, so Miguel returned to the car, dropped the bag in the back and retrieved his note pad. He returned to the house and began writing a note. Then out of nowhere, a policeman ran up the steps to Miguel, pushed him face first up against the door and crossed his arms behind his back.

Then suddenly I felt the presence of someone right next to me.

"Put your hands where I can see them! Your license, let me see your license!"

I always kept the bag with my essentials under the driver's seat, so I began to reach down. My heart raced. This was no *CHiPs* episode—this was *real.*

"Freeze! Not so fast, amigo! Nice and slow."

I turned my head only to be faced with a bulging waistline in a blue uniform and a hand hovering above a gun. Slowly, I opened my bag and pulled out my license. The officer flipped through it and squinted his eyes.

"What the hell are you trying to pull here, amigo? Where's your license?"

My throat seized, so I sounded like a chipmunk. "That *is* my license, sir."

"What is this, Chinese? What does it say on the front?"

I pointed to the date on the cover. "That's the expiration date. It's according to Japanese calendar. So it's the year Showa 62, the 62nd year of the emperor. It's now the year 59."

"What the hell is that supposed to mean?"

I had to make up a date. "Well, it expires, ah ... in 1987, April 11."

"Right." He looked at the pile of bags in the back seat. "What's in those bags?"

"Clothes and some camera equipment."

The other police man brought Miguel to the car. "Hey Steve, this one says they got six cameras in the back."

"Yeah, this one's got a Japanese license, if you believe that," the officer next to me said, adjusting his deep purple sunglasses. "Okay, get out of the car, slow." He then opened my door and turned me around. "Hands up against the car and spread 'em." He frisked me, then turned me around to face him. "Six cameras, huh?"

"We're photographers."

"Right. Open them and show us the cameras."

Miguel and I took out our bags and produced the cameras.

"What do you need all those cameras for? Where did you get them?" the other officer asked Miguel.

"We bought them."

"Where?"

"At Yodobashi Camera in Downtown Tokyo."

"Right."

Officer Steve edged me away from the car. "I want you guys to sit down on the sidewalk, comprende? Now, where's the other guy?"

"What other guy, you mean Poi?"

"Yeah, where is he? We got a report that three Mexican hoodlums stole a car in Seattle and were headed south to L.A."

"*She's* supposed to be staying with her sister in that house over there."

"Right. Hey Wong, look at this guy's license," Steve said to the other officer. "You read Japanese, right?"

"What, just because my name is Wong? For your info, I'm Chinese. Wong is a Chinese name, okay?" He peered over his sunglasses at Steve, then pointed at us. "Okay, guys, let's start at the beginning." He spread his legs. "Give me your names."

"Teja-José Manuel Arboleda," I said.

"Miguel-Diego Teja Arboleda."

"Oookaay ... where you guys from?"

"I'm from Oregon, and he's from Massachusetts," Miguel said.

Steve folded his arms. "No, no, no. Where are you guys *from*?"

Miguel looked at me and smiled. "Oh, right. We're from Japan."

"Japan, huh?" Steve said. "You don't look Japanese. I was in Japan in the service. I know some Japanese. Say something."

I jumped in, "*Kimitachi yo, nanto bakana koto iuuka?*"

Miguel nudged me. Steve nodded his head slowly. "Right."

Wong pointed at me. "You sound like an American."

I wanted to tell him the same. "I *am* an American. But Miguel is German."

"And you live in Massachusetts and he lives in Oregon? Sure." He pointed at Miguel. "Now, where's the other guy?"

"Who are you talking about?" Miguel asked.

"Your amigo. Mexican male, about 5'8", Chicano."

Miguel chuckled. "You thought we were Mexican?"

"That's right," Wong said. "Now, let's start from the *real* beginning, shall we? Name."

The neighbors started arriving home from work by the time the officers finished with us. Miguel and I hadn't even eaten lunch, and I was tempted to ask them if they would join us at the Dunkin' Donuts up the street.

"Quite a story, guys!" Steve stood up and patted his paunch. "I thought *my* family was messed up!"

I stood up and stretched my legs. "So, you guys really thought we were Chicano?"

Officer Chin pointed at me and smirked. "Well, you fit the description! Now, you see that sticker on the main door of that house? It says, 'neighborhood watch.' Folks in these neighborhoods are wary of ... foreigners. You might wanna wash your car or something. Shave. Go out and treat yourselves."

\* \* \*

The next day Miguel and I traveled further south to the resort town of La Joya where we camped on the beach and caught grunions spawning on the sand in the high tide at night. We sat by the fire and listened to tape-recorded radio mystery theater and drank wine coolers. We hadn't recuperated yet from the Los Angeles experience, and were weary of everyone that looked at us, but we dressed down on purpose and held back from shaving as an experiment to test the boundaries of criticism. The comments and looks from the local aristocrats would help us determining where we might want to live.

We walked into a four-star restaurant overlooking the bay, prepared to be denied a table.

After passing over us a few turns, the concierge sighed and looked us over. "Oh ... may I help you?"

Miguel spoke confidently, adding a little upper class British. "Yes. A table on the balcony, if you would be so kind."

"Oh ... I'm afraid, they are all taken. We have a table over there." He pointed toward the kitchen.

"My, my, how awfully dreadful. That definitely won't do. There does seem to be a table free on the balcony, we'll take ... that one."

"Yes, but ... ," the concierge sputtered.

"Thank you, you know, I always love the view." Miguel walked onto the deck and sat down. As I followed him, critical eyes followed us and mouths whispered. When I sat down, the concierge flittered off.

"Mick, ah ... everyone's wearing formals," I said.

"And we're not! Take a look at this menu!"

The more we drank the more nervous the other customers became. We took off our shoes and laughed out loud.

"This ... is life!" Miguel cheered.

"To life!" I echoed, raising my glass.

Our neighboring patrons buried their arrogance in their silverware, muttering their concerns. But their attention only fueled our design—Miguel and I conspired, criticizing the wealth and waste of the privileged few, and the consequence of America's impotence regarding race and culture. Then, to add confusion and mystique, we switched from Japanese to German to English, comparing Asian philosophy with Western.

I relieved myself in the bathroom and looked in the mirror. For the moment, my smirk gave way to seriousness, and my skin, darkened even more by the California sun, fell heavy against the white wall behind me. What was I doing in the presence of strangers, jading my image to effect more hate? Had the sun been in fact been cruel in darkening my complexion? Was my image in old clothes and a new beard my own effacing method of testing the limits of inclusion? Could I hate myself so much that I was willing to blame it on a conspiracy, an agenda? Or was America, after the thousands of miles I had traveled, really as judgmental and horribly exclusionary as it seemed? And would I ever have the luxury of planting myself firmly, and know that the earth beneath welcomes my roots?

Miguel and I slept deeply that night. As we drifted into sleep, we heard out on the edge of the waning tide, families with flashlights scouring for more grunions. Their laughter and play reminded me what it was to be filled with happiness.

*  *  *

In San Diego we made a U-turn for Los Angeles. Miguel flew back to Oregon, and I sold the car to a used car dealer and took my flight to Tokyo.

# Top of the Hill

It wasn't until the winter of my senior year at Clark that I realized how many friends I had lost. My work had come first, managed by a calendar and a watch. I had been freelancing as a video production specialist and struggling to produce my thesis—a documentary on divorce from children's points of view. I shared my findings with Mama, and we both realized how therapeutic the project was for both of us.

But the city was full of too many skeletons and reminders of her past. She would run away, leave Boston, in need of a big change from the segregation and conservative atmosphere. She thought about Germany or the west coast. Somewhere else. Somewhere that bustled with a more vibrant cosmopolitan life. She needed to be inspired, to finish writing her novel and build a career.

"I don't know, Teja." Mama fidgeted with her tofu and egg sandwich. "I really don't where I should go. I mean, this is a nice apartment, but I can't stay here." Her voice and disposition had changed since I last saw her. Something irked her deep down inside. "I just need something else. Besides, I can't stand the people downstairs on the first floor. The husband is always beating on her—shakes the house! I can feel her being slammed against the wall. Then he yells at her, she screams, the police come, but nothing changes. Then his buddies pick him up and they go get drunk."

Once, when she was at the store when I was visiting and sick in bed, I heard and felt the beatings. Soon after, the husband stormed out of the house just in time to get picked up by his buddies. He leaned back as if to embrace the sky and yelled clearly for all the neighbors to hear. "I'm jahst ah fahkin' Irish guy, ahright? If I wanna fahkin' get fahkin' drunk and beat my fahkin' wife, it's none of yah fahkin' business!"

I helped Mama move to New York City in October 1984. Jack, Papa's best friend from the 1960s, came to help move her in. Jack was proud of his Black heritage and spoke and walked a certain way to validate his presence and identity. In his direct manner and loud, penetrating voice, he told us stories of life in America and his native South, and how life in Harlem had changed. It was almost as if his recounting helped fill the void that was created by our absence during the years in Japan.

The next day, Mama's new landlord came to the apartment. After a brief introduction, he made his concerns to us very clear.

"Was that man who helped you move yesterday your friend?" he asked, looking around the apartment for clues.

"Yes, why?" Mama said, not suspecting anything.

"Well, I'm sorry to say—this is an established building, and it's not that I personally have anything against him, but the others in the building, they might not be too … comfortable with … "

"So, if he *acted* White, it would be okay?" Mama said with a jab.

With that, in her studio apartment, and only a mile from where she first set foot on America 25 years earlier, Mama set out to start a new life once again.

\* \* \*

A month before graduation I received a "soft" job offer at a video production company in San Francisco, California. I immediately sat down to write letters to Papa, Miguel, and Mama about the good news, and my decision to move to the west coast. That afternoon, I remember walking across the street to buy stamps at the drugstore. A Japanese family stood at the black iron gates at the main entrance admiring Jonas Clark Hall. I slowed down to eavesdrop on their conversation.

"*This is a really nice campus, nice buildings too,*" the mother said.

The daughter, who I figured was looking to attend the college, pointed at the masses of students traveling the walkways. "*Look at all of them—I've never seen so many gaijin!*"

*So many gaijin?* I thought to myself. *Since when were Americans in the U.S. "foreigners?"*

I stopped just as I was about the pass them. "*Forgive me for being so rude, but here in America,* you *are the gaijin.*"

Their eyes widened and the daughter's mouth dropped. "*What! They speak Japanese, too?*"

I smiled, turned, and crossed the street. I was at first embarrassed to have made them so uncomfortable—I would rather have hosted them for the evening and returned, through them, to the streets of Japan. But the thrill of being able to humiliate others, especially the few who had dishonored me in my childhood was overwhelming.

I saw an American flag posted next to the window at the edge of the drugstore. At that instant I wanted a U.S. flag of my own to wave—to wave unconditionally and watch all of Japan bow to me in apology for its treatment of all *gaijin*. I turned angrily, then took a deep breath to cool down. I would not be excluded in my own country. I wanted to run after to the Japanese family and tell them that they didn't belong here, point at their faces and tell them to return to Japan. Then, as I left the drugstore with my roll of stamps, I began to think of how that reaction would only lead to more conflict. I was in a way an ambassador, and I had to learn to maneuver through the tides of ignorance. I felt my fists relax and my jaw ease up. I sat down and leaned against the trunk of a large maple tree and watched the Japanese family enter Jonas Clark Hall.

The following weeks were mired in hysterics and depression. San Francisco, that faraway, foggy, friendly city that had smiled at me had come through. But the fear of moving, of starting all over again, triggered severe dizziness, bouts of crying, and self-imposed isolation.

I graduated with honors, said good-bye Mama and my last remaining friends and flew to California.

\* \* \*

"Yeah, come on up!" Joe yelled from the top of the stairs. He had graduated from Clark the year before and suggested I check out this apartment. His roommates Janis and Meg greeted me casually at the top of the stairs and Joe took me to the roof through the ceiling in the kitchen. "Doesn't get any better than this!" I turned around slowly and took in the city. We were at the top of the hill on Columbus and Union. A colorful group played kunga drums under the park lights across the street in Washington Square. The tips of the downtown office buildings were eye level, their lights blinking in the low fog that skimmed above our heads. On the other side was the bay and Alcatraz. Little box houses rose up the hill gently to Coit Tower to the east, and behind me to the south lay Russian Hill. "San Franciso," I whispered to myself. Just the sound of the name elicited a feeling of comfort.

"Here you go." Joe handed me a wine glass. Janis and Meg appeared with folding chairs while Joe poured.

"What do you think? Better than *Wustah*, huh? San Francisco is the only place for me."

"I knew when I came last year that I would end up here," I added, feeling the wine ease down my esophagus. "Weird, huh?"

"We all felt it," Janis said.

\* \* \*

The next day I met with my contact who told me the job had fallen through. "I'll keep you on file," he said. "I'll give you a call."

I spent a week in the apartment, eating spaghetti in front of the television. I pretended to see my name in all the credits until they became dull and tasteless like the spaghetti. I imagined the dullness as a good thing, as a reminder to remain humble. I decided I would not treat myself until I had succeeded, no matter how long it would take.

When I finally went outside again I felt guilty for not having explored the city. I decided I would open the city like a present and save the wrapper. Immediately, I met Carla who managed the flower shop next to the apartment. She was a nervous young woman, but smiled graciously and had a great sense of humor. Every Monday she would give me an overstock rose or carnation cutting. Over the weeks I learned that 2 years earlier, at 18, she married an Iranian who sought U.S. citizenship. In return, he hired her to run his flower shop and took care of her. Carla lived with her father, a lawyer who was in his fourth marriage to a woman Carla's age.

I tried to get Carla to quit smoking, but during the first month I realized that was the only thing that kept her going. I could tell by the way she held the flowers with the tips of her fingers and talked to them that she was hiding a lot of rage and loneliness.

In the mornings I placed calls to video production companies, and sent out résumés. Usually by 1 p.m. I jogged up and down the hills looking for work. By the end of the first month my legs were solid and my stamina was at its peak. I ate less, remained positive, and arrived at interviews prepared. But I was offered no jobs, and was even turned down for a position as a waiter at a Japanese sushi bar. *"Your Japanese is impeccable, but most of our clients are Japanese, and you look too much like an American."*

Carla was sympathetic. She took me on explorations, showing me the magic of the city. Occasionally she was able to shake off her depression, and when she did, I could see in her some of my own lack of trust in people and places that seemed too good to be true. I realized I was rushing to belong again, like I had through college, and especially my later years in Japan. I wanted so much for this city to be mine and I was scared I was going to lose it.

* * *

"You only comma here two munt!" Mrs. Salucci waved a wooden spatula at me. She and her husband Guiseppi ran the cozy Italian restaurant below us. "Ita tehka longa time maka home. We come here tirteena iyears, leave Italy wit nuhting! Now we hava business, small, butta family business! Eat! Nobody hire eh skinny man!"

As the weeks passed, my remaining savings had dwindled. How could this happen? Here I was, in the only city I had ever loved, where strangers genuinely said hello on the street, where gay and lesbian couples could hold hands, where Chinese immigrants practiced Tai-chi in the parks and Spanish speakers played chess with Italians, Jamaicans, and Indians. I had finally found culturally rich communities, liberal and accepting, where the air was always fresh and the landscape left you breathless. I could not let my misfortunes take this from me.

I called Miguel in Oregon and cried, knowing somehow I had failed. Papa offered to send me money but I knew it wouldn't last. Mama consoled me, offering advice to return to the east coast, and to consider returning to San Francisco in the future.

Papa came to visit on his way to Europe for a conference. He treated me to my first nonpasta meal since Massachusetts. The scrod, prawns, garlic bread, and Caesar salad were more than I could bear, and the wine warmed the pit of my stomach.

"So you like San Francisco," Papa said.

My stomach hurt from having gorged through my meal and now the chocolate cake teased me like a little brat. "Yes. I can safely say it's the *only* place I have ever fallen in love with. It seems like home more than Japan or the east coast or Germany."

"Even though you don't have a job?"

"Yup. I don't know what it is."

"I feel the same way about this city," Papa said, between sips of coffee. He always loved coffee, and now that I had acquired a love for good, strong coffee, it was nice to share this with him. In my first year in Boston when I was visiting Mama, I found a coffee mug at a cart outside of Feneul Hall in Boston. It matched Papa's favorite mug in Japan. *This is how cultures develop,* I thought to myself. *Parent to child, even the simplest things, and without words.* I was sure Papa knew what I was thinking. "Sometimes," he said, "I wonder if I should just buy some old Victorian house with a fireplace and a yard and move to San Francisco. Or Vancouver. Hmm. What will you do now?"

"I don't know," I said. I watched a cable car full of passengers make its way up the steep hill. *Mostly tourists. What do they know?*

"If you have to come back to Japan, you know there's always room for you."

"I know."

* * *

By the fourth month I was forced to pack my bags again, and use my open return ticket to Japan. I decided to be logical and leave my emotions behind. "Feelings are thoughts," I reminded myself, "and thoughts can be controlled."

Soon I would be with Papa again. Just maybe, Japan would welcome me back this time.

*   *   *

I carried my suitcase up to my old room and unpacked. I couldn't believe I was back in Japan with no plans and no job. Everything I had worked for—an impressive résumé, four internships, and a move to San Francisco—was now hollow and broken like an arrow to a stone.

The cicadas prayed on my patience, their constant whining, in the thousands, like the noisy crowds in the Tokyo subway. I lay in bed, already soaking wet from the oppressive humidity, evaluating my options. Boston, Worcester, Tokyo, San Francisco, and the rest of the world became fused into a large ball of intangible contradictions. In America I had at least experienced a semblance of a freedom I had never experienced in Japan. In my mind I scanned back through the hours, months, and years I spent shaping and reshaping a mold to fit my image. As tears ran down my face and onto my pillow, I realized there were no promises to adhere to, no place that was sacred. No hope opened its doors. Even in reincarnation there is a choice, I had always hoped, but here in the confines of a room that was once a safe retreat, I knew my options were limited by the very nature of the country that I called home.

Maybe I could, maybe I *should* live in Japan. Maybe after all the searching and moving and confusion, destiny had brought me back. I didn't need to follow my career options—after all, wasn't "home" as an institution more significant, more worthy? I would make Japan my own and accept the consequence of always being an outsider. The brothers at St. Mary's used to remind us that we were just visitors in Japan, and that we must adhere to the host's wishes. How long must one remain a visitor? Ten, 20, 30 years? Would I still be a visitor, a foreigner, when I'm dead and cremated? Would my epitaph read: "Here lies an alien?" Would I fight for Japan or would I go to war for the United States or Germany?

*   *   *

*"Hideki, how are you!"* I said, figuring a surprise would be in order.

*"I'm sorry, who is this?"* he answered.

*"Teja. I'm back from America."*

*"Teja!"*

*"You never wrote back to me. Busy?"*

*"Yeah, I have a lot of things I'm doing."*

I thought I should work up his appetite. *"Just for the fun of it, you want to go cruising and crank some* rock and roll *like the good old days?"*

*"Well, I have a new car, it's an Italian car, to go along with my new love—Italian opera."*

*"Italian opera? I don't know anything about Italian opera."*

He never called back that summer. Neither did anyone else. I gave up trying. It was as if somewhere between youthful innocence and adult ignorance, I had misplaced a box of treasures, and I wasn't about to retrace my steps to look for it and risk looking desperate.

Then I received a call from Harlan. He was the one who was voted "Most Likely to Get Stoned and Marry a Japanese Woman." In high school he dated a Japanese girl, and back then they vowed to get married. I was curious to find out what the outcome was.

We talked in my room for hours. As he spoke of his life in America, his eyes were sunk deep into their sockets and his shoulders drooped forward. Only his bright blond hair reminded me of his vibrancy in high school.

"I got out there and within my freshman year I got smashed. I mean fucked up. I bailed out of school and then surfing became my life, man. Won a lot of awards. Number two state champion. Santa Monica, babes, drugs ... shit, I don't even remember a lot of it. Then I came back to Tokyo in the summer and Eriko broke up with me. I went back to California and got real heavy into drugs. I lost more than 25 pounds. A year later I was living on the floor of my buddy's apartment. I fucked up, I tell you. Eriko's gone, I had no job. Tell me, how did you stay so straight?"

"I don't know. Never did drugs. Got drunk a few times, that's all. A few friends. Never really dated. I was lonely. Really lonely. And it's such a big country." I thought of Kansas, Colorado, and California. *Could I be happier in Japan?*

We talked until the moon appeared, almost touching the branch of the *ginko* tree. *Just like the old days. Japan has its beauty too.*

*   *   *

Again, I was trapped in the house, sitting in front of the television. Reruns of old American television shows made me vaguely homesick, and sometimes just downright sick. I waited for nightfall to cool my diversion, when I could have dinner with Papa and talk about the world outside of Japan. I held my frustrations inside, and sometimes I called old friends who always seemed too busy with work. My sense of time melted, I ate less, woke up late, and took naps. Even my breathing was irregular. My arms became curiously numb, and soon the sensation spread to my legs and my face. Within a week, my whole body was buzzing. I lost 10 pounds in the first month and woke up from nightmares every night. Eventually, I could think only of suicide.

I cried all morning the night I told Papa about my condition. He brought me to the family doctor who found nothing wrong. Even a psychiatrist suggested I was fine. So, not wanting to worry Papa anymore, I pretended I was alright.

Tokyo, with all its bustle, was like an old movie running at top speed, in which my whole childhood flashed past leaving me motionless. How could my past desert me? The smiles of my favorite store clerks, the neighborhood policeman, the train station attendant were genuine, and yet I couldn't reach them anymore. Was I no longer welcome here, or was it just my own apprehension? I walked around Jiyugaoka, Mejiro, Shibuya, and Shinjuku, through city parks and along familiar riverbanks. I hated the physical world, and it hurt to think I'd be around to experience this terrible loneliness and isolation for a lifetime. But my body, now with deadened nerves, was too dull to feel any physical pain. I could almost smile at a fish on a hook and know it was me.

*   *   *

Six weeks had passed since I had returned, and it was time to leave again. I packed my bags, folded my futon and hugged Papa good-bye. Maybe New York would finally embrace me.

*   *   *

One thing Mama learned well in Tokyo was how to conserve space. If anyone in Manhattan knows how to stuff 41 years into an 18 x 15 foot room, it would be Mama. Except for the furniture, dishes, and other key items lost since the divorce, her apartment was a museum, stretching from Japan to Germany, India to Mexico.

However, I was lost in the wrinkles of the big city, overcome by its enormity. Manhattan was like a big, gray salad, just about to be tossed. I was humbled by huge piles of garbage, cowered by the crime, provoked by extreme wealth and poverty, muted by police and ambulance sirens, infected with the grime and darkness of the subways, saddened by homeless women with infants begging for change. What made New York so ill? Would I be the same person if I had grown up in Manhattan? I had thought that I would feel as if I was returning to a place I used to call home. But now my childhood memories of this city seemed unreal.

"Well, I love it," Mama said. "There are people from all over the world, speaking many languages and you're right in the middle of it."

"In the middle of a battlefield," I said. "Just because there are all kinds of people walking the same streets doesn't mean they actually *live* together."

I slept on the fold-out futon until late while Mama worked. I took naps and skipped meals, and the numbness worsened. I knew my stay in the studio apartment was limited and that I would be moving again soon.

My senior-year roommate, Dan, invited me to stay with his family in Framingham, Massachusetts, until I got on my feet. It was my only option. Maybe Boston would embrace me. Saying good-bye to Mama, and getting on a bus reminded me of the first few days back in America when I arrived for college.

*   *   *

Now, in the uncomfortable hush of the suburbs, sharing the basement room with Dan, I was less than optimistic about finding work. I sent out résumés that seemed to vanish into the still of the evenings. The nerves throughout my body still buzzed and I cried quietly under the covers at night. What was supposed to be temporary, ended up creating a burden for the family. I chose to leave for Boston with only a duffel bag.

I crashed on acquaintances' couches and looked for jobs during the day. Using my friend Laurie's computer at work, I changed the spelling of my name to "Arboletta," figuring it looked more Italian. I then sent out some résumés with my legal name and some with the Italian version. Within 2 weeks I received responses only from the Italian version. I then jogged to interviews across the city in a two-sizes-too-large borrowed business suit. At every meeting it was obvious to me that my interviewers found my identity problematic. "Your English is pretty good and you're obviously very energetic and have an impressive résumé, but we're looking for something else."

I ran out of couches and favors. Along with the numbness that blanketed my body, I now became dizzy and exhausted. I knew I had nothing left to offer and my body was shutting down.

I sneaked naps in university lounges and took showers in gyms. I slept on park benches and once under a dormant construction truck to escape a downpour. I bought week-old bread from bakeries and filled my plastic water bottle with hotel tap water. I cursed out loud at the tinted glass of passing limousines, and kicked cans and rocks at luxury cars. I elbowed my way through crowds of people at full speed, with my head down, and spit on department store display windows. I scoffed at laughing families and middle-aged White men, and seriously considered the act of robbing. I hated America for all its hypocrisy, promiscuous consumption, racism, and sexism and all within the promise of democracy. I fell lower and harder than I thought was possible, and hate filled me like a good meal.

A poster in the window of a travel agency in Central Square caught my eye. It showed a serene Japanese garden with a Shinto temple in the background. On the bottom of the poster was a note that read: "For only $1,400, visit the gem of the Orient!" How dare they advertise a trip to my home as if it was for sale! I imagined loud, fat Americans in sagging Bermuda shorts, slobbering on dripping hot dogs outside the temple, bumping against each other and farting from the gaseous oil in their intestines, marking their presence like dogs.

I noticed a young man in Harvard Square wearing an American flag T-shirt. The stains from his armpits desecrated the corners of the flag, and I supposed he was making a statement. A Toyota pick-up truck passed by with a bumper sticker on the back that read: "Buy American." Another car had a sticker over the tailpipe read: "Love your mother earth." Drivers with American flag stickers on their windows tossed out cigarette buts and cans. Parents shook their children at bus stops until they stopped crying. Store clerks, ill-trained and lazy, slouched over and huddled to avoid customers. Public phone receivers hung from their cords, vandalized. Tangled graffiti-ravaged trains and storefronts screamed for attention like angry tattoos. Broken car window debris and condoms were pushed up against crumbling curbs. Fat policemen with sunglasses joked with a group of equally corpulent construction workers, while they watched one man dig a hole, like a hazing ritual gone union. White faces suspiciously followed Black youths in stores. Men grabbed their crotches, burped, and ogled women. Eyes followed me.

I took a stool in a dim-lit bar in Somerville. Shamrock icons dressed the far wall and middle-aged White men, many in green jackets with the Celtics logo, sat like diseased birds in a cage. Except for the heads that turned and the eyes that squinted with disapproval, the room was quiet. The two men to my right puffed on cigarettes like they needed nicotine for survival, and Mel, the bartender, avoided me as long as he could. Finally he edged up to me and whispered, "Are you sure you're in the right place?"

"Yeah. I'd like a beer," I said.

"Just one beer."

"I don't know yet. Let's see how it goes."

He took a deep breath and widened his eyes at the two men. He then turned back to me and spread his hands on the counter. "Let me see some I.D."

I pulled my passport from my back pocket and straightened it out. He stared at the cover and cocked his head. "What *is* this, a joke? No I.D., no service!"

"It's a passport."

"Never seen one. I need a driver's license."

"I don't have one."

"Can't let you drink then."

"You want me to drink and then drive? What are you, stupid? That's a passport! Haven't you ever seen a fucking passport?"

"Marty, get this guy out of here!"

A man three times my size picked me up by the jacket and walked me outside like a marionette. The other patrons laughed and coughed through their cigarettes, and I prayed they would all choke to death. I spit on the dusty pavement as I walked away. "Fucking America! Fucking land of the fucking free!"

When I did sleep, I dreamed of stepping in front of oncoming cars, committing hara-kiri and jumping from buildings. I would wake up sometimes sweating, bewildered by the state I was in, convinced none of it was real. I'm not sure why I kept moving, or even why I sensed hope, but I did know that my family could never see me like this.

Certain thoughts and memories, like trinkets, kept me warm. Once they had been disturbing recollections, reminding me of what I didn't have, but now, bundled under the few possessions I had, they were beautiful. I saw my friend Cheryl and the rest of her family cheering as Mr. Spoza tore open his Christmas present. I was only a guest back then, so there weren't any presents for me, nor did I have any presents for them. But now, in my imagination, I was one of the family. The warm glow of incandescent lamps and candlelight mixed with the green and red holiday design filled me like the hot mug of cider in my hand. As I fell into deeper sleep, I dreamed that it was never quite that good, certainly not as good as Christmas in Japan, under the bending tree with the gold star atop. The smell of home and a smile comforting me to sleep. We didn't need many presents. The sound of Mama's voice and Papa's guitar lulled me to sleep. Miguel put his arm around me—the best oldest brother a *koohai* could have. This was my home. The smell of *soba* and the tree-lined streets of Denenchofu.

* * *

I slipped into a gymnasium at Boston College and took a shower. I ran the soap over my body but felt nothing. I had become so used to the numbness that the occasional clear moment was a shock. Later, I crossed the street to look at the job listings board in the communications building. There I found a flyer requesting applications for a company I had briefly worked with when I was a freelancer in college. Within a week I had secured a job as a video technician. During the following week I bumped into an old college dormitory friend, and we got an apartment together with his girlfriend. Soon after I obtained a weekend job as a video production instructor at a community center in Somerville, and an evening job at a video rental store in Harvard Square. By the end of October, I was working 14 hours a day, 7 days a week.

My numbness disappeared completely by early November. And for many nights, in my basement room next to the boiler, I cried, knowing that if it were not for luck, it would have been too late. For the next 4 years I shut out any memory of the summer and the fall, and finally felt free of that part of my past. I had reached an almost religious fervor—my feet were light on the ground, my back straight and my thoughts nothing but positive. I couldn't stop smiling, and welcomed the stares of strangers who seemed to avoid me when I acknowledged them. Only a few could see my happiness as genuine, but the frowns and mutterings of others (some of whom I had connected with when I was on the streets), I perceived as merely temporary. While in liberation of my painful experiences, I could not connect with their misfortunes anymore. I whistled while I walked, greeted cashiers and waved at drivers endangering me on crosswalks. The world was a new place, tranquil and accepting, and I was sure it would stay this way.

# 20

# Letting Go

A college friend introduced me to a tall, lanky, friendly looking man named Bruce, who was looking for someone to develop a video division for his media production company. Intrigued by his quick wit and ambition, I obliged, and over the next 6 years Bruce would become my closest friend, and a catalyst for a significant change in my understanding of identity and stereotypes.

Bruce considered himself Black, but often challenged others to skip references to physical attributes. "Why does he have to be *Black*?" or "Why does she have to be *fat*?" he would say, responding to someone making a comment about a passerby. He was generous, open-minded, and patient, and yet was faced everyday with the prospect of having to dodge or take the pounding of another racist comment or look. He was convinced he could change Boston and would turn down any negative comment regarding it. So in the evenings and weekends, outside of our regular work hours, we colluded and designed a plan to change the world.

Our business goals, although idealistic, were based on two directives: to market artists through video and photography and help improve the image of women and minorities in the media. We challenged potential corporate clients at sales meetings to consider non-White, female actors for key roles in business instruction videos. We keynoted at casting agency seminars, stressing the importance of steering away from stereotypes and embracing inclusion and diversity. We wrote pilot scripts for television shows that challenged Hollywood's racist, sexist grip. But for the first couple of years, we obtained little support or understanding. In meetings, corporate clients sat bewildered at our plans. Casting directors and White actors would argue: "It's difficult for everybody to find acting work, so why should minorities complain?"

195

Eventually we began to make enough of a stir in the production community—we were on to something. We didn't have the technical resources, but we had ideas that challenged the status quo. By attending sales meetings with dramatic and comedic outline for scripts, we succeeded in obtaining some large corporate production contracts. We hired nontraditional actors and completed competitive, successful productions. On a roll, we were convinced Boston was about to change.

In the evenings, in the living room of Bruce's Jamaica Plain apartment, we analyzed television shows and commercials, deconstructing their content and locking on to their racist, sexist devices. The success of television to this degree created pure motivation for us to challenge their influence. We didn't get angry; rather, we laughed hysterically at their blatant ignorance. Sometimes well into the early hours of the morning we schemed alternative versions that would kick the pants off every Hollywood or Disney executive. Through our late-night brainstorms, our comic sense ripened into hilarious routines, and we diverted our energies into creating comedy skits and ideas for television shows. We sent out well-designed, well-written proposals, met with interested parties, and learned to schmooze, but as the months rolled on with no responses, we began to wonder if we would ever be heard.

*   *   *

Spring was making its way back—a time I always equated with leaving the places I had called home. I was also born in the spring, and so my birthday always left me feeling ungrounded. In May I received a letter from the IRS indicating I didn't exist. My social security number, they claimed, was invalid and my tax returns could not be processed.

"Don't look at me. I just did the numbers for you on the forms," Dale said. He was film technician at work, and had done my tax return forms for me. "How the hell could you have an invalid social security number?"

"I don't know, it was given to me by my college when I was accepted back in 1981. I was living in Japan, and I didn't have a social security number—it wasn't required by the time I left the States."

"They probably just put a number in so they could process it. It says here you gotta apply for one."

"Yeah, like I'm going to see any benefit from it by the time I need it."

"Yeah, yeah, yeah. Everybody complains about that, but this is the good 'ol U.S.A. you're talking about. The number one country in the free world."

"Number one *what*?" I asked. "Gun-related deaths? Teenagers on drugs? Pregnant middle schoolers? Lack of discipline? Want me to go on?"

"See, that's why they screwed with your social security—you're too much of a risk. You're being watched you know. You oughta check your phone for taps."

The Social Security Office was packed, buzzing with Russian, Spanish, Portuguese, Chinese, and a bunch of other languages I couldn't understand. During the 2 hours I waited for my number to be called, I made acquaintances with the others in my corner. Next to me sat a woman wearing a *sari* and holding a squirming little boy. She and her husband had come from India, and although he was promised a job when he arrived, he was still unemployed. A Chinese couple shared an orange with us and explained that they had been trying to bring their families to the United States for many years, but immigration laws had made it more and more difficult. A man from Nicaragua told a story of how he escaped political persecution and spent 16 months getting to the United States. They laughed at my story and joked that I was probably the only person in the room who had been born a U.S. citizen and didn't even legally *exist*.

As I rode home on the bus with my new official card, I thought of the others still in the waiting room. Unlike mine, their trek was necessary for basic survival. The brief moments of laughter we shared made me sad and uneasy, and I had forgotten how to appreciate my privileges. I visualized laminating my card and fitting it neatly into my wallet—always accessible, but not too obvious. Now that I could pay taxes legally, I knew I had truly become an American Citizen.

*     *     *

"Let me give this numbuh a call," Lou, the real-estate agent, said. His cramped office smelled like fast-food. "Somerville's, not exactly Cambridge, ya know, but close enough, ahright?"

I had been looking for another apartment with Charlie, my friend and colleague from work. We wanted the intellectual atmosphere of Cambridge, but not the rental prices.

Lou spoke like a weathered used-car salesman. "Yeah, hi, this is Lou from the real estate agency? Yeah, I got a gentleman heah who's interested in seeing the apahtment ... his name is ... *what's yoah name again?*" he whispered loudly, ... "Teha Abode ... *again?* ... Teya Adoleeebro ... *huh?* ... *Oh ... Teja with a 'J'* ... Teja with a 'J' ... then Ar ... bo ... lee ... da ... Is he what? Black? *She wants to know if you're Black!* Ah ... well ... *are you Black?* ... No. No, he's not Black. Great! 5:30? He'll be theah."

Sometimes the mind is slow and sometimes you believe in the benefit of a doubt. And sometimes you just block information because it's too damn reminiscent of everything that's wrong with America. I'm not sure why I remained optimistic when Charlie, Lou, and I went to check on the apartment, but I had been feeling so lucky lately that I couldn't envision things getting worse.

"Oh ... is this them?" Lorraine gave Charlie and I the once-over.

Lou smiled and nodded his head rapidly. "Yeah, the two guys I told ya about."

Charlie and I walked upstairs while they spoke.

"Aah you suah he's not Black? He's ethnic or *something*," I heard Lorraine say.

"I donnow. He said he wasn't Black, though ... and I think Chahlie is Jewish."

"Are they *gay*? What am I supposed to do now?"

"They look fine. They have jobs."

Lorraine ran up the steps and edged her way between Charlie and I. "It's really not a very nice apahtment. It's kindah small, so."

"No, actually it's twice the size I thought it would be," I said, admiring the woodwork and the ceiling fans.

"Well, theah's a Haitian or something family next doah, and theah not very clean. And a group a *gay* guys next doah. I'm suah you could find something else around heah."

"Hey look, great balcony!" Charlie said.

"Lorraine said it was just rebuilt," Lou said. "Great for barbecues, huh?"

Lorraine jumped at the door to the balcony. "You ciahn't use the balcony."

"I want it," I said. "Charlie?"

Charlie opened one of the living room shades. "I love it. Back balcony, too! We'll take it."

\* \* \*

Walking through the community was like marching through a minefield. Besides the Haitian family in the building to the left of us and an apartment of four gay men next door, none of our neighbors paid us any attention. Doors and windows closed whenever I waved hello to someone across the street, and passersby pretended not to notice me on the streets and sidewalks. Even Lorraine remained unavailable until the last day of each month. Then, with rent in hand, I was directed by her to slip the check under her screen door. The instant her hand grabbed it, she would deadbolt the door in my face.

During Chanukah, Charlie was tempted to place menorahs in the windows, but was defeated by the blinding, flashing Christmas lights that encased the row of triple deckers. Our street had been transformed into an authentic landing strip for a giant Santa Claus. Charlie chewed his nails over the Christmas bulldozing, then unwittingly began dating a Christian who loved tinsel.

Many Boston-area artists and yuppies like myself moved to Somerville in the early 1980s to maintain the affordable Cambridge tie. Along with this population shift came an exotic mix of bohemian intellectuals, three-piece-suit lawyer trackers and doctoral immigrants, except for some reason, in our neighborhood. Subsequently, local newspapers reported a rise in nazi and racist graffiti on storefronts and graveyards, and violence and harassment against foreigners.

\* \* \*

One afternoon, on my usual weekly trip to the supermarket, I strolled along a side street in my favorite neighborhood. Old Victorian-style houses and capes were complemented by drooping willows and sturdy pine trees. I approached the corner to the shopping plaza when a pick-up truck veered and blundered toward me. I froze, and as the truck passed within inches, the driver flipped his middle finger at me. "Yeeehaaa!" Then three large guys riding in the back of the truck howled and raised their fists. "Get outa thah fahckin' way, *spik*!"

I was losing hope for America, for myself. I felt trapped again in the garbage of my own country. Although my friends had become, in a sense, my family, I started shutting them out. Our late-night gatherings were becoming difficult for me to swallow.

It was just after Thanksgiving that we held a party to finish the leftovers from the feast. Earlier during the day, I watched some neighbors drench their house with yet more Christmas lights. They cursed at each other as they tangled the cords beyond repair. Now, in the evening, I lay on the living room floor listening to my dear friends' joking. Throughout most of the party I tried hard to smile, but the recent incidents were beating me down. And it was late—more like early morning—by the time we usually ended our get-togethers. Two years into my life in Boston, and the feeling of euphoria and optimism after the cold summer of 1985 had vanished with any hopes of finding a real home, a *real* sense of belonging.

My friends were the only thing keeping me from falling into a chasm of loneliness again. Now safe inside, surrounded by cheap wallpaper and flimsy walls, I could no longer hold my anguish inside.

"Guys, I can't live in America anymore," I said, barely containing my tears. "I can't stand it. I have to leave. I can't walk down the street and not wonder when I'm going to be harassed. I say hello to a woman, and she thinks I'm attacking her. I say hello to a kid, and the mother thinks

I'm a kidnapper or child molester. I walk into a store and I get suspicious looks. I'm sick and tired of seeing mainly White people on TV. I thought this country was supposed to be different! I have to figure out a way to get back to Japan before I completely lose it. I don't even know who I am anymore." I cried hard that night. Steve, Julie, and Bruce listened patiently and nodded with understanding. I wished hard they could *really* understand.

I couldn't stop thinking of Papa and Mama, especially now that Papa was remarried. His wife was Japanese and brought a new dimension to our international family. I had received a long letter from him and an envelope of photographs of the wedding. His wife, in traditional Japanese makeup and attire, stood next to him, composed and serious. His dark Western-style suit looked good on him. It was neither odd, seeing them together, nor was it difficult—the process of remarrying had taken so long it was expected. Nonetheless, I wondered what complications would arise from yet another intercultural marriage.

They had looked for an apartment in vain for months, turned away because of Papa's skin or the fact that he was a foreigner. It seemed as if our old neighborhood had become more exclusive over the years. There were no legal ramifications against such discrimination—Japan is not a litigious society, and the government routinely sanctions racist behavior. They finally found an apartment when his wife looked for housing alone. By mentioning Papa's profession, she won their approval, and by stating that he had lived down the street and the neighborhood was familiar with him, she was added to their gold list.

Mama kept quiet about the marriage, and I wouldn't have known how to bring it up. Papa's wife was conventional, in a strict Japanese sense, and had requested that all ties, including financial ones between Papa and Mama, be broken. The tension that grew from this was equal to the cultural conflict it symbolized.

* * *

Miguel called from Oregon, frustrated. He had received his master's degree in architecture but learned there wouldn't be any work for him there. Most of his friends had left the state to find jobs elsewhere, so he braced himself for another move. He decided to come to Boston, as the building boom was still at its peak. It was obvious, however, that having to make the decision to leave the west coast was tearing at him. Several years earlier when we visited Mama for Christmas, he had made up his mind that he disliked Boston. He was to stay with me until he found an apartment and a job. It would be good to have family nearby again, but we both knew it would be a challenge. More than 3 days together, and we would be at each other's throat.

We hugged each other for a long time at the airport. My brother! My big brother, here in Boston! I wanted to yell out on the streets that my brother, Miguel, family, was here! We would reconcile our differences and build a family again. That night I promptly took him to a Japanese restaurant and stuffed him with sushi. We walked around the neighborhood and joked in Japanese, and told stories until early morning in the living room. I wanted so much for him not to know what I had been through, but inevitably, as honest as we were together, I confided in him.

One month passed and he continued to look for work. It was obvious from the beginning that our family name was a hindrance, and he would come back from an interview, defeated and angry. He was sensitive, more than I was, to subtle negative looks and comments. He defended himself by announcing his evaluation of Boston whenever he felt appropriate. When the landlady, suspicious neighbors, or any general logistical chaos of Boston frightened him, he lashed out unapprovingly.

"See that construction they're doing over there?" Miguel pointed to a pile of rubble at the intersection of South Huntington and Huntington streets. An odd group of workhorses, men working signs, and pile-ons were scattered haphazardly across the street. "It's been there since I got here, with no trace of workers and snarled traffic because of it."

"Union," I said. "Typical American, typcial Boston union job."

"In Japan they'd be done, no complaints, no garbage left behind and swept clean."

"And no obese policemen chewing the cud with a lazy crew of 15."

"And these guys probably won't even do a good job."

"Actually, they've been working on it for 7 months. First they ripped out the old trolley tracks, with no notice to the public, putting all the stores out of business and inconveniencing the residents. Then they decided to put the trolley tracks back in. So they ripped up the street again, waited for winter to pass, then spring fever hit, so they went to Florida to catch some rays, came back, worked a couple of days, eventually they put the tracks back in. Now they've decided to take the tracks out again. Maybe."

"So, tell me, Teja, how does America survive?"

"Unions."

As an architect and naturalist, Miguel's criticisms came from understanding the dynamics and pitfalls of bad design and bad attitudes. He demolished gaudy, ugly buildings with his eyes and waved ugly personalities into the gutters with his hands. "The John Hancock is an all-glass building, so why do they have all the lights on during the day? It's a waste of energy! Look at it! It's a phallic symbol. The architect obviously had penis envy of the Prudential Tower." I began to understand that he would never feel comfortable in Boston. He wanted more than just a job and an apartment—he needed a community, a true supportive, like-minded community, something he had always wanted. I did too, but I had given up early, or maybe I found it easier to adjust.

*  *  *

"You need a girlfriend," John advised. He ran the convenience store and gave advice about women like he was charging for it. "When was the last time you had a girlfriend?"

"Senior year in high school," I said. "Is that bad?"

"No, it's not bad. You just need a girlfriend."

"Common scenario: A woman flirts with me, I ask her to coffee, then she freaks out! What is this with American women?"

"You're too nice."

"I'm too nice? Asking someone to coffee is too nice?"

"Well, in America, a lot of young women find gentle men to be less attractive."

"Well there goes the notion of chivalry out the window. What am I supposed to do, *hiss* at them?"

"They might like that. Try not asking. Tell them you're going to *take* them to coffee."

"Oh. You mean like *take* your dog to the vet. Sorry, I'd rather be single."

Among my acquaintances and friends, many had relationship problems. So I thought I was content living as a bachelor without these hang-ups to quell. Besides, the late hours I worked with Bruce took away any desire for intimacy. Bonny, Bruce's girlfriend, however, was clearly upset about his limited time with her. During one evening, 1 hour before Bruce and I were to leave for some television production work, Bonny showed up with a friend.

"Teja, I want you to meet Barbara." Bonny nudged her friend toward me and whispered out loud to her, "He's *very* single."

Barbara didn't say much at first, she was obviously very shy. She laughed nervously, as Bruce, in his usual outrageous mockery, made suggestive faces at both of us, implying some electrical connection had taken place. But her eyes, green and large, seemed to cut through his folly. When she spoke, her hands were delicately expressive and when she relaxed she moved smoothly. It was obvious she was well-read, but in the middle of a serious discussion, she could switch, surprising us with her unusual sense of humor. Soon she became part of the regular weekend hangout at Steve's or Julie's for group snuggles in front of the fireplace, hot chocolate and spicy chicken wings, ice cream bashes and bad movies late into the night. Within 1 month, on the living room floor of Steve's house, at 3 a.m., I found my lips against hers. She pretended to sleep, so I watched for her eyes to open. When she finally opened them she looked at me and smiled softly. I knew I had fallen for her.

*  *  *

I moved to a small studio attic apartment in a two-family house in Jamaica Plain, about 1 mile from Bruce's place. The rent was reasonable and the view was perfect. Off the kitchen door, the deck looked over the neighboring houses, and the overhang of the maple tree provided ample shade. The skylight in the main room sometimes offered a private view of the moon at night, and bathed me in sunshine during the day.

I quickly became acclimated to the neighborhood, with its predominant Hispanic, Black, and southeast Asian makeup. In the evenings there was often Salsa music, and kids from all backgrounds played together in the park across the street. Jamaica Plain, like Somerville, had also seen a dramatic rise in the number of resident artists and musicians. But there was a definite relaxed atmosphere, diverse and colorful, many mixed and gay couples. On weekends, in the center, there were always street vendors selling African and Asian paraphernalia, musicians playing jazz or classical music. There were natural food stores and vegetarian restaurants, an arts center and two theaters. Generally, people were cordial and friendly, and certainly no one stared. I began to discover that there was a part of Boston, the heart of the city, where I could blend in and no one would notice.

I was undoubtedly pegged as Hispanic by the neighborhood youths and in the local Spanish-speaking markets. Barbara always got a kick out of shopping with me.

"*Hello, how are you!*" Consuela said. She usually never spoke to customers and worked quickly, so I was caught off guard when she greeted me. Barbara had taught me a few phrases in Spanish, but when I actually had to say them out loud, they came out sounding like I had a speech impediment.

"*Good ... how are ... you?*" I answered, hoping she would leave the conversation at that.

"*Oh, I'm not so well. My aunt just had surgery and my dog has the runs. I've been working overtime so I haven't been able to spend time with my brother who is staying with us for a couple of weeks. Look at the crowd behind you! Oh my heavenly God, this is going to drive me to an early grave! Oh, look, you got the good coffee!*"

I nodded, smiled, and thanked her, guessing that somewhere in her monologue she had complimented me.

*"So, don't be so rude, introduce me to your friend!"* she said, stuffing my groceries in a plastic bag. Her eyebrows danced as she waited for me to answer.

I looked at Barbara. "What did she say?"

"What? I'm sorry, I wasn't listening," Barbara said.

"Consuela. What did she ... "

*"She doesn't speak Spanish?"* Consuela looked sympathetic.

I forced my eyes on Barbara's. "What?"

Barbara looked down, not to embarrass me. "She thinks *I* don't speak Spanish."

I looked at Consuela, knowing that what I was about to say would make me the laughing stock of Jamaica Plain. "I'm sorry, I don't speak Spanish."

Consuela's eyes widened and mouth dropped. "Yu eh don espeake Español?"

"No, I'm really sorry. I don't. But she does." I put my arm around Barbara.

Consuela shook her finger at me. "Yu eh don espeake eSpanish, but *yu* areh Latino!" she continued stuffing my bags. Then she stopped, looked up, and squinted her eyes. *"What is your name?"*

I understood that much. *"Teja Arboleda."* I rolled the "r" and softened the "d" perfectly.

Her eyes widened and she smiled. *"Arboleda. Arboleda! See? You are certainly Hispanic!* And she espeake? She eh don looke likeh Latina."

She went back to packing my bags. *"But where are you from?"*

Barbara jumped in to translate. "Where are you from?"

"America," I said.

*"Yes, yes. No, where are you from? Costa Rica, Puerto Rico? No wait, I have a friend ... Honduras, Columbia!"*

"Where are you really from?" Barbara said.

"Japan," I said, looking for a proverbial hole to crawl into.

*"Japan! Japan! You are so funny!"*

"Ah ... she thinks you're lying," Barbara advised.

"Thanks, Barb."

*"You know, we could be relatives, but I don't know how to help you,"* Consuela said. Then she put her hand on Barbara's. *"Make sure he gets the translation."*

* * *

I had become too comfortable with my surroundings. Having learned to automatically avoid certain dangerous neighborhoods left me in stark denial of the consequences of cultural trespassing. Perhaps I was finally adjusting, possibly even happy with my world, my friends, and of course

Barbara, that I lost some of the sensitivity and awareness necessary to survive in a volatile country like America.

It was a beautiful day, the kind where when you leave the office building, you wonder how many days or months you've lost sitting under florescent lights. I decided to use my break to buy some lunch materials and eat on the grass behind the building.

For a daytime grocery shopping spree, the supermarket in Woburn was unusually crowded. I watched the cashier lazily packing a customer's groceries while chatting with a friend. She rolled her eyes and stroked her blond hair to the rhythm of her gum chewing and yawned in the old woman's face. Ahead of me was a large man with a sunburned nose, wearing a Red Sox baseball cap. His balloon-shaped belly stressed the buttons on his Oxford. Behind me was someone who might have as well been his brother. I placed my humus, pita bread, and carrots on the conveyer belt and picked up a magazine that claimed the world was ending next week.

"Hey Rick!" The gentleman in front raised his wobbling arm above me, releasing an underarm body odor so bad that it needed its own category. "Take a look at this one!"

The one behind me picked at my bag of pita bread and leaned over behind me. "Yeah, what the hell is this?"

"You imagine people actually eat that crap?"

"Well, that's what these fahkin' immigrants feed on!"

They both laughed and coughed, their bodies, which were four times my weight shook the checkout lane dispensers. I closed the magazine and placed it back in its slot. Then I looked at the guy in front of me.

He ignored me. "Maybe that's why their so fahkin' skinny!"

I looked at the cashier who had stopped chewing her gum. She looked at me, shrugged her shoulders, and rolled her eyes. I turned to the guy behind me and looked him in the eye. He smiled sheepishly, then the one in front of me picked up my container of humus and laughed. I turned back to him and squinted.

His finger was an inch from my eye. "Take your fahkin' humus and pita bread and go back to fahkin' Mexico!"

The world turned shades of blue and the floor became sand. My hands clenched into fists and my right shoulder coiled back for murder. He laughed in slow motion, and there was no sound. In this silence, the cashier, the traffic outside, the day—everything vanished. Hate and adrenaline pumped through my veins. My years in Judo and wrestling shot back like a freakish nightmare. His life was about to end.

By the time I relaxed my fist, I was aware of his laughing again and the two of them were already walking out. The cashier closed her eyes slowly and resumed chewing her gum. When I finally returned to work after a long detour, I sat in the lunchroom next to the vending machine and drew a blank. "Feelings are only thoughts," I reminded myself.

* * *

"I don't wanna be White." Bruce looks at me, I look at him, we look at the crowd, then continue. "I wanna be an ethnic." Look back at the crowd, look at each other, resume. "Maybe an Indian, or Hispanic!" Start the dance. "Maybe a Jew, just like a dream come true ... I wanna be an ethnic too! More Blacks, more Jews, more you-know-who! I wanna be an ethnic too!" Crowd cheers. "Hi! I'm Tom!" Bruce says. "Hi! I'm Harry!" I say. Audience responds, "Who's Dick?" Bruce and I look at each other. "You are! And we are ... the Daring Ethnics! To boldly go were no other ethnic has gone before! *I'm getting ethnic in the morning! Ding dong the bells are going to chime!* Eeeek! He's ... ethnic!"

Bruce and I were on a role. The material we gathered from our painful experiences were too dramatic to remain serious, so we developed stand-up comedy routines, and formed a duo: The Daring Ethnics. We used the tired, racist antics of Hollywood stars like Al Franken, Jackie Mason, and Don Rickles as targets for our campaign. With our attack, punctuated by pratfalls and slapstick, we had Boston-area audiences doubled over in hysterics. We picked on audience members to act foolishly, which only added fodder to our character studies of racists, homophobes, and women-haters. I don't think they knew we were using them as the subjects of our discontent, but they toasted to our antics with beer and cigarettes, and howled at the prospect of being guilty as tried.

From the very beginning, however, it was clear we were not welcome by the Boston-area comedy clique. The all-White, male, woman-bashing, racist, sex-and-alcohol-joke specialists were obviously threatened by our politically correct approach to cultural criticism. The whole comedy scene was ugly—like walking through a Penthouse magazine soaked in beer. Most comedians' jokes stayed within this realm, predictable and appealing to equally shallow patrons. I often wondered how it is so many famous comedians came from Boston and whether their success was indicative of Americans as a whole.

Although we met with some success, our stage time was consistently being pushed back, sometimes eliminated. No one from the clique ever spoke to us and the club managers grunted when they saw us coming.

Bruce and I were on the way to a gig one night, driving through the back roads of Cambridge. The traffic light had turned to yellow, so I slowed down to stop. A taxi driver honked at me from behind and yelled something. I rolled down my window and gestured for him to slow down and turned on my left turn signal. In the mirror I saw his headlights retreat, then he started edging around me in the oncoming lane. I knew he was looking for trouble. I looked at Bruce, then when the light turned green, I swung left into the street where the taxi was headed, thus cutting him off. He gunned his engine and swerved around in front of us and slammed on his brakes. He got out of the taxi and walked toward us, cracking his knuckles. I closed my window and locked the door.

"Hey, shithiead!" His shouting was barely muffled through the glass. "Where the fahck d'ya learn how tah drive, fiahckin' Afghiahnistiahn?" He punched my window and spit on it. I blew him a kiss. His forehead veins popped and he pulled his hair, then pounded the hood of my car and kicked the tires. He bent down and looked into the car, saw Bruce, then quickly retreated to his taxi. "Go biahck tah fahckin' Piahkistiahn' you fahckin' fiahggit!"

That night we were hot, and the other comedians hated us for it.

# 21

# Check One Only

I kissed Barbara goodnight and walked my bicycle to the gates of the campus. As I mounted my bicycle and turned on the riding light, a faint premonition suggested I take an alternate route. I had been in a odd mood all night, so I decided I didn't need any more strange ideas. I brushed off the brief notion and proceeded east on the bicycle path parallel to Washington Street and behind the housing projects.

My bicycle light danced along the hedges and guardrails, and the wind, chilly and moist, found its way into my jacket. I loved the sound of the gears against the chain, well-oiled and tight, purring with the steady rhythm of my peddling.

I maintained a good pace, challenging my stamina just slightly more than necessary. I would be home soon and had ice cream waiting for me. I approached Center Street at the main gate to the housing project and behind the Jackson Square train station entrance.

Out of nowhere, to my left, a man appeared and stepped into my path. Before I could grip my brakes tight enough, another man gripped my brakes and the tires skid. Another man jumped in from my right, grabbed my shoulder, and used my momentum to propel me off my bike. I slammed into the top of the cast iron gate where an arrow-shaped tip ripped through my right shoulder. I landed on the pavement with my knees and fell forward, bracing my face with my hands. There were now three men. One ripped my knapsack from my back, another removed my watch, and the third retrieved my bicycle. A sharp pain shot up from my legs and I screamed.

"Shut up an keep yo face down!" the closest yelled.

I turned and looked up at them. One was going through my wallet, another searched my bag. I could see their eyes under their hoods, and their face masks were pulled down, covering only their mouths. "I said, keep yo face down or you dead, muthahfuckuh!" The one on my right pulled out a gun and held it up.

"Okay, okay! Take the money and the bicycle. Just leave the wallet!" I yelled.

"Keep yo face to the groun and count to a hundred, or I'm gonna shoot!"

I buried my face in my arm and waited until their footsteps faded. I heard a train approaching the station behind me. I tried to stand but my knees wouldn't move. Then I noticed the right arm of my sweater was soaked in blood. With my legs dragging behind, I pulled myself along the pavement to the edge of the street. Two women in a Toyota were attempting to park at the curb, then saw me. "Help!" I cried. They locked their doors and started to leave. A well-dressed couple crossed behind me. As I crawled into the train station, a group of people rushed by me, staring, and pointing. Three policemen near the token booth stood drinking coffee and chatting. "Help!" I gurgled. One of the officers looked down and pointed at me. "Hey look, deahs anuduh one." He sauntered over, picked me up, and sat me down on a bench. The other two officers took sips from their cups, studying the situation. I peeled back the collar of my sweater. Dark blood oozed from the deep puncture in my right shoulder. A piercing hot flame exploded in my knees. I screamed again, and doubled over. When I was propped back up, I noticed that another young man was sitting next to me. His face and hair were bloody and he held his arm, gritting his teeth and shaking in pain.

"Ambulance will be heah shortly," the officer said, slurping his coffee.

I was in a wheelchair in the hallway of some hospital, listening to the announcements and calls over the PA system. Doctors and nurses rushed by me, tangled in stethoscopes and clipboards; one looked at her watch and cursed. A nurse wheeled me to the registration desk where a large woman with heavy makeup and lethal fingernails sat at a computer.

"Name?" she asked. She didn't look at me, but her chewing gum kept her occupied.

"Teja Arboleda."

"Huh?"

"It's on the form you got there."

"Oh ... look at that. Citizenship?"

"U.S."

She batted her eyes lids, and rolled her eyes slowly until they met mine. She snapped the gum in her mouth.

"No, honey. C-i-t-i-z-e-n-s-h-i-p."

"American ... oh, you mean *race*!"

"Riiight! What are you? Hispanic? Black? White? What! I don't have all night, does it look like I have all night?"

"You don't have to put it down."

"Yes I do or my boss will kill me. Why, do you have a problem with that okay fine." She began typing in her computer. "H-i-s-p-a-n-i-c. Okay. See that wasn't hard, was it?"

I was in too much pain to argue. Instead, I imagined her suffocating under her own weight and having to check herself into the hospital. I would be at the computer to type in "imbecile."

The x-rays showed a slight crack in my right knee cap and a severe bone bruise in my left leg. I also had a sprained neck. The hole in my right shoulder was sewn and followed up with a tetanus shot. I left the hospital with my right leg, right arm, and neck each in a separate brace.

A week later a detective called, asking me to help identify my assailants. At the station he presented me with a neatly organized binder filled with mug shots. All of the faces had dark skin.

"Recognize any of the faces?" he asked, taking a drag from his pipe. His stomach hung over his belt like a petrified wave, and I wondered if having a gun meant less energy was needed to chase a criminal.

I studied the faces. Although I could remember my attackers faces clearly, I didn't recognize any of them in the mug shots. "No, sorry."

"They were Black, right?"

"Their faces are not here."

"Were they Hispanic or Black?"

"I'm not really sure. They had dark skin … "

"So they were Black."

"I think one might have been Hispanic."

"Well either you're sure or you're not sure."

"It depends on your definition of Black and Hispanic, doesn't it? Maybe they were White with Blackface. Amos 'n Andy on the lamb, you know."

"I'm only trying to help you here, kid."

"I'm only trying to help us all."

\* \* \*

The shock of gunfire ripped through the neighborhood. Again. I clenched my teeth, and I thought of returning to Japan as a refugee. Soon a pair of police cars would squeal down the street followed by an ambulance. The scenario had become so common in Boston, and the newspapers revelled in headline reports of gun violence heating up in the grip of summer. Pictures of Black youths, angry and sweating under dark hoods, left White Boston naked with fear. There were reports of kids killing kids, drug deals, pie charts dividing the neighborhoods, and graphs rising higher with the weeks. How could America be so complacent? Guns and drugs would never be tolerated in Japan.

I thought of how Americans like to boast of their freedom, often casually claiming it as a given birthright, like cars and *The Love Boat*. Often ignorant of the reality of other countries, Americans are sure that in the United States individuals are truly sovereign without limits. Yet in the confines of their enclave, their neighborhood, their streets, they protect their own, shelter their children from kidnappers, preen their lawns, wax their cars, and rarely venture beyond the familiar. Violence in a medium-sized city like Boston had become commonplace, irrelevant to the sanctioned idealism of freedom. Women continued to be stalked, raped, and killed by husbands and boyfriends; elementary school kids learned to duck at the sound of a gunshot; swastikas were smeared on storefronts; police traded guns for drugs with gangs. In Japan I was never afraid. In America, the land of my birth and citizenship, I always will be. America will never be the land of the free until every person can truly understand the real meaning of freedom.

*   *   *

The second I opened my door I knew what she was. Her uniform and clipboard had been seen all over the neighborhood during the last week.

"Hi. I'm from the Census Bureau for the 1990 national census, and I need some additional information that wasn't filled out in the form you mailed in. The office needs these completed as soon as possible. It looks like here, all we need is your race."

"Oh, I didn't fill that out."

"Right. So if you could please."

"You don't understand. I filled everything else out but that. On purpose."

"Why didn't you want to fill it out?"

"It's not appropriate to ask me what my race is."

"It's not … appropriate? But that's all we need to complete it. I can't go back to the office without this information."

"I'm sorry, but you'll have to. I wouldn't know what to put down anyway. Goodbye."

A week later she returned.

"Hello again, I'm from the Census Bureau and…."

"I remember."

"Ah … my employer suggested I return. He asked if you might be able to help me with this little matter."

"It's not a little matter. I'm sorry, but these racial categories should be illegal."

"What are you talking about?"

"I am of many so-called races. What am I supposed to put down?"

"Other. Right here." She pointed to a little box which read: "Other race (Print race)" at the bottom of the page.

"What is that supposed to mean? Am I supposed to just make one up? And why is it at the bottom? Look, White is at the top. Doesn't that say anything to you? I'm sorry, have a good day."

She returned yet again, the following week.

"You again," I said.

"I'm so sorry." Her eyes swelled with tears. "My boss is really upset."

"Well, I'm sorry too. But you know my answer. Human beings are a lot more complex and interesting than just some color-coded boxes. If I put down my race, I would need extra paper. Either that or put down "human." Can I put down 'human' in the 'Other' box?"

Her mouth broke into a little smile. "No."

"Then please, tell your boss if he wants to talk to me, he can come here. Otherwise, I'm sorry."

She turned to leave, pressed the form against the door frame, and checked the "Other" box. Since I was standing on my staircase, I could look over her shoulder. She wrote "Hispanic" in the adjacent box. She gingerly closed the gate, avoided my eyes, then hastened to the other side of the street.

"Hey, you can't do that!" I yelled.

"I'm sorry, just doing my job," she said, shrugging her shoulders.

Eight months later I started receiving Spanish-language junk mail.

\*　\*　\*

The charred skeleton of a car remained at the end of our street. No truck, no police, no headline. "Yeah, this happens once in a while," a neighbor told me. "My brother's a cop. Rich kids from Weston and Concord deposit the car here, torch it, then collect insurance, blaming car thieves from our neighborhood. Can you believe it? Makes us look like animals. They're so stupid, they don't realize the serial number can be traced."

I had to walk past this eerie sculpture everyday for 3 months. With each passing, its ugliness gradually turned to beauty. Not the kind of beauty one might find in an antique shop but one like the subject in a painting. An American icon, a shadow of Henry Ford, rusting on Cornwall Street. Children playing across the street, just out of reach, were too innocent to grasp the irony of this presence. If the car had been torched in the rich neighborhood where its owner lived, it would have been long gone, swept from its pristine environment and dumped into some metal yard far away from the eyes of the rich, possibly even here in Jamaica Plain. I thought of how marginalized—how separate and unequal America had become. It wasn't just politics or economics anymore—America had become an each-man-for-himself nation.

I had to at least try to justify the burnt car. Maybe on a macrolevel it wasn't so bad. It would be gone someday, remembered only by *where* it was. It could be that the very ground I walked and lived was once a native American burial ground—what right did I have to point fingers?

Besides, maybe things were on the upswing.

The maple tree in the yard blushed a bright red. This was the time I enjoyed most in New England, with the radiance of fallen autumn leaves and the fresh smell of a cool breeze, just in time to savor the days before another harsh winter. I always took comfort in the approach of the cold months. Maybe I equated them with some residual but somehow romantic melancholy, like the memory of a good conversation. I had promised myself every winter that next year things would be different, better. A fireplace maybe, friends, and hot chocolate in a quiet place, and the chill would be just right.

I walked through Jamaica Plain at any time of day or night. The guns were down the street the other way, and besides, I was sure I had already run out of bad luck and bad people.

It was 11:30 p.m. on a Tuesday night, and I decided I needed a bag of Smart Food. A hooker greeted me at the end of the street. *A hooker? Since when were there prostitutes here?* "Hey there, wanna good time?" she asked.

I broke into a jog and crossed the street. Ten minutes later I turned the corner on Center Street to the convenience store. Flashing blue and red lights splashed the adjacent buildings where a crowd of people had gathered. Three police cars surrounded the entrance to the convenience store.

"What happened?" I asked a woman in a housecoat and slippers.

"Damn near killed somebody," she said. "Five minutes ago some guy held up the store with an assault rifle. Third time this year. What do they need assault rifles for, you know what I mean? This is my husband, Gerry. I told Gerry we gotta move, we're old but we gotta move, right Gerry?"

One month later it happened again. Then, one morning I found my headlights punched out. "Yeah, they drive by in cars sometimes with a bat," my neighbor explained. I swept up the broken glass. A young boy, around 7, passed me on the street. Our eyes locked. He reached into his front pocket, then threw his hand in the air. About 100 pennies rained down on me and the car. He looked away and turned the corner.

I never walked the streets at night again. Imprisoned in my apartment and in my car, the winter crawled along, deadening the anxiety of the past summer. The community seemed untouched by the recent events, or maybe my own perceptions were exaggerated and my assumptions were arrogant. In the coffee shops and in the arts center, others seemed so much more relaxed and unscathed. "Oh, I just don't go out when it's dark, that's all," a woman in the copy shop admitted. "I don't even drive at night."

*No driving! How un-American!* I worked the car over the embankment of snow the plows had deposited in the middle of the street. Three boys swaggering and crouching under black hoods turned to look at me as I approached. Their faces were stern, intent. One pulled out an a shiny object, held it up with both hands outstretched like a gun, and pointed it at me. I ducked below the window and stepped on the gas. Seconds later I sat up and barely managed to maneuver the car away from a utility pole. In the rearview mirror the kids laughed, slapping their knees, clutching their stomachs.

* * *

Barbara and I decided to live together outside of the city. I had been working at the public broadcasting station in Boston, across the bridge from Harvard Square, and Barbara took a job managing a bookstore in Waltham. We found an apartment convenient to both and moved in the spring of 1990.

Bruce and I quit the comedy scene, realizing its limitations and predictability. We needed fresh ideas and a new venue. Besides, the Boston comedians' gang virtually kicked us out, threatened by what they called "politically correct bullshit."

I decided to pay a final tribute to a comedian whose lack of awareness, insight, and sensitivity reflects the success of the entire entertainment industry. The famed Al Franken was to speak at the Harvard School of Government and show politically relevant clips from the renowned NBC comedy series *Saturday Night Live.* Steve and Barbara joined me at the hall, which was packed with 400 bright, eager college students; media profession-als; and a video crew. The clips were mediocre at best, showcasing the actor's skill more than the message or content, making political criticism purely personal. Mr. Franken then entertained questions. "I love your show. How do you come up with these ideas?" someone asked. "Do you have to memorize that much stuff every week?" another audience member asked. I waited about 20 minutes, just enough time for the crowd to get to know Mr. Franken. Then I approached the microphone in the aisle.

"Mr. Franken. I have watched the show for many years. It is a long show, longer than most, 1½ hours, I believe, so it must be a powerful show. My question is: As a producer and the head writer of the series, what do you plan to do to represent minorities and women more justly on your program?"

The audience hushed. *A serious question!* I reminded myself that the two video cameras were catching everything.

"Well ... " Al Franken began in his nasal command, smirking sheepishly and scratching his bushy hair. "I'm looking for a couple of Blaaaks ... I am looking for a couple of Hispaaanics, oh and I'm looking for a couple of gaaays ... and maybe a Hmong tribesman. Does that help a bit?"

Half the audience laughed, the other half hissed.

This was good. I had some of them on my court. Next move. "Well, let's put it this way. How many minorities do you have as writers on your show?"

"Ah." He adjusted his thick, black glasses and exposed his massive teeth. I waited for an answer as he thought carefully.

"Okay ... well, how many women do you have as writers?"

"Ah ... two, but they don't get paid to be writers."

I gained the women. Mr. Franken became visibly upset.

He waited for the crowd to simmer down. "Well, actually, I was considering hiring my son, he's Jewish, you know, like me, so that would probably do something."

We volleyed for another minute until my time was up. After I sat down, he continued making racist, sexist, and gay jokes. Each time he did this, he laughed, looked for me and pointed. "Oh I'm sorry, where's that ethnic guy?" For the next 45 minutes I never let my eyes leave his, until he decided to depart early, bent over with his foot in his mouth.

Steve, Barbara, and I sat in an Indian restaurant still in shock by the evening's event.

"'That *ethnic* guy?' What the hell was that supposed to mean?" Barbara asked.

"It's unbelievable that he's that popular," Steve said.

My nerves still tingled from the rise in adrenaline. "Well, I've made a decision tonight. In 6 months I'm quitting my job and I'm going to dedicate my life to fighting that man and everything he represents. Ethnic guy, huh? It's people like him who have desecrated the image of minorities and women on television—set back the clock for a population that's changing so rapidly—we're not going to take it anymore. And the sad thing is, half the people there didn't even have a clue as to why I was attacking him. I'm quitting my job. I've got to do something about this."

# 22

# Losses

The Gulf War had become a sickening media event. Fancy titles, trite roundtable discussions, and footage of flag-waving Americans filled airtime on certain stations, while the other broadcasters were relegated to situation comedy reruns. President Bush was determined to create patriotic nationalist riots against an enemy that most Americans didn't even know existed. I had never seen so many flags mounted on cars and briefcases and "Saddam, I'll kick your ass" baseball caps. I asked some middle school kids to locate Kuwait or Iraq on a globe. They responded with relatively little success, but were certain we were defending democracy. I began to question if Americans really needed a war to feel proud. Is blind killing of "different" or darker skinned people easier, more justifiable than killing people who look like the "majority?" After all, we tend to be horrified over the killing of a monkey or a dog, but not so much an ant or a flea.

I was angry at the ignorance and incompetence of our country, the lack of public awareness, education, and truth. Americans were spoon-fed lies about our role in the history of the Middle East and our part in the creation of our own enemy. Politics and reelection campaigns concealed the real motives of the west, and proved again our unwillingness to seek the truth.

In defense of peace, I had seen much, heard much, and argued much. An Episcopalian minister at a party in Waltham preached anti-Iraqi rhetoric that reeked of Arab bashing. A 7-year-old boy on Cape Cod shamed "those Arabs" for their "evil ways." Drivers in Massachusetts pinched pennies over fuel prices while Iraqi oil field fires glowed in the night like beacons for its dying citizens. Western soldiers, fixed and steady, murdered the innocent with "smart" bombs. Politicians accepted responsibility for successful "missions," when the real mission was to eliminate

216

Hussein. No doubt, Bush needed his enemy to remain, as do our troops today, our ultimate interest. The Middle East, in turmoil because of a handful of tyrants had no hostages to hand over this time, and the West pretended to regret the selling of its arms.

With the hype and marketing of Arab-bashing, America had found itself again, surfacing after the lingering recuperation from the Cold War years. James Bond and Schwartzenegger would no more single-handedly eliminate the Hammer and Sickle Empire, rather mock, caricaturize, and decapitate this new enemy. Corporations like Disney thrived on this phenomenon, emerging with the release of the children's animation movie, *Aladdin*. The Arab-American community protested the racist lyrics in the opening song, and the Disney company, with batting eyes and a feign of innocence took a bow. PBS aired *Are You Being Served*, a British situation comedy series in which in a single episode Arabs were mocked, chastised, and prostituted. Three years later, the whole country jumped to a conclusion as a bomb devastated a federal office building in Oklahoma City.

It was near the end of Desert Storm, and I drove to my old stomping ground in Jamaica Plain to pick up a pizza for a meeting with Bruce. A large man, dressed in fatigues and black boots, eyed me as I entered, then stood up abruptly. He walked over to me, and jabbed his finger into my chest and pushed me toward the door. "Go back to Iraq you son-of-a-bitch!"

At this point, and for my own sanity, I had learned to laugh at ignorance and misdirected aggressiveness. And now, in the heat of an election year, I had plenty of material from which to work. One evening, I sat in my office laughing at a David Frost interview with George Bush on PBS. In his reelection campaign, Bush discussed the Republican Party's success on improving the economy.

David Frost asked Bush, "When people say are you're better off than 4 years ago in general, the public economically would seem to say no to that. Do you think they have a kinder, gentler nation than 4 years ago?"

"In some ways," Bush replied, "but I'll tell you what, a guy that has a mortgage on his house and has a job, and 93% of the people are working in this country, he can refinance his mortgage and he can say he's better off. Suppose you're an ethnic guy living in Poland, I mean living in Chicago and you've been worrying about your family for decades over there, they go to bed at night saying, 'Thank God the United States stood firm, and Poland is free or Czechoslovakia is free,' so it depends who you're talking to."

*What?* I couldn't even afford a mortgage in Boston, let alone worry whether or not I was ethnic enough to be Polish. Or maybe he meant Polish "ethnics" as opposed to Americans ethnically Polish three or four generations ago. Or perhaps Bush assumed that everyone not White,

Anglo Saxon was ethnic, making him ethnically challenged. And if Bush did have Polish in his ethnic blood, was his mortgage less of worry if he couldn't trace his ancestors?

Ultimately, Bush's failed operations in the Middle East and Quayle's reference to Blacks as "your people" managed to steer away significant minority votes. The winter fell heavy and big changes were in order. There were new promises and fresh expectations. Soon racial gerrymandering would be a key phrase and Clinton would ask the Democratic party to heed the call of "angry White males" at a state convention in Sacramento. "This is a difficult time for a lot of White males, the so-called angry White males. Most of them are working harder for less money than they were 15 years ago. They come home and sit at the dinner table and wonder, 'where did I go wrong?'"

It was then I began to investigate the underlying complexities of our language, trying to understand how certain keywords have been misused and tangled. Even political leaders didn't seem to understand the words they used when it came to race and identity politics. I thought about the words *race, ethnicity, minority, nationality*, and *culture*. The problem was, I discovered, that without clearing up their definitions, we would continue down the spiral of misunderstanding. I contemplated my own race, my own culture and ethnicity. I drew maps of my heritage and played the words in my head over and over again.

Because the concept of different races was created from subjective views from self-serving individuals, the concept of race as purely biological was invalid. The hierarchical division of races had always been one of the worst downfalls of our civilization, and I was not going to play a part in fragmenting myself for political purposes. I was not of many races, in fact, I was of the *same* race as every other human. But my *culture*—my upbringing and environment—was first New York in the United States, then northern Germany, then Central Japan, and finally back to the northeast coast of the United States. So I was, simply, multicultural. I was also multiethnic, with origins spanning the four corners of the world. I was not "ethnic" as in "different" because every human on the planet is ethnic, and has many ethnic backgrounds. I was a United States citizen. I was a minority and majority as well because, in fact, I did encompass so much. I knew America wasn't ready to eliminate racial categories, in fact for the powers that be, the White category still remains at the top. That is when I started thinking about a multiracial category. This way, the government couldn't force anyone to chose just one race. Then maybe, just maybe, we would be able to see each other as sisters and brothers with more similarities in wants and desires than differences.

\* \* \*

"Teja, I can't find a job here," Miguel said. "I have to go somewhere to find work, so, I'm going back to Japan."

Miguel had been out of regular work for most of his 3 years in Boston. His intolerance for the struggle of modern everyday city living was clearly written in his face, even more so in his words. An idealism, maybe even a wisdom was apparent in his frequent harsh criticism and anger. I began to see that he was from a different time and place, an old soul, lost in the jumble of the new world. As brothers, we were often opposite, fighting different battles, but often to the same end. I understood that even as siblings, our cultures were sometimes at odds—our different viewpoints on politics, nature versus man, our social behavior and spiritual practice, the way we communicated, and so on—was proof that even for a whole society, tradition and cultural logic were not inherited, but gained, cultivated, and practiced. Miguel's wish, the same one for most in the Arboleda family, was to belong. A trade-off was not acceptable. All or nothing for Miguel. I only wish I was so optimistic.

"What will you do in Japan?" I asked.

"Teach English, I presume. Maybe try to find work in architecture there. I'm not sure."

"I miss Japan too." I thought of the way store owners in Mejiro swept the sidewalks in front of neighboring shops and the smell of fresh bamboo. Sometimes it hurt to think of the past, of home and family, and now it was painful.

Miguel was tired. He sat with his back slouched and his hands drooped over his knees. "That's our legacy. We'll be remembered as the homeless clan."

I thought of missing him again, and the isolated moments of longing when we lived apart after he left for college the first time. "You think you'll come back?" I asked him, hoping he'd say, without hesitation, "Yes." If he was sure he would come back, I wouldn't feel like I would have to consider leaving America. A "yes" would mean it was okay for me to stay.

"If I come back to America—I don't think I'll be in Japan forever—I'll probably go to the west coast. I really need an Asian influence in my life and I'm just more comfortable in Japan."

"Me too. You'll be closer to Papa, though. That's a good thing." I missed Papa a lot, too. I saw him less and less and thought of how much closer we had become when it was just the two of us—we had become good friends, more than what most of my male friends could say about their relationships with their fathers. If he had stayed truly Filipino according to his father, Grandpa, we would never speak as candidly as we do. In that respect, Papa had relinquished much of his Filipino culture. But the distance between us, and Miguel's pending departure, left me struggling for new meaning in the concept of "family." I wondered if loneliness was a creature that was always alive within us, watching, eating away.

"Maybe Papa and I can finally learn to understand each other," Miguel said.

We bowed our heads and fought back the tears.

"I don't know why things always have to turn out like this." Tears dripped from his chin. "Why can't we just find a nice place, the family, a community ... something."

"I don't think we ever will. It's like a cheap dating service—the Arboledas are a difficult match. You know, I'm learning how to be okay with it."

"Well, I don't want to be okay with it. If I find it, I'll send for you guys."

He returned to Japan that winter, with only a suitcase and a backpack, leaving behind piles of boxes, full of memories, frozen in the darkness of a public storage facility in Waltham. I couldn't help see Miguel's leaving as another circumstance, not choice. "It will all work out," Mama always said. "When?" was always my question.

*  *  *

On the morning of February 14th, Valentine's Day, I kept urging Barbara to leave and not be late for work. I gave her a quick, rather passionless peck and locked the door behind her. After I heard the car start, I ran to the bedroom and began what I had planned for more than 2 months. I pulled out the supply of adhesive glowing stars and stood on the bed. There, under the constellations we had carefully arranged several months before, I measured the distance between Taurus and Aries. Then, one by one, I placed more stick-on stars that spelled out: "MARRY ME."

The day at work went quickly. Often, when in the hallways, friends who knew about my plans for the evening, asked me if I was nervous, if I had the ring, or if she had any idea. I wasn't nervous, the ring was waiting in my dark fuzzy jacket I would wear later that night, and she definitely had no idea.

At about 6:15 p.m. I said my good-byes and wish-me-good-lucks and headed out the door. I waited at the crosswalk for the cars to pass. On my left a van was double-parked and a car waited to get around it. I took a few steps toward the divider line. There were four cars coming from the right, and I calculated that they'd pass soon. A friend waved to me from the other side of the street. I waved back. The four cars from the right passed when suddenly my legs were jolted from the ground. The pavement turned to sky. Streetlights and stars formed strange, squiggly curves in the night sky. For a split second I felt completely free, groundless, without gravity and without pain. Then I instinctively tucked my body in and guarded my head. I bounced off something on my right side, then rolled off what looked like the hood of a car. After I landed I inhaled, grasped the pavement, and let out two primal yops.

I dropped to my side and could think only of my premonition the day before, where I saw myself in a wheelchair. In a panic, I checked to see if I could move my legs. Time accelerated as adrenaline rushed through my veins. There were faces around me, peering. Slowly I began to hear voices. Familiar voices. And what seemed to be seconds must have been minutes because everyone I knew was around me. The ambulance and police were already there. My co-worker, Bob, held my right shoulder and spoke to me. I repeatedly asked him to call Barbara at home to tell her to bring my black jacket.

I looked to my right and saw a car parked in the middle of the street next to me with its windshield smashed in. I remember thinking how vandalism had gotten out of hand in the city, and wondered why, in the age of Black & Decker and designer jeans, would Americans drive a car in that condition. It took me several seconds to realize that my body had gone through the windshield.

Then a woman with a horrified look on her face leaned over me. Her tears landed on my chest. She kept calling out to me, "It's my fault, it's my fault, I'm so sorry." I reached out and held her hand. I told her not to worry, that I was fine. Then the pain started. I grimaced with every throbbing jolt and squeezed the woman's hand even tighter. A bright, blinding light appeared, growing larger and warmer, shimmying like swirling tinsel. I closed my eyes and relaxed. When I opened my eyes again, I was being hoisted into an ambulance.

In traction and a neck brace, I was wheeled toward the x-ray room. In the hallway I heard the sweet voice I was waiting for. Barbara came over to me and smiled. "Ha-ha," I thought to myself, she still didn't know. Then I noticed she brought the wrong jacket. Without the ring how could I ask her? Then I realized the fuzzy jacket I wanted wasn't even black, it was dark brown.

The x-rays looked promising and the doctors said it was miraculous that I was even alive. One physician mentioned that if I wasn't so flexible and light I would have been paralyzed with multiple broken bones and a ruined spine. I did have massive bone bruises and sprained joints, but I was fully conscious. I wanted to cry, not because of the pain but because I kept thinking what Barbara would do if I had died, only to find the ring in my jacket back home, and the message in the stars above our bed.

The nurse, whom I humored by telling her the plans I had for that evening, smiled, shook her head, and told me that by stepping in front of a moving vehicle I was taking severe and unnecessary measures to make a point. I was discharged and ordered to report in the morning.

Barbara was still quite shaken and couldn't stop talking once we got home. I asked her to give us a moment of silence. As I lay on the living room floor, moaning in pain, she poured some wine, lit a candle and some incense. She handed me my Valentine's present, a hardcover copy of *All I Really Need To Know I Learned In Kindergarten*.

I asked her to get the fuzzy jacket from the closet. Then I asked her to sit down on the couch and close her eyes. In a very stupid move, I slowly got to my knees. (How could she say no now?) I produced the ring box, opened it, and faced it toward her. I asked her to open her eyes. Then I asked her to marry me.

When the lights finally went out that night, it took her only a second to read the message in the stars.

The next morning, promptly at 8:30 a.m., I received a call from the driver's insurance company trying to solicit my waiver for insurance coverage. Then 2 days after the accident, at breakfast, as I struggled to raise a spoonful of cereal to my mouth, a severe, swirling headrush threw me to the floor. I was admitted to the hospital immediately and remained there for a week. A stroke was suspected, possibly a blood clot in an artery from the impact of crashing through the windshield. As I lay in my hospital room between tests, I wondered when the driver would show up.

"She's not going to show up, you know," Barbara said. "She's probably been advised by her attorney to claim innocence."

"Yeah, but the police recorded her saying it was her fault."

"But in this country, it's never your own fault. She just doesn't want to be sued."

"I'm not planning on suing her, I just want her to come here and apologize. Isn't she concerned about how I'm doing?"

"I'm sure she is, but her lawyer probably advised her never to visit or contact you. See, I know what you're thinking, sweetie—in Japan her whole family would be here."

"She and her whole family *would* be here. Everyday! Bringing flowers, baskets of food, apologizing in unison, making sure I was taken care of. What the hell is wrong with Americans, can't they take any responsibility for their own actions?"

"In America, even if you're a cop caught on videotape beating a motorist, you're innocent, right?"

"Do you remember, I told you I was back home when the Japan Airlines 747 crashed in the mountains in southern Japan in 1984, and the president of the airline went to each victim's family's home and apologized, bowing on his knees? That's respect and honor for you."

"In America the word 'honor' is reserved for judges."

The next week I hired a lawyer and embarked on what became a two-year battle to receive compensation for the hospital bill.

No respect. No responsibility. No formal apologies. I felt like America had fallen to its lowest standards, where the idealism of individuality had given birth to a selfishness that would feed on itself until the country would be morally bone-dry.

* * *

Bruce and I sat in the corner of the Cambridge restaurant in which we had filmed a video years before. We had both changed so much since then we jokingly looked for wrinkles and signs of wear and tear. Now in our early 30s, we both exuded a confidence that was almost surreal, and not at all a reflection of who we thought we would be.

"I'm changing my name," Bruce said.

I knew instinctively that my food was about to sit idle and get cold in the process of this conversation. "Changing your name? To what?"

He handed me a sheet of paper on which some foreign words—his name, I presumed—were printed.

I stared at the words, and read, "M-b-w-a S-a-u-t-i." What does it mean, what language is it?"

"Mbwa is Swahili for 'dog,' and Sauti means 'voice of my people.' Dogs are faithful and man's friend. I'm going to change it officially."

"Do I call you Mbwa?"

"That's right. Everyone except my immediate family."

"Why?"

"The African people have been subjugated for too long, and as an African, I'm … "

"Since when do you consider yourself African?"

"We have always been African."

"We?"

"And that was taken from us. Nothing will change that. It's just words. My homeland has been raped by Western interests and my people were raped and my culture is still being raped. My former name only served as a reminder of our people's enslavement. My new name at least liberates me from ownership in that respect. Andrews is from Andrew's, the possessive—belonging to some Andrew guy, whoever the fuck he was."

"That I know. Arboleda is not a Filipino name, it's Spanish, by force under the guise of religion and Catholic oppression. But Bruce!"

"Mbwa."

"Mbwa, you've never even been out of the northeast, let alone Africa. How could you be African?"

He pointed to his heart, then his temple. "Africa is in here, and here." Nothing can take that away from us."

"I know *what* you're saying, but I'm not sure if I agree."

"As Africans, we must take back what was taken from us. Our culture, our music, our women." He stroked a green, black, and red flag that he had sewn on his fanny pack. "My country of Africa will soon rise again, and all of our people will be free only then."

"What about, let's say, eighth generation White South African. Are they African?"

"No."

"What are they supposed to do then? What are they?"

"They must find their homelands, and return there. Leave Africa to the African people."

"I don't think that's really possible, do you? That they all just pack up and go back to somewhere in Europe probably, where ethnic conflict and migration has changed the terrain so much you wouldn't even know where to start?"

"That's their problem. They did it to my people too, splitting our land for their greedy capitalist power trips."

"You keep saying 'my people.' Am I no longer one of 'your people?'"

"Your struggle is your own. But we cannot afford a part-time supporter."

"You know, the reason why I consider myself Japanese is because I spent so much time there as a kid, that I not only speak Japanese, but when I'm in Japan, I eat, walk, talk, interact, move, and sneeze Japanese. You have never been to Africa. In fact I have, even if only for a fleeting moment. How can you claim an African culture as your own? Just last year you dreamed of limousines, a mansion, a billion-dollar media production empire, marriage to a German—from Germany, not German-American mind you—and now, suddenly, you embrace Africa and denounce capitalism, and blame everything on White Europeans?"

"I must sacrifice for the betterment of my people."

"I see you made a flag for your fanny pack. What is it?"

"The flag of my people."

"What flag do you think I should have or make?"

"You'll have to decide for yourself. Make one up."

"Can I write my own anthem?"

"Sure. Just don't leave it to Rogers and Hamerstein. You'll end up with a line dance of White women as your intro."

A week later Mbwa brought me to an African paraphernalia shop in Harvard Square. He explained to me the uses of different kinds of drums, their names, and where they were from. His recent collection of library books on African cultures seemed to be paying off. The clerk at the counter completed the transaction for some kind of flute Mbwa had picked up.

"Where are you from?" The clerk looked at me. His accent was heavy and melodic. Before I could arrange my answer into a logical sequence of events, he snapped his finger. "I know, I know. I'll make a guess. You are from ... Egypt?"

I shook my head and looked over at Mbwa.

The clerk studied my face. "Libya? No, Algeria. No. I have a friend in Morocco. You must be from Morocco! What is your name, please?"

"Teja Arboleda."

"But you look like a Moroccan, no?" He smiled at Mbwa. "Doesn't he look like Moroccan?"

Mbwa smiled and looked down at his flute.

"Pray, what is your name, my friend?" the clerk asked Mbwa.

This was the moment of truth I had been waiting for. "Mbwa Sauti."

"Mbwa Sauti! Oh! African name! Swahili! I'm from Ghana. Where are you from, please?"

"Oh ... I'm from here."

"From here?"

"Well, from New Jersey."

"I have never been to New Jersey. It must be a very nice place, this New Jersey."

Later that month, Mbwa called me to tell me he had to change his name again. Apparently the word "Mbwa" suggests, "You are a dog," and that, as a name, would not make as a good a first impression. So he lengthened the name to "Ukumbwa," which vaguely means, "I am a dog."

Ukumbwa filled his apartment with books on African history and politics, African languages, and Pan-African newsletters. He tagged every item in his house with the Swahili translation cards, and cultivated a small African clothing wardrobe. Our staple of comedy routines and talk of television made way for his continued detailed analyses of the struggle of his people. As Ukumbwa pulled away, I felt I was losing the strongest advocate and confidant I ever had. He nodded in communion with darker-skinned brothers and sisters as he passed them on the street and solicited exclusive friendships with others of his kind, rapidly withdrawing from our friendship. Early in the summer of 1992, out of work and frustrated with Boston, he moved back to New Jersey, to his parents' home.

# 23

# The Testimony

I drove east toward the bridge that connects Hilton Head Island to mainland, South Carolina. During slavery, this passage was precarious and rare, leaving the African inhabitants relatively isolated. But now, with a BMW tailgating me at 65 mph, the history of my ancestors mixed with the hot, moist breeze that circulated in my rented hatchback. For a week I would finally be with relatives whom some of my family had been so eager to forget.

The trees were thicker, greener, and lower in the south, caressing the roof of the car as I passed below and swaying in the rearview mirror. Mansions set back behind iron gates clashed with the terrain like Christmas ornaments in July. Then, as if emerging from the It's A Small World ride at Disney World, tin and plywood huts appeared, scattered near the roadway, rusted and stained with mildew. The crass differences between the wealthy and poor sickened me. No doubt, the land of my African forebearers, in all their struggle, was confined by this systemic divisiveness—we live with blinders, trained to see only what we want to see. For me, driving through the stretch of road that brought me to the burial grounds of my heritage, I saw my own image not as a young man but as an old man with stories and echoes of secrets.

It was 2 days before Independence Day and there was already a buzz about this year's annual reunion and celebration. There would be more food, more people, and the certainty of good weather. "It will be a big family reunion, you'll see," Uncle Mark prompted me in his rich Gullah accent. In the warm, southern night sky, bright, crisp stars hung close enough to touch. The freshly watered grass squeaked under my sneakers as we walked outside his house. "A big family we have." He spoke in no rush, and took deep breaths. "Big family. But things are changin' around here. You'll see."

We walked behind the house toward cousin Ann's. In the middle of the open field, he stopped. "Do you see those trees over there?"

I squinted. The moonlight was just bright enough to make out a silhouette of a treeline.

"We've been fightin' for that land since my grandfather passed away. White folks come and take it up. They have been pushing Black folks, Gullah, off the land by raising taxes. White developers told them their land is worth $1 million. But when they refused to sell, taxes skyrocketed. Aunt Ann Marie's cousin Susan? Three years ago she paid $800 in taxes. Now she pays $7,000. Developers go around and measure every inch. And if it's over what records say, they literally move the stones and rocks. So now they build condos and golf courses on the seaside, and their taxes are less! Your Aunt Millie? You'll see her tomorrow. She has been fighting to keep the Gullah graveyard behind her home ever since the White folks decided they want to build a development on top of it."

The next morning I explored the island, videotaping the contrast between the have and have-nots. Fat White tourists in undersized shorts and bright-colored shirts hid behind sunglasses, and clutched tennis raquets. They smiled and laughed a lot, flicking credit cards with the tips of their fingers, while dark-skinned cashiers calculated their own losses.

Hilton Parkway, the main road that travels the length of the island, is graced with manicured lawns, private fountains, grand entrances to former plantation mansions-turned-condos, and sprawling, gated golf courses. Middle-aged White men reclined in electric-powered carts, while Black caddies steered or carried the weight of the game on their backs and shoulders. Not long after, the Clintons would grace Hilton Head, teeing off and waving, blind to the truth that lingered beyond the weeping willows and silverware.

Inside the glamour of the beltway remained the last breath of Hilton Head's Black children. Dilapidated shanties sat dormant, like ducks in the line of fire. Crooked trailers and sad mobile homes tangled in the underbrush lay broken, barely escaping shame in the eyes of the disapproving rich.

At the base of a newly built private school building meant for rich White kids, politics of old were celebrated in fresh asphalt and shiny gravel. A common Gullah graveyard with reminders of a holocaust grew smaller, buried in the enveloping folds between a country club wall and a gas station. Black men and women, out of work, rocked back and forth in the afternoon sun, chiseling their prayers in the air with their defeated breath. Children played on dirt streets, sometimes barefoot, their smiles and laughter a shining moment. Many Blacks travel to the mainland, sometimes remaining there for weeks, to scrub the bidets of White women and the stained collars of their husbands. They hold the White children, nourishing them, while their own remain behind.

But there were others. Black professionals with cedar wood decks and Volvos, a sign of the transplanting times. African names were chic among the young. They recited their names, proud of the sound but often ignorant of the meaning, and only a step from their given name that could never know them. Success was happening, even to some ancestors of the Gullah. For Whites, these Black professionals became shining, necessary examples of the inevitable changing order.

\* \* \*

Aunt Millie fed me well that evening. She had spent the day at the river catching crabs, and now, in her backyard overlooking the graveyard, she ripped their tight skin off, humming gospel songs.

She touched a tiny lung in the crab's innards. "Remember, see this thing? If you eat it you can surely die. Learn how to remove it, and you'll live forever."

Her house consisted of two sandwiched mobile trailers on stilts. "For when it rains," she explained, pointing at the long iron poles that held up the units. "Now, get inside and eat my food."

The crab and dough fused, rolled over, and bounced in a pool of boiling oil. "Your father, Bobby, used to love these. It was hard to find in New York, but when I used to take care of him, I fattened him up! Now look at you! You're so skinny, all bones, just like your daddy when he was when he was a kid. He was such a good boy, very obedient, quiet—he just loved my crabs and fish, and he always finished all the food on his plate. So if you don't finish what I'm making here, I'm going to have to smack you!"

The next morning, after an equally filling breakfast, she took me on a tour of the graveyard. Broken clocks, glass, and metal lay strewn over each grave, traditional Gullah reminders of the deceased and their few possessions. "It's been vandalized, though, I don't know who, but every year, there are less reminders, pieces missing, clocks disappearing. Now they want the land for greed. It's getting more difficult every year to fight and I'm going to get old someday."

Later in the day I met with Uncle John and his son David who were both excited to show me a letter they had received a week earlier. "Look, it's from a Driessen ... in Michigan! He is putting together a family tree from all over the country, and he wants us to write back. I wonder if he knows we're Black! We should invite him down here and see what he says!"

"No," said David, "he probably already knows. He just wants to complete the tree. But how do you know he's White?"

"He's in Michigan! We don't have any relatives in Michigan. I know my family and I know where they all went. I'm 71 years old!"

Copies of the letter had been passed around, and were causing a stir for those Driessens who were planning the July 4th reunion. There was talk about "the White Driessen," which led to discussions about who was darker and lighter, who had more White blood and who was probably closest to the anonymous relative in the north.

Denise Green, her brother George, and her father-in-law, Charles invited me over for lunch that afternoon. They welcomed me in Denise's house, full of interest in my research.

Charles started with slow-building emotion. "Your Grandpa Federico used to come over on weekends and fish with me, you know. That was when he first married your Grandma. Federico was always very stern, I remember he never laughed. That was when I had a farm, you know, sold much of it since then, actually had to because of the taxes. But I remember everybody's name—you see, that is how important family is to me. I will always remember the name and face, and your father, Amadio—Bobby we all called him—came here too, when he was a little one."

George stared at me intently, studying my face, while Denise nodded her head. "You know," she said, "we've been able to keep the family together pretty well—we have hundreds here every year for the reunion, but the rich Whites are killing us. The highway used to be a simple one lane, two-way road. Today it's a two-lane highway and now they want an elevated highway so they can tee off 30 seconds earlier. They left no sidewalks and you can't cross the street. Half our family is across that damn street. You have to drive 10 minutes and do a U-turn to get there now!"

"Resorts!" George belted. "Golf supply stores, surf shops, Burger Kings, bankers and lawyers, car dealers!"

"Whites tell the Blacks, 'Well, *your* living is better and you got jobs! Got cars and live in better homes!' Better homes? What, from a shack to a plastic trailer?"

"While they got their condos and private pools," George said, pointing out the window.

Denise nodded her head rapidly. "We're losing our land and livelihood. No more hunting and fishing, which we depended on for generations, because it's all private now! No trespassing signs, you know? No more farming. Now we gotta buy our food from the supermarkets who take our food from the rivers."

"There is a lot of anger," Charles said. "It is not apparent, and a lot of alcoholism. They hide their frustration about the Whites pushing them off their land, but when they get going ... ! We only have one Black councilman and he is not taken seriously. He knows why he's there. See, we've been poor, but we managed. Slavery, the Depression, war, resorts, racism. And we are still poor. They got their big White hands all over us, dividing us. Now, how do you know you're poor until someone tells you or shows you?"

"Ahmhm." Denise shook her head, her jaw stretched out in contemplation. "You know, I came from the mountains of South Carolina to get married on Hilton Head. Now you look at me, what do you see? I've got light brown skin like you, so when I came, all the Blacks say, 'What 'chu bringin' roun' a buckra here for?' Buckra means White—you don't want to say that word—well, they thought I was White! I'm a lot darker now, but I'm still an outsider to the native Blacks, just like the Whites from Hilton Head—they also have a tough time proving they're from the island. Now you get some of our own blood into fighting about 'who is Whiter, who is lighter, and who is brighter. And then, who is darker.' Do you see what I'm saying?" She folded her arms. "So, how do you feel on the island?"

"How do I feel?" I asked.

"What do you think people think of you?"

"What do *you* think of me. I mean, I think I know what they're thinking—they know I'm not White, but, 'is he Black?'"

"If I didn't know you I would think you're Asian. Like Federico, your Grandfather, you're only a little bit dark, but Asian. And certainly you're not as dark as any of us! But also I can see you have Black blood."

"So, should I not say anything?"

"You mean, should you not bring it up at the reunion? No. Unless they do. But they know who you are, just don't be hurt if some of them don't say hello right away."

This was the moment I had waited for and suddenly I felt ashamed. I wanted so much to be accepted, especially in the part of the family that had been shunned for so long. George knew my answer and so did the others, but it wasn't a matter of "yes" or "no," all they wanted was honesty.

George rubbed his hands over his face and took a deep breath through his fingers. "But why did you all forget us?"

A cool breeze filtered through the screen door to the backyard. Right then, I was closer to home but further away from myself than I had ever been.

"I didn't even know you existed."

"So, you shocked?" George asked, leaning back. He was testing me.

"At what?" I asked.

"Did you know we were Black?"

"No. I didn't," I said. "And frankly, I never even think about it. At least not until I was in college. When we were kids, I always suspected Grandma Isabella was Black. But no one ever said so. They said she was a Filipina."

"You know, George, I never really thought about these things until I was older. No one ever told me about you. And since I grew up in Japan, we were away from the family, so I never really got to know Grandma or Grandpa. If I was told she was something other than Black, and I was 5 years old, how would I know the difference? I'm here now, and I'd like to clear this, set it straight. I want to get to know this side of the family. I mean, in my case, I was taught you're not Black until someone tells you."

The next morning I woke up late and nervous. Over breakfast, I went through my notes and studied the family tree. I quizzed myself on names and connections, fretting over details. How was I going to do this? I couldn't possibly catch up in 3 days what my family had suppressed for all those years. There I was, a long-lost Arboleda in the middle of cousins and distant relatives and a total stranger.

By the time I arrived at the reunion, the acre-sized yard was filled with people, the older folks sitting under the tents and the younger ones on the lawn, dancing and eating. Esther's house, where this event took place every other year, was crammed with relatives coming and going, taking naps, and admiring the growth of the children. Outside, a team managed seven grills and huge pots of boiling oil, dunking fish, crabs, and chicken on skewers. Almost 300 relatives, all dark, beautiful, and alive, danced and feasted. I was visibly out of place and was regarded cautiously.

"So, who are you related to?" a woman asked, looking me up and down.

"I'm Bella Driessen's grandson."

"Oh, I didn't realize she married a White man."

"Well, technically she did. He was Filipino."

"Oh, okay, so."

"Well, my mother is German."

"Hey, you know, so was Henry Driessen. You know, the White man. Great-great grandfather Driessen."

"Yes, I've seen his photographs in everyone's house."

"Uhmhm. Now, meet my daughter. Lukresha? Come here, baby. Meet your cousin ... Teja."

Lukresha, in the middle of dancing with her girlfriends, hopped over to us. "Hi! What's your name?"

"Teja."

"Oh yeah, you're the one from China. But you look Puerto Rican or something. Your Mama's a White woman they say?"

"Ah ... yeah."

"So, are you surprised your relatives are ... this way?"

"Maybe you're surprised to find me ... this way."

"Uhmhm hm hm. Well, I just wanna know if you can dance." She smiled. Her friends laughed, slapping their knees.

"Of course I can dance."

"You know, we wanna make sure you still got some of this in you." She gyrated her pelvis and her friends shrieked, "You go, Lukresha!"

"White boy's got no rhythm and they got stiff butts. If you can't dance, you're a White boy." Lukresha started back to her group. "You dance, you're in."

The D.J. faded songs from L. L. Cool J to Prince. I joined Lukresha and her cohorts on the patch of dirt where they danced.

"Hey, now you talkin', Mr. I'm-not-really-Black-but-I'm-Black-Chinese man!" Lukresha chided. "Now, move your butt some more, we wanna see some butt!"

I moved my butt to the music and clowned ever so slightly. Some people pointed at me, and talked, sometimes smiling, laughing, well-intentioned.

The women's comments made me feel conscious about my lack of body mass and to remedy this situation, I was fed the greasiest of crabs, fish, hot buns, and beans. The men invited me to drink wine and beer, making me tipsy but unconditionally happy. I sat with the elderly under the tent, answering questions about my family connection. I mingled with young adults and talked about current issues, politics, and race relations.

I met David in the living room of the house. He wore a yellow and green dashiki and a subdued green hat and sat at a round table with about seven others. I stood on the periphery, watching as they listened to David intently, with respect and genuine inquisitiveness. The group discussed pan-African issues and David's tours as a guide for trips to Africa and the middle passage. His voice was commanding, crisp as he illustrated his recent voyages to investigate his roots. Fascinated, I joined the group, sitting two people over from David. He didn't acknowledge me at first, but then he changed the focus of his speech to the condemnation of White Europe.

"So, what do you do?" he asked me. His eyes never left the table in front of him.

"Well, I formerly worked in television, but now I'm working on a play about my heritage."

"Ahmhm. What sparked your interest?"

"Well, I wanted to tell the story of my rich cultural backgrounds."

"And which backgrounds are those?

"German, Filipino, African, and Japanese."

"So, what are you? You're not Black, that's pretty obvious."

"Well, actually, I'm a mixture. Besides, if I wanted to call myself Black, I should be able to do so, shouldn't I? Or German, for that matter."

"You know, the Germans don't really have a culture. Not like the Blacks have their African culture. Your culture is in your blood, brother."

"I don't fully agree. I believe some groups of people have a stronger connection to their ancestral culture than others, but that's circumstantial, environmentally based. If you were adopted by White parents, what would you be?"

His lips formed a smile, then quickly disappeared. "We have held onto our culture despite all the obstacles. We are stronger than ever and we still don't get the respect we deserve. Take for example the Jewish people. Many claim they had been persecuted more than any other people, that more of their people were tortured, raped, and massacred than any other, so they deserve all the compensation and a homeland! That would be nice! Well, what about Africans or Native Americans? You know, Jesus was Hebrew, and Hebrews were a Black people. They were dark like Abraham. But you won't find *that* in the Bible."

The buzz of conversation continued into the evening. By nightfall, almost everyone had left, the music had died and a multitude of fireflies dotted about, their brightness competing with that of the stars. I finally said good-bye at 12:00 a.m., drained but happy. I only hoped I carried the weight necessary to make up for many years of neglect.

\* \* \*

"Rise and shine young man, got food waiting for you here!" Aunt Millie called out to me and made scraping sounds on her large blackened iron pan. "Too bad you had crab and fish yesterday, because that's what we're having here today." She squinted her eyes and studied me in her peripheral vision. "I don't want to hear any of the vegetarian stuff you folks up in Boston eat, no, no, no, no. You eat everything up, or I'm going to have to come over there and," she waved a spatula at me.

I played with the grits and greasy bun and the oil ran down my fingers. I figured that for a few days this heavenly food couldn't hurt my normally low-fat diet.

I thought of how people often referred to the food they eat as an emblem of their culture. In Massachusetts I had been on a diet of spaghetti for 7 years. Certainly through my sustenance I didn't inherit Italian culture, language, or art. Besides, pasta was invented in China, and here, under the direct order of Aunt Millie, I was to bring some of Hilton Head back to Boston.

Aunt Millie wiped her hands on her apron and pulled out a piece of paper from her pants pocket. "Now, lookit' here. I got a call this morning from the Danish Driessen gentleman in Michigan. He wants those questionnaires filled out for his research, uhmhm. So he looked up my number in the telephone book, and guess what? He called me! So I asked him if he knew we were Black and he said he knew! Isn't this exciting! You know, maybe he can come down next year for the reunion! We're going to have to send him pictures of us immediately!"

She returned to her cooking, smiling. She broke the lull of her gospel humming with shouted questions. "Are you eating? If I don't hear you chewing while you're talking, you're not enjoying it. So, am I going to have to stuff it in your mouth?"

"Aunt Millie," I said, "Your food is the best in the south. In fact, I would drive from Boston to this table for breakfast every morning if I could. Now, it's a good thing I don't live too close because you'd fatten me up so much I'd get no more acting work!"

After breakfast we sat on the porch and she told me about the earlier days growing up in the south, migrating to the north for odd jobs and finally returning to Hilton Head. To her, the island was more than a home. In her words, it was God's choice, a spiritual connection that was rivaled by no other feeling. She would die on her land, maybe even be buried with her ancestors behind her home. She was part of the last generation of her kind, fighting a losing battle with an enemy that always was.

I traveled down the road to interview Uncle Jacob. In his mobile home, set back from the highway, we sat and talked in his eat-in kitchen, barely conscious of the slow, gentle angling of the sunlight over the tabletop. He had been around longer than most on the island. Lean, wise and without an ounce of fat on his body, he was well into his 80s. His hands were tough and his eyesight keen, and he rambled on for 2 hours about the evolving landscape he called home. In his younger days he had raised pigs, chickens, turkeys, and cows; fished for profit and sustenance; and cleared rattle-snakes from the yards of White folks. He was from the days of herbologists and medicine men, when Blacks owned almost all the land, when most didn't have glass windows and had to stave away mosquitoes with cow manure and smoke. His means of survival had been minimized by real estate development, and now had to rely on buying shrink-wrapped fish and crabs from his own streams in the glossy aisles of neighboring supermarkets. Some days he supplemented his income through odd day jobs, hauling junk and building fences and walls for newcomer White folks. His smile changed me when I asked him if he was angry with the blatant racism and a hard life. "I thank God everyday for the sun that comes up," he answered. "Then I thank him again every night before I sleep."

*  *  *

On the last full day of my stay I said my good-byes and drove the length of the island one last time. Access to the ocean was mostly private, and I found myself irritated and claustrophobic. I finally found an open field where a Black child and his grandfather were flying a kite. I thought I recognized them from the reunion, but I wasn't sure. I lay on the grass and watched the clouds transform and glide like amoebas. Each moment I identified and named a cloud, but it changed shape, fusing, and separating like a soul with no home. For the first time, I saw myself in the clouds, not as a body, but more like a player: changing, moving, and wandering the planet. I thought, if spirits are carried by the clouds that travel the globe and if my spirit has seen many lives, then I have traveled the world hundreds, maybe thousands of times void of borders.

# One

It was the year hate rose up from the ashes of blame and scapegoating, licking its lips, hungry again.

It was the year of the Los Angeles riots. Race relations exploded in a fiery mayhem, leaving the nation afraid and exhausted.

It was the year David Duke, a former Klansman with two face-lifts, became a national figure by playing on White paranoia, then running for president.

It was the year Louisiana resident Rodney Pieres aimed a .44 caliber magnum revolver and blew open the chest of a Japanese boy asking for directions in a Halloween costume.

It was the year France's LePen stirred up his right-wing National Front Party crowd, echoing his hostility toward dark-skinned Muslim Arab and African immigrants.

It was the year Italy's Senator Umberto Bossi gained party platform for his Lombard League by denouncing dark-skinned immigrants.

It was the year Serbian President Slobodan Milosevic led his people to war in the name of a virulent ethnic nationalism.

It was the year that Austria's Jörg Haider declared that the Nazis "had a proper employment policy in the Third Reich," boosting his Austrian Freedom Party to a higher share.

It was the year a unified Germany's hate crimes soared: A Mozambican immigrant thrown out of trolley car to his death in Dresden; a Vietnamese nearly stabbed to death in Leipzig; stone-throwing skinheads converged on a Soviet-Jewish children's home; a mob in Rostock besieged and burned a house for asylum seekers to the applause of 2,000 bystanders.

It was also the year Barbara and I married.

* * *

Just as the heat from Los Angeles settled in Massachusetts, we arrived in Germany. I could have shown Barbara every corner of Hannover that night—the detailed architecture of the buildings, the magnificent gardens, the smooth, granite cobbled streets, the old town center. I was a little kid again, and I remembered that I always dreamed of walking with my wife down the streets of old Hannover.

Opa turned Oma's wheelchair to face us as we entered their apartment. Oma broke into tears and touched my face, her soft fingers like refugees from a lifetime of factory work. She looked me straight in the eyes and caressed her soft, frail hand on my cheek. Then she took Barbara's face and studied it and smiled, nodding her head. Opa shook my hand tightly and he gave Barbara a kiss on the cheek.

"*Are you tired, are you hungry?*" Opa slurred, fighting his age and gravity.

Oma slowly raised her hand and pointed to a plate of leberworst on the dining table.

Opa picked up the plate and sniffed the meat. "*Smells good, Teja, Barbara, real German Leberworst, your favorite, I bought it this morning just for you.*"

Opa squeezed the liver paste from its sausage tube and handed me the plate. "*You're skinny like your mother. Barbara is too skinny also. Eat.*"

Oma nodded her head and chuckled. Less than 1 year ago following the stroke, she lost her command of speech and mobility on the right side of her body. As a couple, they were lucky—Opa was one of the only remaining men in the old age home and was still capable caring for her. Still, it was clear that he would remain alive only as long as she would.

Opa leaned over to Barbara. "*Where is your family from?*

Barbara looked at me. "He slurs his words. What did he say?"

"He wants to know your heritage. *Opa, do you mean her grandparents? She has some German background.*"

"*See, I told you all along, Teja—German women are the best!*"

Oma giggled and struggled to wave him away.

Opa lit up a cigarette. "*So, you're going to Czechoslovakia for your honeymoon? Why would anyone go to Czechoslovakia for a honeymoon?*"

Oma looked at me and waved Opa's comment off again.

"*You're still smoking? We wanted to see part of Eastern Europe before everything changes,*" I said. "*We're going to East Berlin, too.*"

Opa took a long drag from his cigarette and coughed hard. Oma waved away the smoke. "*Do you remember we took you and Miguel to a gated border near the mountains and you stuck your hand in through the big chained fence and taunted the guards? Oma thought they were going to take you into the east and make you a good little communist soldier.*"

Oma turned red and shook on the edge of laughter. Her eyes became glossy and her cheeks became flushed. Opa smiled and took another drag. *"Now you want to go there and say 'hello?' You're just like your mother."*

*"We'll be back in a week, and then we'll take our time here."*

*"Just don't be late for your party—everyone's excited to see you."*

*   *   *

We hopped on the sleeper car and inspected the blankets and pillows on the top two bunks. An elderly woman joined us in the compartment and took a bed on the floor level. As we headed southeast, our jet lag got the better of us, and we fell asleep to the rhythmic rumble of the train.

*"Wake up please, passports, please!"* Two police officers stood inside our cabin with clipboards and walkie-talkies.

We produced our passports and handed them one of the officers.

"What time is it?" I asked Barbara.

"5:30."

"We must be at the border."

The officers handed back Barbara's and the woman's passports. They held mine up to the light, shook their heads, and then left the cabin.

Barbara's eyes widened. "Where are they going with your passport?"

"Don't know," I said. "I don't think I want to spend a night alone in an iron curtain jail cell."

"That's not funny, Teja. We're on our honeymoon. We'll go together, you know, get the honeymoon suite."

*"Good morning!"* The woman spoke in German. *"They're just overly sensitive, that's all. You'll be all right. And if not, I'll take care of it. I'm from Prague. I know these things."*

*"Good morning,"* I said. *"You speak German. Have you been in Germany long?"*

*"I am now a German citizen and I just visited my son. My home is in Prague. Sometimes I stay in Prague, sometimes I stay in Germany. All the same."*

The policemen returned. One stood at the door and the other walked up to my bunk. He spoke in German. *"Where is your other passport?"*

*"My other passport?"*

*"This passport is no good."*

The other officer came into the compartment, flipped through my passport, and pulled at my photograph. They switched to Czech. *"No."* They walked out again.

The woman whispered to me. *"They think it's fake."*

They came back again, this time a third officer stood at the door. *"Do you speak German?"* they asked the woman in Czech. *"Please translate."*

*"They want some other identification with a picture,"* the woman said.

I pulled out my driver's license from my wallet and handed it to the officer. He looked at it, then passed it to his partner behind him.

*"Okay. You can go,"* he said and handed me back my documents.

I looked at Barbara. "Wow—I can't even get a drink at a bar in Massachusetts with my passport. But a driver's license? I wonder that says about our national identity?"

After the police left, the woman offered us each a peach. *"So, you're going to Prague for vacation? That's very interesting. As you know, Czechoslovakia is changing very quickly. It's good you are going now."*

We arrived at Hlavni Nadrazi, one of the main train stations in Prague. There, we sought out apartment rental solicitors. Within 1 minute we were haggling over rental prices with a tall, slender old man with deep wrinkles named Bedřich Hruska, who spoke in broken German. He took us by subway to his station chatting all the way.

The apartment building was dark gray, flushed with cracks and crumbling concrete. His unit was about the size of the average bachelor pad in Tokyo. It had an entry space with an electric stove and some bottles of tea bags. The main room was large enough for a twin bed, a small table, and a standing clothes closet. In the bathroom he turned on the shower. *"Look, hot water!"* Water trickled, gushed out, then leveled off. His smile broadened and his shoulders straightened as he sucked in his pride. *"Now, if there's no hot water, just wait, it will come!"* He handed me the keys. *"Now, on the last day, I will come and you can give me the keys."*

One hour later we headed back downtown. The train glided on the rails as if on ice through well-lit tunnels. Other passengers studied us with cautious measure. One boy was particularly interested in my green jeans, and a little girl was fascinated with Barbara's flowery pastel shirt.

The subway system was in plain contrast to the order of the city. The ticket vending machines were quick and easy to operate, large information signs were clearly labeled in four languages, and on the platforms, digital clocks displayed the exact time remaining before the arrival of the next train. I thought of the debris and rodent-infested, illogical, and unpredictable mass transit systems in urban jungles like Boston and New York. I don't know why I always expect more of a superpower like the United States—I thought I would have gotten used to it by now. And here, looking like an arrogant, rich foreigner in new jeans, I only wished I could explain to the passengers how embarrassing it was to come from the wealthiest country in the world, where public transportation smelled and operated like a garbage truck.

We emerged from the subway onto a main street. Old, ornamental buildings bursting with architectural intricacies remained the color of soot covered with decades of neglect. The only color was in the army of foreign tourists in bright T-shirts and neon-colored sneakers running about, snapping pictures with their plastic throw-away cameras.

We broke away from the trendy sights and wandered the back streets. Quirky, compact houses and apartments squeezed together like huddled children on twisting, cobbled streets. Layers of paint as different as the ages peeled and cracked along the edges of iron framed windows. A Coca-Cola can sat comfortably on the ledge of a stucco wall, and a crow perched in a tiny tree in the courtyard of a family graveyard. Prague had kept its beauty well, but it was only a matter of time before money and the West would change everything.

We ate in faraway neighborhood restaurants under the watchful eye of residents where the food was meek and fatty. There were no tourists here, and at once, the true story of Prague's condition was pictured with broken windows, a war-torn cripple, and a tattered homeless woman with her child.

But at the center of the well-planned attraction, Prague teased its residents with the beat of Western pop culture. Here, one floor below the apartment where Kafka weaved his tales of horror, a brilliant café flourished at his feet. Blocks away, Mozart settled, wrote *Don Giovanni*, and claimed, "Yes, my Praguers understand me." One year after Hollywood's *Amadeus* was released in major theaters in America, MTV teenagers flocked to pay him homage.

Karl's Bridge reached over the Vltava River to Prague Castle, and the water below rose and rushed, almost washing away its own name in a tide of Westernization. Kiosks and flamboyant booths lined its bulging middle, streamers hung with masking tape from elegant gargoyles, and sale signs covered the curves of its sensual lamp posts. A chubby little kid in U.S. fatigues balanced a family-sized ice cream cone. A German couple grabbed lustfully at each other, catching the attention of young locals.

We wormed our way through the crowd toward some live music that sounded all too familiar. There, at the apex of the bridge, was a group of American kids in tie-dyed shirts, flowing skirts, and sandals, performing an Arlo Guthrie tune. A cardboard sign next to a metal can read, "Need a miracle, drop a Korun, drop a Mark."

"What, is The Dead in town?" I asked Barbara. I thought of the groupies Todd and I had bumped into in Salt Lake City, Utah.

"I guess so," she said, raising her eyebrows. "Why else would these kids be here?"

"Maybe they're as lost as I am."

As the world seemed to grow smaller, American culture grows larger.

They finished the song and the crowd clapped. We left when the singer acknowledged his audience and pointed to the coin drop. "Thank you. All we need is enough to get back to America."

On street corners and in parks, we listened to the old and young debating the future of the country. Within a week the country was going to vote for a split. Czechoslovakia would become two separate countries, divided by language and heritage. Soon after, Western venture capitalists would storm into the city, dividing it even further, leaving Prague to stumble for its lost identity forever, another victim of the West.

* * *

As our train rushed west toward Berlin, the roots of old Europe flashed by like a stream of abstractions. Rich green fields, sprawling farms, and ancient villages converged and disappeared with the dirt roads that connected them as the train sped north into a newly freed country. Stucco and wood-framed houses with red tile roofs flanked the banks of the Elbe River. The former East Germany was alive, visible and as real as its people.

Berlin, in full bloom of dichotomies and contrasts, thrived in the aftermath of communism, with tourists pouring over the concrete reminders of a country still wrestling in two worlds. The façade of success, decorated in painted brick and glass, roamed the periphery of what was the East, like a mirror of the West, looking in. In ashen decay behind this layer of icing lay the reality of a society in distress. And on the rim between these former enemy lines, brief stubbles of the wall jutted up in shock, like sudden souvenirs for photo opportunities.

Only steps away, lovers strolled through the *Tier Garten*, a large public park that butted up against what was the Wall. We roamed the luscious gardens, hand in hand, imagining the defeat of the millions who were separated by greed and politics. Then, out from a grove of bushes, strolled a completely naked man, reading a book and walking as if in the privacy of his own bedroom.

Barbara cupped her mouth with her hands, quenching a squeal. "Oh my God! That man is … !"

"Oh, look at that," I said, nonplussed. "Don't worry, he won't bite—this is Germany."

Barbara's eyes were as big as her interest. In the clearing lay a group of naked picnickers, breasts and penises hanging out with the mustard and cheese. With her hands still wrapped over her mouth, Barbara bent over and laughed uncontrollably.

"You know, it's the Puritan Americans that have a hang-up with body parts and they call themselves European. Bah!"

"Yeah, but ... "

"There's nothing to be ashamed of, especially not *that* guy. I just wonder what the Germans beyond the wall would have thought."

"I wonder what my mother would think—she's got mostly a German background."

"Well, obviously something happens when you cross the Atlantic Ocean. Most Americans who like to boast their German heritage don't know anything about it."

"So, you can be butt-naked in any park?" Barbara asked, looking back at the display of flesh on a bed of grass, like ham on a tossed salad.

"Not every park, not everywhere."

"Women can't even breastfeed in public in America or burn a bra. That's like burning the flag."

"You know, in Japan, a woman can breastfeed in public," I said. "It's considered natural, normal. In fact, public baths are sometimes open to both sexes. Body parts aren't necessarily seen as sexual."

"At least, not when it's taking place *in* Japan," said Barbara, pointing to a man aiming a videocamera at three naked women lying under a tree. The back of his T-shirt read in Japanese, "Losing is for weaklings. Japan Kayaking Club."

Downtown Berlin was like New York City on a good day. Quick-gated business professionals negotiated sidewalks strewn with drug addicts wilting on park benches. Homeless people begged for change and store-display video monitors blasted the latest music video hit. Teenagers ordained with spiked, neon hair and pierced navels dragged on cigarettes while mothers kissed their babies in frilly-laced carriages. High rises, corporate towers, chic restaurants, and peep shops crammed for space. Nouveau riche college students in black silk sampled the latest beer and a McDonald's employee washed the yellow plastic logo below the over-hang.

"Just like America," I said.

Barbara nodded. "Just like Germany."

We took a table outside a small restaurant whose interior was plastered with photographs of famous people who had been patrons. With my coffee, the waitress gave me several packs of sugar. On the cover of one of the packs was the name of the coffee and a cartoon depiction of three Black sambo dolls with protruding lips and the big white of their eyes.

"Just like America," I said.

"Just like Germany."

That night we went to see Barbara Streisand's version of *Prince of Tides* at a local movie theatre. A soft-drink commercial preceding the previews depicted three sexy young campers being chased by a group of angry dark-skinned natives with large bones in their noses, loin-cloths, and spears. The campers were caught, then barely escaped being cooked up in a large iron pot. The tag read: *Afri Cola—no comfort without danger.* The audience laughed, spilling popcorn and dignity. I grabbed my armrest, my knuckles white, and proceeded to watch the movie in anger. Why couldn't Barbara Streisand have picked a Black man, an Asian, or some other kind of man to play her lover? Would it really be that difficult? Just for Germany? Just for America? How narrow-minded could we all possibly be? I thought about Woody Allen and Steven Spielberg and how close-minded people like them must be, unable to acknowledge the existence of the diverse cultures and people that made their fortunes possible. I felt sorry for the studio executives, the filmmakers, and advertisers, burdened with negative karma from ignorance and racism. And I felt guilty, paying for their successes.

\* \* \*

Oma brushed her hand over mine and cried. Barbara gave Opa a kiss on both cheeks. *"You married a wonderful woman, Teja. We waited for this moment for a long, long time."* During the last 3 days in Germany, our reminiscing was sweet, like the kind words of a final farewell. I would never see them again.

\* \* \*

Returning to the United States from a foreign country is somehow more abrasive than leaving. Quietly, we readjusted, catching up with news and acquainting ourselves with domestic married life.

The ills and ignorance of society spilled forth in my writing. The blatant irresponsibility of popular culture killed me slowly, like a social cancer turning my hopes for the worse. Billboards, television ads, radio, Howard Stern, Rush Limbaugh, Disney, Hollywood, *Baywatch*, Al Franken. I discovered that my rage was unmanageable in its little cocoon, the soul of an artist's fury. I swore I would take on the world, turn the tide of the racist wall of Al Franken's legacy and beat the fires of hate. In our travels, something had flashed, like a shiny nail on the skin of a balloon. Growing, from one in millions, I would march forward with a final warning. *We are closing in, we are closing in.* Tomorrow would be too late, the world would have changed and where would we be but lost? In 20 years most Americans will no longer be what many choose to refer to as a pure White majority—a fact reflecting the inevitable, beautiful, necessary, and good. I would say again with confidence, "We are closing in."

In July 1994, I testified at the Senate hearings on Directive No. 15: Race and Ethnic Standards. I concluded my speech with fire in my belly, "I argue that the multiracial category be included in the year 2000 census. In the end, the government has no right to limit people to one simple box. America certainly is not ready for the elimination of race categories defined by skin color, facial features, or other common biological differentials, but at least we can take a step forward to support the millions of Americans who don't consider themselves one race. Look at my face, just *look* at my face. Can you honestly say, without disgrace, that there is such a thing as a pure culture or pure race? I rest my case."

# Cool Winds Return Home

Grandpa *had* achieved his version of the American dream. His family had survived thousands of miles of isolation; now here, he had constructed his American dream. Under one roof, in America, he had a big car and a big television. But dreams can only live with eyes closed. When he opened his eyes, he was spit at, shoved, neglected, avoided. He was called "Kook," "Chink," "China-man," even "Nigger" by other White Americans, yet he never realized that his family in the heart of New York City was the catalyst in turning his neighborhood brown. Outside, on the driveways and in garages, the neighborhood packed up, leaving their homes in regret and defeat to dark-skinned home-buyers.

He was getting old and knew he could never return home again. All he ever really wanted to do was to live and die in the Philippines, and here in America he was dwarfed by all that surrounded him. He never learned to settle down. As he tried to become the perfect American, he aged, void of roots and culturally naked.

It was in 1983, in the middle of a college winter when it happened. I was asleep in my room, warm under the covers. At about 3:30 a.m. I felt a cool breeze brush across my body. I sat up sharp and looked around. The windows were shut tight. Then I felt the breeze again. I knew something happened far away, but I didn't know what. When I finally fell back asleep, I dreamed of flying over a large body of land just under thickening clouds.

The next morning Papa called, then Miguel called. They had experienced the same cool breeze, at 4:30 p.m. for Papa in Tokyo, and 11:30 p.m. for Miguel in Oregon. Grandpa had died exactly at that time. And he had come to visit us. According to Filipino tradition, a spirit visits the family of the deceased in the form of a cool breeze.

Grandma died shortly after. Her diabetes had gotten worse and the pain of her cancer made her cry out. She decided to return to Hilton Head Island to seek solace among her people. No more hiding, no more lies, no more secrets. There in the stale room of a nursing home, she remained for the last 2 months of her life.

She had been ridiculed, brainwashed, and tormented by self-hatred, and yet she rose above the barriers in the few moments of clarity in the end. A head nurse. A caring mother. A devoted human. A Black survivor.

To survive the torment of the color of her skin, to suffer the gift of intellect and beauty in a world that judged her by her heritage, to endure the isolation from family and the loneliness of a loveless marriage, and to die proudly, in the arms of her ancestors, Grandma was finally home.

Oma died in 1995, and Opa died soon after. He had stayed alive long enough to care for her, and then, the purpose of living ended. The longest marriage a couple could have, full of love, support, challenges, and reconciliations.

And secrets.

The day after Opa died, Mama left New York city for Hannover to take care of the funeral. The day after the funeral, Mama's cousins, aunts, and uncles told her for the first time that Opa was not her biological father. There remains no one who can recall who her real father was. He could have been anyone, they said. Italian, Russian, whatever, but the man who raised her, Opa, loved Mama like she was his own child.

\* \* \*

I thought of all the secrets and the lies that transcend the physical body we call family. Like the ever-changing shape of a young cloud: growing, melting, rising, and falling back to earth like the tears of another generation.

\* \* \*

When I die, will I know the truth of who I am, where I came from, and where I'm going?

# Home

"I don't know where I'm going to end up, Teja. I really don't know." Mama adjusted her leather pants that had expanded in the dry heat of our kitchen. The snow outside drifted in the wind like a million nomads. "I'm glad I bought my little plot of land on Isla Mujeres, but I don't think I can retire in Mexico—what would I do? Maybe I could open a little shop on the island, for tourists … I don't know. My friend Donna moved to Costa Rica—said the economy was fine, I could find a house cheap, and there's free health care."

"Costa Rica? Now, what ever happened to India?"

"Oh, no—the heat."

"You could always retire in Germany."

"No. I'm not going back to Germany. The antiforeigner attitude would be too much for me to handle. Besides, people are too stiff there."

"Well, I guess it's the States, then," I said. "But do you think you'll stay in New York City? I mean, really."

"Well, it's very cosmopolitan, there are people from all over the world speaking different languages, there are always things to do, you know. I mean Boston is a desert in that respect."

Barbara leaned back and folded her arms. "In Boston you're not *allowed* to speak a different language. But just because New York has that, it doesn't mean people actually *speak* to one another."

Mama picked at her scrambled eggs. "I don't know."

\* \* \*

"I'm engaged!" Miguel's voice carried his eagerness well over the 12,000 miles of telephone signal. "Yumi and I are getting married!"

He had mentioned her only a couple of times, and I hadn't expected it would get this serious.

247

"She's Japanese!" I said. It was inevitable, I thought, that one of us would marry a Japanese woman. "You're marrying a Japanese!"

"No. She's Brazilian."

Stupid me. After all this time, traveling with my show and workshops, teaching people how to disprove stereotypes—to blunder like this! Well, better with my brother than a client. "Oh, you mean, Japanese-Brazilian."

"From Sao Paulo. She works here in the factory where I teach English."

"So, do you speak in Japanese, English?"

"Mostly Japanese, but her Japanese isn't very good, which is really a problem here because they think she's Japanese. She's teaching me Portuguese and I'm teaching her English."

In the late 1950s, during redevelopment after World War II, the working poor of Japan immigrated to an economically powerful Brazil. Soon, Sao Paulo would become the second largest community of Japanese outside of Japan, and bring to Sao Paulo a change in cultural values and language. Brazil accepted these immigrants with open arms, and in return, newcomers like Yumi's parents embraced their new home, customs, and lifestyle. At first, her parents started their own farm, living out of a cottage with dirt floors and no running water. Yumi was born and learned to speak, eat, and socialize in Portuguese. Her growing up didn't reflect the reserved, formal, societal intricacies of Japanese culture. Rather, she was raised to be demonstrative, outwardly affectionate, vocal, and physically hearty—traits her parents were able to pick up comfortably when they first moved. During the 1970s, Brazil became the leading industrial power of Latin America. Yumi's parents opened a store and eased into a middle-class lifestyle. Some of her cousins became dentists and engineers. But in the late 1980s, income maldistribution, inflation, and government land policies led to severe economic recession.

At that time, Japan was experiencing early pangs of zero population growth, and a native workforce that was no longer interested in menial labor. Japan looked to expatriates to fill these positions with the assumption they would easily assimilate. Yumi's family took this opportunity to return to Japan, the home her parents had forgotten and the home that had forgotten them. Now, fluent in Portuguese and outwardly gregarious, the new immigrants, although Japanese-looking, proved as different as Europeans or Africans. Now, under the nervous flickering of fluorescent lights, Yumi and her family assembled electronic car parts, destined for the Western free world.

"So, are you planning on staying in Japan?" I asked.

"No, absolutely not. You know, Yumi works in the evenings at a sushi bar, and Japanese men treat her like shit. They'll reach over and touch her breasts with justifications like, *"Brazilian women are like Amazonian sex animals!"* She's very patient, though, gotta hand that to her. I would have killed one of those men by now. No, in fact, one of my Pakistani friends was illegally arrested the other day—the police thought he was a drug dealer and an illegal alien. Did you know the Japanese government has warned police to wear special rubber gloves when arresting Middle Easterners, Central Asians, or Africans? It's just sick. In fact, Amnesty International has lodged quite a number of complaints regarding Filipinos, Indian, and African foreigners locked up in isolation cells without a trial, their passports confiscated. I could be next. Yumi could be next."

"So, where are you going to go?"

"I don't know. Germany? Since I'm German, I'm getting my EC passport, although people who look like me aren't exactly backyard guests. We've thought about Portugal or Spain, but what would I do there? And not America, I would never raise kids in America. Certainly not Boston, although maybe the west coast ... I don't know, Teja."

*  *  *

Ukumbwa sat in our living room and stacked his books on African history next to the coffee table. He removed his green and black woven cap and let his dreadlocks fall down to his shoulders.

"Wow, it's been that long, huh?" I said. "The last time we saw each other you had pretty much a buzz cut. And now a beard and mustache too."

"They give me shit about it at work. As if special needs kids only respond to White guys in ties and slacks. The principal really hates it when I come to work in a dashiki. I just tell him it's even more 'formal' than a Filine's Basement oxford. Besides African clothing like this ain't cheap, you know."

"Well, you know, you have to stay true to your African self," I said, remembering our encounter with the taxi driver.

"And you, your Afghanistani self."

"Touché bro. I've been thinking about our conversation when you changed your name. Tell me, how do you define 'African?'"

"Simply, a person from Africa."

"What about Egypt? Some northern Africans don't consider themselves 'African.' Isn't it just politics we're talking about? Haven't there always been conflicts in Africa, even enslavement of Africans by other Africans?"

"Conflicts, wars, and slavery on African soil was invented and controlled by white Europeans."

"I agree that White Europeans destroyed much of the sanctity of the African people. The Native Americans as well. And the Middle East and parts of Asia. Much of the world, in fact. But are they completely guilty about Africa, since the very beginning? Even *before* Europeans lost their color after their migration from Africa? Most other cultures have done equally as atrocious stuff."

"Africans are different."

"Different? You mean biologically different?"

"Yes. Our blood runs deep, and maybe our blood had been tainted by the rape of the White man, and yes I do occasionally find a red hair growing on my head, and I'd rather rip it out for blood, than cut it with scissors. Africans are different. Biologically, sociologically, and politically."

"Well, that certainly gives cannon fodder to the likes of David Duke and the Census Bureau. So, all Africans agree on everything. What about female genital mutilation? That practice wasn't imposed by White Europeans. And that is sexual enslavement of women, en mass in many parts of the African continent and elsewhere. So, outside of White influence there was never any subjugation you're saying?"

"No, of course not. But my people have been divided and conquered and made to live conflicting lives, but that will change."

"You are saying that a people's identities are determined by their ... what?"

"Their heart, soul, their homeland, the ground they worship."

"Betcha Michael Jackson worships his estate."

"Michael Jackson is a confused young African who is a self-denigrating victim of Western capitalism."

"Now, since I grew up in Japan, I love Japan, and I've spent more time there than I have here, I am what, then?"

"You are who you need to be. *Where* is your spirit?"

"Well, I'm also part German. And Filipino. And African. Gullah, actually. So can I be African?"

"No. You are not African like I am. Living, breathing, fighting for the survival of my people."

"So, as a continent, a politically divided continent, like Asia and Europe, Africa ends where?"

"The Sinai Peninsula. And of course the Caribbean and other areas where we have been enslaved away from our homeland."

"So all Asians are one people?"

"No, of course not. Neither are all Europeans."

"But Africans are?"

"We *know* we are."

"Africa is a huge place, though, how do you choose where your home is?"

"Africa is my home."

"To return to a home you have never been to. It's poetic."

"My people will welcome me with open arms when I return."

\* \* \*

Papa had come to visit us after a business trip to the UN headquarters in New York City. Several months earlier, while at a public phone across the street from the UN, his suitcase and laptop computer were ripped from his hands by two innocent-looking passersby. He hated returning home to America. He had been annoyed with rude service personnel and the general disorderly mess of American urban design. He tolerated it, or at least kept a straight face not wanting to upset me. He should have known I felt the same way.

Papa had grown calmer over the years, more patient and accepting. He used to critique and advise on everything, he now sat back and didn't interfere. I had started writing *In the Shadow of Race* and was hopeful that for the first time we might talk openly about what had fueled so much of his anger.

"My father was never around," he said. "In fact, we hardly ever spoke, and I can't honestly say that I ever really knew him. You and I talking like this? It never would have happened between Grandpa and me. He was required to leave his family at an early age, find work and a life in America, and by the time he returned he was an outsider. He became a very lonely man who expressed himself through his wrath. Then he married Grandma, uprooted her from South Carolina away from her family, and then eventually lived on Staten Island where there were very few Black people—she lived completely in a White world. Grandpa then moved us to the Philippines. He disappeared pretty much for the 12 years we were there, leaving Grandma isolated, and as you know, her alcoholism worsened. When they came back to the States, they had no more ties, no more solid roots. For my parents, an interracial marriage in America and the Philippines was very difficult, but even so, your grandfather was a racist in his own way. In fact, Grandpa didn't accept Black people as equivalent to everyone else, and had a derogatory attitude toward them. But he never expressed this to Grandma or her family. He thought of my mother as different, or at least different enough for him—a light-skinned Black was safe."

"So, Grandma considered herself Black," I said, "and Grandpa took that away from her."

"In a manner of speaking. Grandpa must have thought that by taking Grandma away from her drinking, she would be cured. She could never truly return home. And for Grandpa, it was unusual at the time for immigrants, Asians or Europeans, to go *back* to their home of origin. If anything, they brought their family with them, away from poverty. Grandpa had to return to save face, as he promised his mother. He had gotten the taste of a better life, so eventually we bought a house in New York. And then of course, the family disintegrated from block-busting. That killed Grandma slowly. The only solace she got was when she returned to Hilton Head to die."

I noticed that the maple trees in the backyard had started to bud, and then a cool breeze roamed through the kitchen. Papa took a sip from his coffee and looked out the window. The sunlight created an odd shadow on the wall of his thick glasses. He spoke as his eyes danced the contours of the distant Massachusetts treeline. "I always wanted to buy an old New England Victorian—two floors with bay windows, fix it up, and move it somewhere, not to Japan but somewhere else. You know, it's tough to even get a mortgage in Tokyo? Ayako had to buy the house."

"Believe me, I know you wouldn't want to live here."

"I'm aware of that."

"Where would you go?"

"I don't know. We'll probably stay in Japan. She wouldn't survive living in America. I don't know."

*       *       *

That summer on television, I watched a convoy of police cars trailing a white utility vehicle along a highway in California. O.J. Simpson was arrested and the nation was divided again. Here was, yet again, another chance to reinforce the negative stereotypes of Black men.

I started auditioning again for television roles, but the producers and casting agents were only puppets of a larger machine under the pressure of profit motives.

At one of the Boston area's most prominent casting agencies in Harvard Square, I prepared for an audition. I read the list of characters I was to chose from for a cellular phone commercial. In the list 40 characters, two of them, a taxi driver and a convenient store clerk, had the word "ethnic" penned in next to them. With the help of two Black actors to back me up, I summoned the casting director.

"What does 'ethnic' mean?" I asked her.

"Oh, you know, just 'ethnic.' I don't know. That's what they asked for."

"Well, if you don't know what it means, why have it? I mean, who's ethnic in this room? Seems to me if the three of us are 'ethnic' then there are only two parts for us to audition for. Are the others White? In fact, I think I'd like to audition for the doctor. And David here has been thinking the lawyer might be nice."

"Well, what do you want me to do?"

"Take some White Out, and please white-out the words 'ethnic.'"

The casting director complied, then huffed off to the casting room.

A week later I auditioned at a video production company. I read well and I was told I looked the part. I was asked if I would be available for the shoot, usually a sure sign that I got the job. Then the director held his hand as if to ask a question.

He looked over at his producer. "Do you think Teja should read in his normal accent?"

I leaned over his desk and stared him in the eyes. "Gee, I wonder what kind of accent that would be? German? Japanese? Surely you're not thinking Spanish, because that would be just a little cliché, don't you think?"

A month later I was called in for a McDonald's commercial audition. I arrived ready and warmed up. I signed in, and as usual, entered my name, social security number, address, age, and skipped the race category. I picked up the script and scanned it. It called for some shy, skinny guy, sitting on a park bench, trying four times, unsuccessfully, to pick up sexy, voluptuous women who passed by.

"Boy, this looks like pretty stereotypical stuff, doesn't it?" I said to a woman sitting next to me. She turned away from me to remain in character. Then I stood up and realized that I was surrounded by about 30 White, hard-bodied, striking, blond, blue-eyed women in miniskirts and midriff-exposing tops. They leaned forward frequently with their breasts bulging frequently to challenge the others. Almost in unison, they popped gum in their mouths, rocked their long, shaven legs, and checked the terrain of their makeup.

I was angry and deeply ashamed of my profession. A flood of negative history washed through me like sewage. My head spun as I took steps to the office that looked out into the room of actresses. I felt sorry for them all—selling their bodies for a quarter pounder and fries. Once in the office, I cleared my throat.

"Gee, I wonder how diverse the female cast is today."

The secretary who was on the phone cupped the receiver. "What?"

A spoke a little louder. "Gee, I wonder how diverse the female cast is today."

The secretary swung around in her chair, and placed her hand over the receiver again. "Teja, what are you talking about?"

"Okay, let's try this again." This time I spoke loud enough so that all the auditioners could hear me. *"Gee, I wonder how diverse the female cast is today!"*

"Teja, quiet down!"

"You know," I licked my lips, knowing this would be the last time I saw the casting agents who I had always thought were the most progressive in town, "I'm really sick and tired of this, aren't you? I mean really. Look at them! Are all of them White? Correct me if I'm wrong, but they look like Hollywood prostitutes!"

"They're all White, Teja."

"That's it. You can count me out."

As I left the casting agency, I heard the secretary calling for me. I took the stairs down the five flights of steps to escape her. I walked passed the Hancock building and cursed its phallic design and the perpetual wind tunnel it created. *Money.* I thought to myself. *Ronald McDonald. Why don't they make* him *wear a freaking miniskirt. Expose his nipples and sell some fucking hamburgers.*

The next day I spoke to the actor's union. They had heard the whole story and were advised that I hadn't stayed to hear what the agency had to say: yes, there *were* some *Black* actresses auditioning, but they were scheduled to be there later in the afternoon. *What, were they still getting off from the back of the bus? Oh sure. They might* stand out *in the sea of White women. That's why you never see dark-skinned ballerinas doing Swan Lake.*

\* \* \*

I had been traveling extensively, from state to state, throughout the nation, performing *Ethnic Man!* And with each trip, drivers, clients, audience members, and strangers on the street would voice their opinions about the state of the union, immigration, race, sexual identity, class divisions, wealth, poverty, and all the things that fuel this country's engine. I listened with great care and, in turn, offered them my story.

### Macon, Georgia

A driver picked me up at the airport. His dark skin bled handsomely through his translucent white pressed shirt and his tie complemented his fine slacks. No sooner had we settled in behind our seatbelts did he start pouring out his life to me.

"I've lived in the Macon area for 18 years. Was a bus driver in Houston before that and a taxi driver in Seattle even before that. Came to Macon, got married, and then divorced. My kids love me though. They come 'round now and then. In fact, my son ought to be taking over my business someday once he gets his life in order. He's all confused because the other kids make fun of him, datin' a White girl and all. I don't have a problem with it, nor my ex—she sure doesn't, but this girl's parents sure shittin' about it, you know what I'm sayin'?"

I nodded, knowing more was to come. After all, we had 1½ hours to get acquainted.

"This skin color thing breaks my heart. You know this country, God bless her, has got to learn to forget the skin color thing. It's driving people to an early death, that's what it's doin'. That O. J. thing? If he was a White man, he'd be free by now. Used to work for a White man, a Jewish man, who was real nice to me an' everything. My cousins were always tellin' me, 'watchu go an' work for a Jewish man an' everything.' I jus' tell 'em I like my job and it's none of their business anyhow."

"You tell 'em."

"Look at my skin." He pressed his arm against the dashboard. "Now, you tell me, which one is black. Go on, tell me."

"Damn close, but I'd say the dashboard."

"What, are you a comedian?"

"Actually, yes."

He nodded his head and adjusted his large body in his seat. "And that woman over there?" He pointed to a mother on a porch, holding her baby. "Is she White, or is the kid's diaper white? Go on, tell me."

"The diaper, but *before* it's brown."

He laughed through his teeth and honked his horn. "So you *are* a comedian. Where are you from?"

"All over," I said, testing his tolerance.

"Everyone's gotta come from somewhere, where you from?"

"Born in Brooklyn, grew up in Germany, then New York, then Japan for 14 years. My father's African-American/Native-American and Filipino-Chinese and my mother's German/Danish.

He raised his eyebrows, squinted his eyes, and turned slowly toward me. "Yeah. You're from all over."

The rolling fields passed by us like green ocean waves. "You know," I said, "in the Philippines there's an old saying. God was baking man in the oven. The first one he left in too long. He came out Black. The second he left in too short. He came out White. Then he left the third one in just long enough. He came out Filipino."

"Well, then God must still be working on it. Either that or he gots to get himself some new oven! Seems to me, there's all *kinds* of baking going on here in America!"

\* \* \*

*Lewisburg, PA*

A woman's crying caught my attention in the middle of my performance. Then, during the discussion period, she cried again, and stayed in her seat.

"Would you like to talk about something?" I asked.

"Well, I just want to say that I've never talked about this before, and I'm so angry. This has been a secret with me for a long time. Now, look at me. I'm just a White girl, you know, I got blond hair, blue eyes, middle-class family all that. I used to date this Black guy. He was part of a fraternity, all Black. His brothers and family gave him shit for him dating a White girl, and my friends gave me shit for dating him. He left the fraternity and hated himself so much he committed suicide."

"How long have you held this inside?"

"This was 3 years ago. I didn't tell anyone why he killed himself, but I know. Everyone was speculating that he died from an overdose or something stupid like that, just because he's Black. Now I have to live with this, and everytime I hear someone shooting off about who should not be dating whom and all that, I just wanna scream! I loved that man, and we were going to get married. I don't know why you with all the shit you lived through aren't screwed up, but you should be."

"Sometimes I scream," I said.

\* \* \*

*Logan, Utah*

A woman waited for most of the audience to leave before she approached me. She had been crying but kept a straight face. "My son was in the hospital," she said. "Some of the kids in school were always making fun of him, and then they challenged him to a fight. See, I'm White and I'm married to a Black man. Jayson is our son and we always have to explain or defend ourselves concerning him. His school forced him to put down Black on one of those forms and he came home crying. They beat him badly at school."

\* \* \*

*Detroit, Michigan*

"I agree with everything you're saying, chief—the race thing, the ethnic thing, it's really bad news. You know, I hate to see people fighting over stupid little things like the color of skin. See, that's just ignorance. I myself have a varied background, Irish and German, and I'm proud of it. I'm just, you know, a White guy—turn red in the sun. But I have a problem with only one thing: Gays. Gays and Lesbians should all be shot and killed. I hope you read the Bible, because the Bible clearly shows that God did not intend a man to be mating with another man, nor a woman with a woman. It's a sin."

"Been to San Francisco?"

"They're all sinners there."

\* \* \*

## Tacoma, Washington

A woman in fatigues stood at the back of the theater with her arms crossed. Her eyes pierced through the thick of the crowd and she shifted her head. "You know, I was going to pop you!"

"You wanted to 'pop' me?" I asked, wondering how many others had wanted to "pop" me.

"Yeah. As a Black, African-American proud-to-be-who-I-am-and-no-one-I-mean-no-one-is-going-to-mess-with-me individual, I was *this* close to taking you out. If I didn't stay for the rest of the program, I would have been waiting for you right there, outside. Because when you started with the word 'nigger,' in your show, I flipped. You see, I *hate* that word."

"I do too," I said.

"But, see, now I understand. Because that's what someone *called* you."

"When I was a child."

"And you really didn't know your Grandma was Black?"

"No one told me."

"Well, you just show me where they are and I'll go pop them instead."

\* \* \*

## Poughkeepsie, New York

Two students with equally dark skin sat next to each other. The one on the left spoke with a heavy British accent. "I'm from London, England," he said. "Now, in this country, before people hear me speak, they think I'm Black, or African-American, but in London, they naturally assume I'm from England."

The other student raised his hand. "Yeah, but I'm Black, or African-American. If you're in this country, you're Black, and there ain't no way around it."

"Yes, but in London they don't say I'm African-British, they just say I'm British, period.

"But they call you *Black*, right?"

"Yes, but that's *after* British."

\* \* \*

## Springfield, Missouri

His skin was so pale it reflected the stage lights considerably during my performance. He sat in the front row, and wore slacks and an oxford shirt while everyone else was fairly casual. "My name is Tom and I'm going to run for president someday. I'm a student of political science and I'm a Republican and a Christian. The most important issue to me would be to eliminate affirmative action. I think the system is out of control and I just don't see a need for it."

A Black woman sitting several rows back moved her neck side to side and looked at the ceiling while she answered him. "What do you plan to do about all the minorities and women who are still faced with glass ceilings, lower wages, and higher layoff risk?"

He turned around in his chair and quickly formulated a speech. "Oh, no, no, no. It's not like it used to be. Blacks are finding work at an alarming rate and attending college, too. And there are more corporate female professionals than ever before. We're living in the past and we have to make schools and the workplace more competitive."

The woman turned slowly toward him and closed her eyes. "So, just give up on support for people who can't make it because the system is still run by a majority of White males? You *do* know that, by the time you get to running for president, most of the country will be non-White? Who do you think would vote for you?"

"Oh, I will have a tremendous amount of support, I just know it."

\* \* \*

*Arnold, Maryland*

A young woman in the audience stood up and squared her shoulders toward me as if to test me, to guess her identity.

"I'm adopted," she said.

"I can see that," I joked.

She smiled and tossed back her dark, wavy hair. "What do you think I am?"

"Well, if I were to rely completely on stereotypes, but that's not what I normally try to do, mind you, I would say you are Hispanic. And if I tried to guess, in more detail, I would have to say ... African-American, Southeast Asian, and German."

"Oh my," she said. "I *thought* you might know. Being adopted makes it a lot more complicated, doesn't it."

"Well, I think you need to remember that you are who you are based on your cultural upbringing, your surroundings, and your peers. Your heritage has something to do with who you are, in a way, biologically, but not culturally. In fact, my mother just found out after her parents died, that the man who raised her was not her biological father, but she was brought up German. So, she's German by culture, even if her biological father was Italian, Greek, Irish, Russian, Chinese, or whatever. And I grew up in Japan, hence I'm part Japanese by culture, although I don't look stereotypically Japanese."

\* \* \*

*Appleton, Wisconsin*

"My wife and I are both White, and we live in a White neighborhood."

"And you want to adopt a child, preferably Korean, Chinese, or Brazilian."

"How did you know?"

"I didn't. I was making an assumption."

"Well, what should we do when the child grows up and is confused? I mean, she's probably going to attend a predominantly White school, and all her friends will probably be White."

"Well, I think you're doing the right thing. First of all, I think people should adopt a child because you can give them love and a safe, happy home, not because they are a certain color, you know, like picking out a favorite Crayola crayon. Second, in your community, you will be a shining example to the others that love doesn't have color or cultural barriers. Third, if I was this child, I would love you because you chose to take this difficult course."

\* \* \*

### Chicago, Illinois

"I'm the vice principal at the technical school and my wife and I live in a really nice, quiet, safe neighborhood. Lots of kids, with trees and fields to play in. Now, in terms of trying to make a healthy, diverse community, we, meaning my town, have invited the parents of the Black kids in our school to move to our neighborhood, you know, away from where they come. But they don't. Why do you think that is?"

"Have you all considered moving to their neighborhood?"

\* \* \*

### Hartford, Connecticut

A woman with long, striking, deep black braids, and dark, shiny skin to match stood in line wearing a robe of thick, bold, green, black, and gold stripes. She waited to speak with me. When she finally approached me, I had already made my assumption. She corrected me before I opened my mouth.

"I'm Korean," she said, waiting for me to flinch.

"That's what I thought," I said. "I saw you standing there, and I said, 'Hmmm, she *must* be Korean.'"

"My grandmother raised me. She was Korean. My first language was Korean, and I still speak it. I consider myself Korean, no matter what anybody says. And that's fine, because, now that I know, I consider you Japanese. Right next door, how do you like that! But I don't look Korean, do I. So what is it you were going to tell me?"

"Okay, fine, I thought you were African-American, Black, Haitian, something. But that was my mind talking."

\* \* \*

*Mercersburg, Pennsylvania*

She sat near the front of the audience, deeply entrenched in the discussion. "I'm 17 and I've lived in 12 countries. My father and mother are both White and American, but I don't know what I am. Right now we live in Saudi Arabia. I can't practice my Christianity there, so I go to church in secret. We dress conservatively to respect the Muslim culture. Here in America people ask such silly questions like, 'do you really have to wear those things on your head,' and you want to educate them, but sometimes it's easier not to say anything at all. And even after you explain to them that these things are part of the culture they say, 'Oh my God, that's so awful.'"

Another student spoke up. "My father's American and my mother's Indian, but I grew up mostly in Africa. We eat with our hands and stuff. People look at me and assume I'm just White, and they always freak out when I tell them where I live. Part of my culture is contemporary American, but others are Indian and African. I don't know where I'm going for college next year."

"I'm 17 and I'm an American," a third student said, "but I was born in Taiwan. Then we moved to Italy, then France, then DC, then China, then Switzerland. Next we're moving to Brazil. Not everyone has roots to fall back on—a community—and people who have that often take it for granted.

\* \* \*

**Las Vegas, Nevada**

A skinny girl, looking younger than her 17 years, sat up straight and confident with a soft smile. She sat on the edge of a group of students who represented the Asian population at a youth conference.

"My mother and I escaped Laos 3 years ago. My father, we think, is still there. It took us 1 year to get to America, making our way here, eating and sleeping wherever we could. I became a naturalized citizen. I speak four languages, I work in the evenings, I'm graduating Magna cum Laude, and I'm going to be a doctor."

I nodded and smiled. "You know, the common stereotype is that immigrants, particularly from developing countries, are lazy. The fact is that the average immigrant in the U.S. has three times a better chance of getting a PhD."

\* \* \*

**Jacksonville, Alabama**

"I have the same story you do," a young man said to me after a performance.

"Well, not exactly, but I'm just as messed-up."

"Well, I don't consider myself messed-up. How old are you?"

"Eighteen. Like you, I have a really messed-up family. My father's Pakistani/African-American and my mother is White-Jewish-American/Moroccan. And I lived in France for 7 years. So, how do you deal with all this stuff, I mean, what do you put down? I don't know what to do and I'm really confused. I'm American, but I want to know what to call myself before I turn 34, like you."

"Gee, thanks. So, what's wrong with 'American?'"

"That's fine, but no one's happy with that."

"Could *you* be happy with it?"

"I don't think so, because everyone always thinks I'm something else."

"That's their problem, isn't it?"

"So what should I put down?"

"Don't put down anything if it don't agree with it. And in terms of finding out as soon as you can? Don't bother. You might very well change your mind several times as you grow older, especially when you become that horrible old age of 34."

\* \* \*

### Albany, New York

A Ghanaian family sat next to me at the post-performance dinner. The mother, the father, and their three young children wore their bright, bold-colored traditional garbs proudly.

The father spoke with an assured voice. "I don't like it when American Blacks come to my country and tell me they are African. They are not accepted in my community as African. Do you see my kids? Two of them were born here, and the other was born in Ghana, but they are American. My wife and I cannot help that. They are American. We try to teach them our language and our customs, but they want to be like the other kids in their neighborhood and schools. I think Americans should be proud to say 'I'm American.' And me? I have been here many years. Maybe you hear my accent is strong, but I am becoming American. No doubt. It's natural."

\* \* \*

### Canton, Massachusetts

"What is the most popular television show on this planet?" I asked 120 technical high school teachers. There were only three women and one African-American man.

"*Baywatch!*" one man belted out. The room broke out in a combination of laughter and howls. Several men in the center made suggestive curves over their chests with their hands, and spread their legs wider, shaking them with authority. The women looked straight ahead, hanging on to their last string of dignity, not unlike the string bikini the men were imagining.

I timed my next line just right. "You are correct. *Baywatch* is the most popular program on planet Earth. It wasn't even created for the American market. It was created for all those horny Europeans and Asians. It is a bunch of White women running around with bouncing breasts. This is what America looks like to the rest of the world."

"Yeah!" One guy belted and whistled through his teeth.

"Do you think the show would be popular if it featured mostly Black women, or even lesbians? What if David Hasselhoff was Black and gay? Would you get off on that too?"

The room fell silent.

"That would never happen," one man who had been grabbing his crotch said. "I certainly wouldn't watch it."

Another man chimed in, "Yeah, but those blond chicks are a real turn on."

"You know," I said, "I'm a television producer. If I wanted your daughter to play a 'bimbo' in a bikini with bouncing breasts, would you watch the show with your colleagues in the basement with the lights turned down low?"

*   *   *

*Concord, New Hampshire*

"Who here in the room is an American?" I asked an auditorium filled with 200 slouching high school seniors. No one raised a hand except for a girl sitting in the front row. "Okay, fine. That's interesting, I thought there would be more than one. Oh well. Okay, who in the room is Irish?" Half the hands in the room popped up. "Okay, wow, that's a lot of Irish people here today, from out of town, I presume. Okay, who, among the Irish have actually been to Ireland?" No hands went up. "Speak Gaelic?" Hands remained dormant. "Eat Irish food? Play Irish music? Practice Irish culture?" No one answered except for a few who yawned out loud and burped in an attempt to disrupt the class.

"Oh, is that part of your Irish culture? No? Then keep it to yourself. You're not cool, in fact most everyone around you isn't even paying attention to you. Are you American?"

His eyes rolled up into his forehead. "Yeah."

"But you had your hand up for Irish instead. Tell me something about Ireland."

The boy looked around the room with a frown. "I donno."

"You don't know anything about Ireland? Then why would you say you're from Ireland and not the United States?"

"I donno."

"Who here can tell me something about Ireland? I'd really like to know more about its fascinating history."

One boy raised his hand half-heartedly, and jerked his feet against the seat in front of him. "Ah ... we drink a lot?"

The audience broke into laughter some boys through paper and plastic at the boy.

"Well, did you know that many Japanese drink a lot also, but that doesn't make them Irish."

*   *   *

*Greenville, North Carolina*

"So, what do you call yourself?" a woman called from the middle of the audience.

"You mean, what do I fill out on a form?"

"Yeah. Black or White? 'Cause my girlfriend Latisha says you too *White* to be a *brothuh*. But I look at you, and you too *Black* to be *White*."

"I don't fill it out. My father used to tell me to put down Filipino-German. But Filipino is a nationality, not a race. So is German. My brother is darker than I am and he's a German citizen. So, color is irrelevant. When I was born, fathers were not allowed in the delivery room. The doctor or nurse looked at my mother, then put me down as White. The 1990 National Census taker put me down as Hispanic. Now I'm legally Hispanic, thank you very much."

"Why don't you put down 'other,' or fill it in?"

"Yeah, I guess I could if there was enough room for it. But you see, I don't even believe in the concept of racial division, especially when it's determined by color or facial features, because there are no definitive distinctions. When does Black exactly end, or start? How nappy should the hair be? Is Michael Jackson Black? Was he, is he now or will he be tomorrow? When does Asian, the billions of Asians that there are, end or start? How thin should the epicanthic folds of the eyelid be? Was Ghandi as Asian as Emperor Hirohito? The hierarchy of race was invented by, to use their own patronizing terms, a handful of White guys in northern Europe not long ago. We're only perpetuating their wish—to divide people from top-down on an unscientific platform. My cat Sheila cannot have offspring with a zoo lion because the DNA is too different, but I can have children with my wife because we have the same DNA structure. David Duke could actually have a child with a Black woman, and who knows—power over others is manifested in many ways. It wasn't rare during slavery, and it's not now, but all of this is not to say that as Americans, we are not allowed to decide for ourselves what to be called. If this was truly a free country, we should be free to describe ourselves the way we want to. The government needs to stay out of my identity."

"What is your wife?" a young woman asked with her arms folded tightly.

"Human."

"Now you *know* what I'm talking about."

"Well, I *think* I know what you're asking, but I don't want to assume."

"Well, is she Black, Hispanic, American, or what?"

"As I said, I don't really believe in the concept of races, but she is American."

"So she's White."

"I didn't say that. Not all Americans are White."

"I *know* that. Forget it!"

"Hold on. I just need you to ask me exactly what you're thinking. Be honest with all of us and be specific. The use of language is very important in this discussion. Race does not equal culture does not equal nationality does not equal ethnicity etc., etc."

Her friend sitting next to her picked up for her. "She wants to know, what color is your wife's skin."

"She's light-skinned."

The audience laughed, knowing I wasn't going to play any games.

"You mentioned children," said a man sitting in the front row. "Do you have any, and what do you, or will you, teach them?"

"If we had children, I would teach them as much as I know, and encourage them to learn more about their heritage. I know why my father held his mother's identity from us. As millions of other American Blacks or people of color did, if you could pass, you passed. After all, Filipinos were given 'White' identity status by the West in order to boost their positioning while the U.S. occupied the islands with the military. Now, of course, they're back to being Asian, but at the time, that was the way to get work, support a family, and survive in the racist country we live in. People changed names, Germans changed names, Chinese changed names, women writers used male pen names all to survive. Some people dealt with it better than others. I am not angry with my father, and I certainly don't hate him. I just wish knowing about our heritage, bad or good, wasn't so painful that one should hold a secret for so long. Children need knowledge and storytelling. What a beautiful combination."

"Where do you call home?" a woman asked.

I couldn't answer—I froze. Sometimes I was able to answer this question quickly, depending on how I felt that day. But at this moment, I thought about Japan, and our old neighborhood with the wooden houses butted up next to million-dollar stucco mansions, cicadas droning in the wet heat of summer, giggling school children in uniforms, hot noodle soup in the dead of winter, the toothless smile on the grocery store woman, the sweet adrenaline from a deep, respectful bow, my old bedroom, my home. I thought about Germany and the afternoon naps during quiet hour, the hourly chime of the old clock in Oma and Opa's living room; family get-togethers with strong coffee, cake, and gossip; the gentle curve of the bridge over the Elbe river; luscious grass padding the countryside; the long, winding staircase up to the apartment; my home. I thought about Parkway Village, camping in the circular courtyard, backyard barbecues and Easter egg hunts, the gracious bend of the willow tree, socks and mittens drying on the radiator, the big blue and red toy box, goldfish in the toilet, my first bicycle, my first friends, my home. I thought about San Francisco and the eerie, tangible fog, the smile of perfect strangers, cool, romantic evening breezes, walks along the pier, jogging for jobs up Columbus, midnight café gatherings, Mrs. Salucci's dinners and her waving wooden spoon, tai chi in the park, the apartment coffee pot, my home. I thought of Oma, Opa, and Tante Louise; their tough, honorable vigor; and absolute devotion. I thought about Grandma and Grandpa, and their battle for acceptance, their strength and biography. I thought about Mama, and her precious, nervous smile, her love and gentle words, her poise and persistence, lavish hopes and wondrous dreams, her giggle at the obvious and fascination of the unexpected. I thought about Papa, and his friendly sense of humor, his moral strength and kind, artist hands, his pride and foresight. I thought of Miguel, and his touch with the natural, his diplomacy, his creative genius and humanitarian struggle. And I thought of Barbara, at home waiting for my return, her breath and love, her patience, unconditional support, her humor and laughter, her poetic imagination and musical affection, her steadfast honesty and warm welcome.

\* \* \*

The plane emerged from the wispy echoes of the surrounding clouds and the moon proudly beamed its reflection of the sun against the silver wings. The earth snuggled into a nap below. How fortunate for me. In 11 hours I will be home again.

# the Author

Teja Arboleda is a professional television producer/director, writer, actor/comedian, public speaker, and visual artist. He is the founder and president of Entertaining Diversity, Inc., which is committed to diversity awareness training through entertainment in the format of theater, lectures, and multimedia. He has testified for changes in federal racial and ethnic categories, and has been quoted often by the media including *The New York Times*, Associated Press, and National Public Radio.

Teja has worked extensively in public television. In the spring of 1994, he won an Emmy Award for public affairs programming. He served 2 years as staff editor for the nationally acclaimed PBS documentary series, *Frontline,* and 4 years as assistant director/editor for minority affairs programming at WGBH-TV Boston. From 1985 to 1990, he produced, directed, and filmed music videos, corporate sales and training videos, commercials, public service announcements, and independent films.

Arboleda is also a professional actor and comedian. His fast-paced, ethno–cultural-related comedy style has been highly rated by Catch a Rising Star in Boston. In 1990, he played the leading role in the PBS docudrama, *Matzeliger,* and continues to work as an actor in television commercials, radio, and corporate videos. Since 1992, he has been performing his powerful, acclaimed one-man show *Ethnic Man!* around the United States.

266

## STUDY GUIDE FOR COLLEGE FACULTY

To facilitate its use as a course text, a Study Guide written by Christine Clark, New Mexico State University, is offered with this volume. Topics for discussion include:

- the social construction of race; racial separatism versus diversity
- racial, ethnic, and cultural identity development
- the politics of racial categorization; mixed "race" peoples
- cultural identity versus identity by heritage; the concept of a "cultural home"
- changing identities within cultures

The Study Guide is free to college faculty who adopt this book.
  Study Guide ISBN: 0-8058-2873-7
  1-800-9-BOOKS-9 or orders@erlbaum.com

\* \* \*

## VIDEOTAPES AND MULTIMEDIA WORKSHOP

### *Ethnic Man!* Video Package for Grades 5 Through 12

Now for the first time, Arboleda's nationally acclaimed show, *Ethnic Man!*, is available for continuous use in the classroom. The *Ethnic Man!* educational multimedia package has been designed for use in middle and high school classrooms. It includes:

- a 35-minute videotape of the *Ethnic Man!* program, produced for television

267

- a 12-minute teacher's introduction videotape
- teacher's discussion and activity guide
- audiotape of Arboleda's favorite children's idioms and rhymes from Germany and Japan
- cultural objects flash cards

This educational package can be used as a supplement to a variety of social studies and multicultural curricula, including equality issues, identity formation, social history, tolerance education, antiviolence campaigns, and studies of biography as literature.

To purchase the package, contact Teja Arboleda at:
www.entertainingdiversity.com
or call (781) 329-7040

### *Ethnic Man!* Live Performance Primarily for College-level and Higher Audiences

*Ethnic Man!* is the true, humorous adventure of Teja Arboldea's search for his multicultural, multiethnic identity and the discovery of what it is to be American. Arboleda has been performing this one-man show nationwide since 1993. Performances of *Ethnic Man!* have brought a new, highly entertaining voice this nation's current debates about multiculturalism and diversity.

*Ethnic Man!* can be booked by calling (608) 849-6558 or contacting lecturagnt@aol.com.

### *Language of Culture and Race,* a Multimedia Workshop for College-Level and Higher Audiences

*The Language of Culture and Race* is a multimedia, interactive, and energetic workshop in which participants build a collection of tools for discovering our roots, human connectionism, and cross-cultural communications. In a safe, open, and blameless environment, the session cultivates an intriguing climate in which participants build a conversation about who we are and what we must do together to succeed in play and work.

Techniques in perceiving cultural differences as beneficial and valuable will help attendees prepare for a changing national and global marketplace. The tools they learn in this workshop will help them prepare for a competitive and growing international community.

For more information on the workshop contact lecturagnt@aol.com or call (608) 849-6558.